HOLLOW
Family Tree

Shush! Be Quiet I'm sleeping...

CYNTHIA AND DEANA REFFNER

ISBN 978-1-64258-744-9 (paperback)
ISBN 978-1-64258-745-6 (digital)

Christian Faith Publishing, Inc.
832 Park Avenue
Meadville, PA 16335
www.christianfaithpublishing.com

Printed in the United States of America

Intervened by Love
(June 17, 1980)

God entered my life
Set me free
From darkness
Little did I know
Love had already paid
The price for
My soul
The ransom had already
Been paid by the One
Who had paid the ransom for my soul

Contents

Introduction

THIS IS MY STORY AND life experiences as I recall them. They are not written with any ill will or malice toward anyone. They are spoken with a boldness and truth. The truth of how my life was. You will be reading about some very graphic depiction of what I, by the grace of God, lived in and through. Because of all the drugs I was given while in the hospital when I was young, I am not exactly sure of the order of some of the events. I have done my best to make them as chronological as possible.

It is imperative that I tell the story of my life as I lived it. In hopes that anyone out there in the world who is having difficulties overcoming their own experience with living in child abuse and alcoholism—combined with the loss of a body part or a body deformity or scarring—can read my story and hopefully help you to find your own healing. Through much persecution, perseverance, persistence, and patience, and much prayer with fasting, I was able to be an overcomer. In addition, that yes, it can happen for you too!

Through much travail, trial and error, I have learned to hear God's voice and to obey his commands. Yes, God does command his sheep. I am one of God's sheep, and if you are picking this book up to read it, you probably are one too. He has placed a burden on my heart for His wounded sheep: those in turmoil, as I was for far too many years. My job as a child of God is to "feed God's sheep." Through the years, whenever I was in turmoil, God would always speak to me, "Feed My sheep." So to the best of my ability, under the guide of the Holy Spirit, I will do my best to share my story.

Whether it is the loss of a limb or a breast or the loss of a childhood due to the abuse of alcohol being used in your home, they are

7

all a loss. With any loss, there must be a grieving process that needs to take place in order for you to reach a final destination point of healing.

To all parents of children who have suffered affliction, I pray that this book can help you in your journey. That your eyes would become wide open, with no denial of your child's pain. That you would have the courage to walk through your own issues and receive help where it is necessary. Ignoring the issue and hoping that it will one day go away will not work. Your pain must also be addressed in order for health to breathe into your soul. Just because that child you possibly abused or neglected has moved out of the home, it does not take away the damage that has already been done to them.

If you are a parent who continues to suffer from guilt, it is also important that you seek help. Guilt comes from the devil. It is not spiritually healthy. Conviction comes from God. Conviction does not leave your side until, hopefully, one day you repent of any wrongdoing you may have caused in your child's harm. God is a healing god, the restorer of paths to dwell in.

In addition, "they that shall be of thee shall build the old waste places; thou shalt rise up the foundations of many generations; and thou shalt be called, the repairer of the breach, the restorer of paths to dwell in" (Isaiah 58:12 KJV).

God can and will help you to become an overcomer. Amends needs to be made to your child if you have directly or indirectly caused harm to them. It is part of the healing and forgiveness process. There truly are no shortcuts.

Although I became a born-again Christian at age twenty-two, I still had a long journey to finding a completeness that could make me whole. It was not until sometime in my forties I started to realize that I was still deeply hurting. God took this miserably calloused heart and continued massaging it, until he finally softened and remolded it into a heart of flesh. A heart that could feel love and give love back out. It was not until many years into my salvation I received a long overdue healing and deliverance. God ultimately restored me and gave me a healed heart of flesh. A continual process took time for completion.

As God massaged my hurting aching heart, he began bringing life back into it. God never quit convicting me or dealing with me, not even in my silence toward him. God was on a mission, and he was determined to perfect the work he had started in me.

I kept trying to hear *above* the noise of my hurting hating heart. The noises of this world are difficult to tune out. They try to tell you that you are entitled and that you have every right to hate. I kept asking God, "Please take this hating heart and recreate it." I would tell God that I did not want to feel this way. Somewhere along the line, God took me for being serious about my pained heart.

Because my burns and treatment were not a subject that was up for discussion or debate in my household, the topic was held captive no matter how hard I tried to get somebody to help me feel my way through it all. When I would get the courage to challenge my mom on *how* it all happened or would attempt to question my mom on her memory of the events surrounding *my burns*, I was barraged with numerous different harsh remarks that varied on severity based on her mood. She would say things such as, "Oh, it was just an accident." "It could have happened to anyone." "Don't think you are so special?" "You're lucky your hair grew back." "At least your face is not scarred." "You're alive, aren't you?" The subject would always immediately be changed. Leaving me with a fiery ball of emotions that were ever growing and never addressed. Along with the remarks came the look that said, "Enough already," and eyes that would say, "Shush, I am trying to live my life, and you keep trying to interrupt it."

My mom had this way of letting me know she was living her life as she pleased. That I was "just" a child and that I was in no way allowed to bother her in her adult existence. She also implied that a child's life had little or no value. She definitely spoke loud and clear to me many times that I was to be seen and not heard.

What I know for sure is that this was one of the most agonizing events that I would ever experience. Therefore, for that reason, I have decided to tell my story.

At the time that I am writing this book, I have entered into my thirty-seventh year of salvation. God's gentle drawing of my soul is why I am the person in Christ that I am. His sovereign love has been upon me and surrounded me to such a degree I feel I must give back to His people.

Writing a book is something that I have known for a long time that I needed to do. For the longest time I did not understand the whole reason for the lengthy time-consuming healing. I thought it was just for me. But as I have been writing this book, I realize that in addition, it is also for the victims of severe accidents, victims who have suffered the loss of body parts, or for victims who have suffered through any form of child abuse and/or child neglect, or have had to be raised in alcoholic homes.

I realize that I needed to share my experiences in order to help other victims who cannot seem to get the footwork done that is required of them in order for them to be able to receive the healing God has for them. I learned that in order to receive the help I needed from God, I had to come to the end of myself. Repentance is mandatory. Most people do not want to be told that they need to repent and be delivered. If they have held others hostage with their dark ungodly emotions, then it is not so much the abuse or loss in their own life that is keeping them from entering into the love of God. But rather, it is far more the unforgiveness held toward others, because of what others have done to you, that they have held on to, that is harming them and keeping them in bondage and unable to receive deliverance from God.

Sometimes you just need to have someone drop down a rope of grace to you that you can grab a hold of. My hope is that this writing may be the rope of grace that you need to grasp on to in order to pull yourself up and out of any hatred, sorrow, sadness, loneliness, or unforgiveness you are in.

At some points in my story, it may seem that there could never be any light possible, that the evil or pain was so severe, but I have hope for you. I have overcome, and you can too.

I hope that you will get a glimpse of a better life: enough to give you a jump start on your journey of healing, deliverance and restoration. Enough to give you the hope that Jesus Christ is our living hope. For those who do not know Him, come to believe that He is your hope that can lead you into divine and ultimate healing and salvation. Through salvation and steps made toward redemption, you can slowly become the person that God intended you to be. Always remember: Let nothing be done through strife or vainglory; but in lowliness of mind let each esteem other better than themselves. (Philippians 2:3 KJV)

This may seem like a scripture taken out of context. However, think about it, when we are harmed or hurt by others, the last thing we usually do is esteem that "thing or person" that has harmed us as higher than ourselves. It is when we let go of controlling the strife we feel about those who have harmed us that God can deal with us, and even better, He can begin dealing with "the other" whatever or whoever it or they may be!

There is hope for the abused: mentally, sexually, emotionally, and physically. You just have to reach for it.

There were so many different areas of my life that I could have written about, but it would have been too much to fit in one book. I have done my best to include different experiences that I feel best fit the subject manner.

As God leads me, there will be more to follow, addressing in further detail some of the events of my life that I have left out but have affected me, such as the sexual abuse that I endured for many years.

SECTION I

An Abandoned Life

CHAPTER ONE

Reckless Flames

"HELPPPP! MOMMYYYY, HELPPPPP! MOMMYYY!" I screamed louder than I had ever screamed in my life as I ran out of my room and into the living room.

"Shush, be quiet, I'm sleeping," she mumbled selfishly, not opening her eyes or getting off the couch to help me. How could she not open her eyes? Can she not hear the torment in my voice? "Go play in your room," she said in another mumble.

This would be one of the many hundreds of times in my life to come that my mom would try and shush me to be quiet. Well, I am no longer remaining quiet.

In a panic, I ran back down the hallway, still consumed by an engorging fire as my nightgown melted into my body. I ran to my parents' room hoping my dad was still home sleeping. Had he slept here last night, or had they had another one of their fights? He was not there. Abandoned. What do I do now? All I have left is my mom.

I turned back around and ran down the same hallway I had previously just come up, returning to the living room yet again. *Please let her be awake now,* I thought. I was screaming and crying as my flesh was burning. Desperate pain. The fire was now all consuming and had burned completely through my flannel nightgown. Horrific pain. A pain no one would ever even begin to understand.

Just minutes before, I had gone into the living room and gotten my mom's purse. I had quietly marched to my bedroom, which I shared with my sister, and approached the twin beds. One was my older sister's, and the other was mine. This particular morning I was all alone, all except my mom, that is. She was fast asleep on the couch in the living room, but that was nothing new. It was where she landed every time she and my dad would fight.

My sister was enjoying a stay over at her friend's house down the street. My dad was at work. Who knows if my mom had locked my two-year-old brother in his room, like it was the rule. Earlier in the year, she had received a phone call from the owner of the Laundromat just a block away from our house. My brother had snuck out of the house and had traipsed down the street on a typical early morning adventure while my mom was still sleeping. In all his exploring, he decided to cross over a very busy street and enter the local Laundromat. He then decided to remove his overly full poopy diaper and then proceeded to smear it all up and down the very nice woman's laundry equipment.

I was told by my mom, in her version, that this is how it was assumed I had caught on fire. I was told that her purse was found in my room after I was burned and before she rushed to the hospital with me. I truly do not remember how I caught on fire ... getting into my mom's purse or even really lighting the match myself. My closest memory is actually being on fire. With my memory as detailed as it is, this part of the story of my life amazes me how I could blank out such a detailed event. But here it goes.

I was told that I placed the half-burnt match in my front chest pocket with the previous match. Possibly thinking, "Enough of this," not realizing what was about to happen. The very warmth of a blown-out match had allegedly ignited my nightgown into a flame, one that I would be fully engulfed in, in no time. I immediately became terrified and freaked out and began running from my bedroom. I was so scared and in horrible agony. I began screaming and crying as I exploded into flames.

In a fiery terror for someone to help me, I turned back to run back down the same hall that I had just come from toward my parents' bedroom. Still burning and all encompassed by burning flames, I continued screaming for someone to help me. My dad had not come home from the night before was my best guess, because he for sure would respond and put this excruciating fire out that was so sadistically burning my flesh at this point.

Oh, how I needed some help. In desperation, I ran back down the hall to the same living room I had previously been denied, hoping that my mom would wake up and get off the couch and rescue me from this all-consuming fire.

By the time I returned to the living room, a large portion of my hair had been singed or burnt off entirely from my head. It was my body's skin that was now fueling the fire—that and the acrylic that was laced into the pajamas I was wearing, which was keeping the fire on my body fueled and fully ignited. It was horribly frightening.

Very groggily and hungover, my mom finally jumped up from the couch as I entered the living room yet again. She aggressively tumbled me down onto the large rope rug, as a linebacker would tackle his opponent. She quickly folded the rug over me from side to side to help squelch the fire out.

I was screaming and crying like no normal parent would ever want to hear his or her four-year-old child exude, pure pain exhaling from my every breath. This was the very last of ordinary that I would see in this life, in this body at least.

Oh, how I wish that I could take just one hour of my life back, but that only happens in a dream.

Once the fire was out, my mom left me lying there as she rushed to the telephone and called the operator.

I lay there crying, my emotions turning inward, the agony of what had just become of my body becoming a reality to me. "Somebody, help me."

The operator put my mom through to the closest hospital. I could not just lie there, the pain was too immense. I was frantic. I was in so much pain. My body was naked and all burned up.

"Help me!" I screamed, sobbing. I felt useless. There was nothing I could do to change what had just happened. Fear surrounded me from all angles. The pain was so horrific; in writing I cannot even think of any adjective that can remotely begin to describe the pain I was feeling. I was shaking and trembling with a mixture of intense heat and pure ice all at the same time.

While my mom was still on the phone, I got up, pain shooting through every ounce of my being, and went to my room barely able to walk. Sloping on the edge of the twin bed, unable to stand still, I could hear my mom talking to someone on the phone. As I looked at her, my vision seemed to tunnel and the distance seemed so far. This sensation would repeat later in my life. *Why is she talking so long on the stupid phone? Why won't she help me? This hurts so bad.* Each second seemed like a minute. Even in my torment, I knew enough to be quiet because she was talking on the phone. I had no communication with my mom, only tears.

"Put Oleo margarine on her burns," the hospital attendant told my mom over the phone.

There I was standing in my room completely naked and fully exposed, skin hanging off my puny body. Any movement I made, any breath I took made the pain even more severe. In came my mom with a softened cube of Oleo (½ butter, ½ margarine) in her hands. She tried to apply it to the charred skin, but I wailed, "Don't touch me, don't do that anymore, it hurts." It was at that point that my mom finally realized how badly my body had been burnt. My mom gave up on the Oleo, proceeded to get a white bath towel, and threw it over the backside of my shoulders, which was one of the only parts of my body that was not brutally burned up. She told me to stand there and that she would be right back. Abandoned.

She changed her clothes quickly and came back into the bedroom. She tried to grab me up into her arms so that she could carry me to the car, but it hurt too badly. She quickly let me down so that I could walk on my own. I followed her outside to the car. She opened the car door, and I jumped in myself. I did not want her to touch me because at that point even the bath towel that was around my shoulders was hurting and had begun sticking to the burned part of my body. Once I jumped up into the front seat, I shrugged the towel off my shoulders because it only caused me more pain. At that point, I had stopped screaming or even crying, because every breath hurt. I stood balancing myself on top of the front seat completely nude and exposed.

Unbeknown to me, inhaling the hot fumes of the fire had shriveled up a portion of my right lung to about half of its normal size. A detail I would not learn until I was seventeen years old.

My mom backed up out of the driveway rapidly. The neighbor was walking with my sister to school outside at the same time we were rushing to get to the hospital. Rolling down her window, she hollered out, "You get on to school, and I will see you when you get out." In shock, I do not remember most of the ride.

Once we arrived at the emergency room parking area, my mom carried me in. She was in a complete panic at this point. As she stood me up on the waiting room bench, I scanned the all too public waiting room filled with so many vacant faces all turned toward me. I was shaking in an uncontrollable fierce shiver. Naked with not a stitch of clothes on just a towel dangling halfway my left shoulder, which my mom kept trying to reassign on my shoulder; I kept shrugging it off because it hurt being on me. I was so afraid and in so much pain. "Somebody please stop the pain," I thought. Though I appeared silent, on the inside I was sobbing; desperately wishing I could scream. Oh, how I needed to scream, but I knew that would not be acceptable. It was not long before they took me back to a smaller intake room to do paperwork. Paperwork. The nurse was trying to get my mom's medical information. All of this needed to be done before they would see me as a patient. (This law has now been changed; the hospital must admit all incoming emergency patients, regardless of insurance coverage.) We were sitting in a small room with a metal stainless steel bench that my mom instructed me to sit on. I could not sit. It hurt to move and to bend. Stark naked and in ghastly despair, I chose to stand on top of the bench next to my mom. I had gone into total shock. That was the end of normal for me.

The End of Normal

The next thing I remember is a black oxygen or anesthesia mask coming down over my face. None of the medical staff looked me in the eye or addressed me. They had me on a hospital bed, and I was rushed down the hall and into ICU. There were a couple doctors and a couple nurses, a lot of noise and a great sense of urgency. Many scary strange faces. I did not struggle. I did not have the energy. My mom was no longer there. The attendees took complete control of the situation at hand.

The first time they put the black mask on my face, even at my young age, I knew that a portion of my body was gone for good; it had been eaten up by fire. I really did not think I would live. Looking down at my body, I really did not want to live either. In my heart and mind, I kept that determined attitude about dying with me for months. It was not until many months later when Jesus and his five little angels decided to show up dancing around my bed that night, that great and miraculous night, that I finally got the courage to decide to live in this damaged decaying body.

The next memory I have was the male doctor putting the black anesthesia mask over my face again, which could have been days or weeks later. Knowing how this mask would make me feel, I went down kicking and fighting. The anesthesiologist placed that big black scuba-looking, plunger-looking mask over my face. I had freaked out this time. I remembered it from before how strange it had made me feel. I could not breathe; he would not take it off either. Matter of fact, he held it down firmly on my face so that I could not take it off. I thought I was going to suffocate. When I woke up to all those green bandages wrapped up and down my poor helpless body, I had made my mind up that the next time I was not going to just lie there and volunteer to be a submissive patient.

My memory seemed so foggy. All of a sudden, I remembered the last time I had went under the black mask. So there was a time before? Wow, how many other times had I been under that big black mask and not remembered? I remembered from before that when I came out from surgery, I was in more pain than when I had went into surgery, no matter how many painkillers they gave me.

My memory was not very good because of all the heavy painkillers they were injecting into me.

What I do remember is how they would cut, scrape, and pick on my body whenever they wanted to; this is what I thought as four years old. The big black mask would taste funny it would make my mouth, throat, and tongue go numb. I would see weird black-and-white miniature checkers right before I would get ready to pass out. The big black mask was just plain ol' scary. Each time they put me under, it caused me to dislike adults even more.

Several weeks had passed. During these weeks, the doctors had done a series of cleansing of the wounds. It would entail a team of four to six surgical doctors and nurses who would come up to my bed. They of course would be decked out in their sickeningly green attire—from head covering to facial mask and of course feet coverings. What a scary sight for a young girl. How ironic, green of all shades became and still is my favorite color to this day.

The long heavy curtain that surrounded me would be opened up completely. They would keep my curtains closed most all the time. I am certain it was so that the other children on the ward would not get scared looking at me; even though it was the Burn Ward, no one there at the time was burned nearly as badly as I was.

The white volleyball-looking net that covered the top of my crib would be removed. They would lower the arm on my crib bed and put me onto an operating bed, and in for the count, they would reach in and get me.

Many times, I would get agitated and anxious; most often they would just inject more morphine in my IVs. Once I calmed down, they would then roll me down a hall, enter into an elevator, and take me to what was the stainless steel room.

Once we entered into this room, they would move me over to a stainless steel operating table. Over the table would be hanging a series of high-beam surgical lights. These lights were like heat lamps; they were used as a high-beam light to help assist the surgeons accomplish their job properly, and possibly to help keep me warm. They would usually start the procedure by dousing my body down with a good amount of orange-red Betadine sanitizer sterilizer. This would soak into the bandages, as well as make my body shivering cold. That did not stop them though; they were on a mission, and they intended on completing it.

21

Once they removed as many of the bandages as they could without damaging the wounds, and without drugging me up to oblivion, they would change things up somewhat.

You see, the bandages did not come off willingly. Most often, if not always, they would have to tug and force the removal of the bandages. They would become entrenched in between the hardened dried blood and white and lime-green secretions, most often requiring them to apply painful force, which inevitably would require drugging me up to numb me so that they could proceed with removing the bandages and so that I could withstand the pain. The follow-through of removing these terribly soiled bandages was a horrible job no doctor or nurse should have to endure.

In between all these different procedures, I would be given additional pain med injections anytime they felt I was feeling the least bit of pain.

Once they were able to remove a majority of the bandages, their job would continue with their original intention—to remove any infected scabs, dead skin, or hardened-up plastic (that acted as glass would in someone's skin) from the severely damaged area.

This was in the sixties where many pajamas had an acrylic-base plastic in the material, making it more susceptible to igniting easier to fire. Sometime in the seventies, the government got involved after many reports of people being burned to death and passed a ruling demanding all child pajamas to be flame-retardant.

They would start in by using some very long surgical tweezer-looking instruments and other ominous medical utensils. They would begin mildly and end up becoming more and more aggressive the deeper into the wounds they dove.

Pick, pick, and picking the scabs that had formed on my little body. I would always slide in and out of consciousness. Many times, I would awake out of a deeper consciousness when one or two of the surgeons would tug harder than I could mentally handle. This called for further injections of morphine.

I would plead with them, "Please stop." But with no relief in sight, they would continue. Any movement or resistance on my part was case for additional medication. Knocking me out, yet again. I was miserable, it was miserable; the whole entire event was just plan miserable.

I would act out by begging them, "Please stop." But with each attempt, there was just the same ol' consequence: morphine. I am seriously surprised they did not overdose me and kill me.

Jacuzzi's Not So Cool After All

Once they had removed a sufficient amount of infected scabbing, they would wheel me over (in the same room) to a huge stainless steel bath. This tub was similar to a Jacuzzi tub. It would be filled with warm water and some sort of salt cleanser. The water would be violently whirling around in a very frightening fashion for a young child. They never got less scary—ever.

Each time as they would begin to lower me into the stinging salt baths, I would scream, kick, and throw a tantrum. This of course would lead to more morphine, which I quickly learned to despise. I despised women, I despised men, I despised women and men, and I particularly despised morphine.

I would feel internally violent and full of rage, definitely revengeful. I wanted it to stop, and I wanted it to stop right now.

The result was always the same: I was placed into the water yet again.

The next thing I would remember was waking up on that doggone stainless steel table again. I would awake to the same doctors and nurses. They would be just picking away at all the waterlogged awkward-sized pieces of white clotty and chunky scabs and green puss–looking corpuscles. Mixed in with all this was a whole lot of blood and secretions both clear and cloudy. It was disgusting. It would make me feel so filthy. There were many larger hardened pieces of scab that had never been affected by the soaking of the water. I did not understand why they kept it up, because the more they picked, the more it bled—what a mess. One that would repeat itself over and over again for months to come.

Pulling, tugging, jerking, methodically yanking, removing, discarding, and chunk after chunk they would continue to work furiously.

It was the strangest thing for a young abandoned child to watch. My deepest agony yet, it was even more excruciating than the initial burns. This would carry on for several hours at a time. Going down into the salt baths for a second time in a day sometimes. Painfully angry.

I just wanted to scrub it all off and make it all go away. That did not happen.

Oh, the unendurable stench, the smell mercilessly gagged me. I would look around at the nurses and doctors, and I could see how they were desperately trying to hide their body's natural reaction to throwing up as they worked reverently to clean up the disastrous mess my body had become.

This cleanup process was unrelenting, each time taking them hours to complete. The procedure was so actively difficult to perform, hours and hours on end of extreme heat beating down on the bodies of those servants of the medical field's bodies. There would be beads of sweat falling off their foreheads. When this would happen, they would excuse themselves, step out of the area, clean up, and enter back in and continue working diligently. The nurses would rotate in and out, just to get a break from the intimate act at large. The doctors never did; they remained steadfast until the final task was completed. Men are so resilient that way. God made them that way for a reason. Hard workers they can truly be.

The room would feel solemn, the doctors and nurses shaking their heads in a negative manner, at times gagging, not having conversation beyond a few comments over long periods.

When they would speak, I could of course hear their comments, and it would frighten me immensely. I felt like they were being mean when they would throw their thoughts so indiscreetly out for all to hear. Giving no real care that I may be able to hear and understand them, despite all the drugs I was under the influence of.

I realize I was young; however, I had grown up so fast when my body burst into flames that very early spring morning.

Having been introduced to such trauma had caused me to be overly sensitive to just about everything going on in my life, both within me and around me. It has been called oversensitized now in the 2000s.

"Poor little girl," they would say carelessly. "I will be greatly surprised if she makes it," another nurse would blurt out. One doctor spoke something that imbedded fear into me. He very quietly whispered, "I don't know, she might be better off dying." Words I would try to forget from that day forward, yet words that would haunt me on and off the remainder of my life.

Grandma's Got Some Explaining to Do

I would awake off and on in Burn Ward to see my grandma sitting by my side. She would be sitting alongside my bed in a chair. She tried to explain to a four-year-old where I had been and what had happened to me. She explained to me that I had spent weeks in my special room (ICU) as the doctors were trying to help me get better, as she would put it. I was extremely scared, ridiculously nervous, severely anxious, and frightfully fearful of what was going to happen to me next. I thought to myself, "Do I even want to live?" There were so many thoughts racing through my mind—far too many for a young girl to have to deal with. These fear-laced emotions soon would turn to anger.

I am certain my grandma could discern the fear in my eyes; after all, she knew me best. Nonetheless, she continued to try to explain what had happened to me, making sure I was informed; that is just how my grandma was.

During all the many weeks of memory fog, the doctors had performed two different plastic surgeries and grafting. This first surgery, they took skin from my left hip and rear area; the second time they removed a five-by-fifteen patch off the right side of my outer thigh and buttocks.

My grandma's presence was the only comfort I received. She had the most beautiful cobalt-blue eyes. No pain medication in the world were as comforting as those shiny gorgeous eyes. What was not so comforting were the green bandages that remained wrapped all up and down my body, from head to ankle, pressing up against my blistering third-degree burned excuse for skin. I hurt. I felt all weird and peculiar both on the inside and on the outside. I looked like a four-legged monster, with nothing left but a few singed pieces of hair on top of my head. What are all these plastic cords that are attached to me? Who was going to help me? Where were my mommy and my daddy? Somebody needs to help me now! Though I lay there all drugged up and calm on the outside, I was raging with uncontrolled emotion on the inside.

This was the beginning of many years filled with an urgent sense of anxiety in my life. I felt unusual inside from all the morphine that they were constantly pumping into me. Little did I know I had been in the hospital Burn Ward for weeks in a drug-induced coma. I guess one could say the doctors had done their job well.

You see, seventy percent of my body had been burnt that early spring morning I went running so violently through my home. Forty percent had been third degree. That portion nearly took my life.

What I was not aware of is that there had already been multiple efforts by the doctors and nurses to remove as much of the lifeless, morphed, hardened dead skin and particles of plastic that had been burned up and yet was stuck into my remaining flesh. They could only do so much each time they worked on my skin. So days and weeks later, they were still trying to get me stable and my body out of rejection mode. It was only by the grace of God I had made it thus far.

Overwhelming Stench

One of the heftiest emotions that I had was that I stunk, because I did. Each time the physicians would unwrap me from the bandages, a decaying strong stagnate odor would be completely overwhelming. I smelled putrid and vile. A very gross and unbelievably potent stench of dead infected skin would radiate from my body. This was so shaming. As a four-year-old little child, I felt so helpless, so imprisoned in my body as well as confined in my cage of a crib. I was so humiliated that the appalling smell was searing from me. It was the elephant in the room that no one wanted to speak of. To watch the eye language between the nursing staff was very defaming. I knew those eyes were rolling, because of me, and the odor I was protruding into the room.

Later on as I returned home, if for one second I thought someone could smell me, I would avoid eye contact with them. This was my way of ignoring the problem. It is called self-preservation.

After each undraping of the bandages and picking session, the nurses would follow a careful regimented procedure. They would finish the procedure by carefully, light-handedly applying a thick layer of yellow salve-like lanolin-vitamin E ointment all over my infected areas. Then they would wrap my delicate body back up in many layers of a loosely woven white cotton dressing followed by many layers of a heavier, weightier cotton dressing followed with the heaviest, a white eight- or nine-inch-wide Ace bandage-looking dressing. This would hurt incredibly. Any weight that was placed on my burns only caused me more induced pain. Resulting in a whole lot of additional weight being placed on my wounds, which was incredibly miserable. Once the burns were thoroughly covered, they would then wrap me with yet the final layer of material, this one being the ugly green color I described earlier.

When it was time to change the dressings, the green outer dressing would come off without any problems. The white Ace bandage-looking bandaging usually came off without a hitch. The white gauze dressing would inevitability have embedded itself into the grooves of my open, oozing wound. The nurses and doctors would try their best to remove as much of the bandaging as they could. However, the wounds would bleed off a huge amount of discharge. The puss and blood would ooze through the dressings and would stiffen and harden, encasing the bandaging and would be irremovable. The thickest part would drain to the lowest point of my concaved side and would be entrenched and trapped into the cloth dressing. This would cause a whole lot more work for the physicians each time they would remove my bandages to service the wounds.

I was feeling dark and lonely, scared and angry on the inside. Abandoned by love. At four years old, I knew enough to know there was a problem, one that was not going away soon.

They kept me in this heavily medicated fog for weeks on end. A lot of which I cannot recall. It was in that time that I suffered a deep-rooted loneliness that I would later receive help for in 1994 by way of an antidepressant called Zoloft. I remained in need of antidepressants for eighteen years.

As days and weeks passed by, the doctors and nurses would continue to perform a series of scab picking. Yes, I said scab picking.

As weeks passed, the doctors would come in and see me, assessing how I was or was not doing. I believe they knew at this point I had a staph infection, they just had not released this very important information to my grandma; that is why they were doing all the extensive picking and salt baths.

Maddening Salt Baths

Having been near death for many months of my young life had changed who I was as a person. My small little body, oh the pain, every breath, every slight movement. The heartache I suffered from by feeling and seeing the ruin that had happened to my body. I could feel the loss as the healthy layer of my body had been taken from me. That would be a feeling of loss that I thought would never leave me. A loss that years later God would walk me through, helping me to grieve the loss of my body.

Each event only seemed to deepen my mistrust in adults.

They would start in again. Pick, pick, picking the scabs that had formed off my little body. I would slide in and out of consciousness many different times during this horrific procedure.

Many times I would awake from a drug-induced unconscientiousness and would begin kicking and screaming. I would plead with them, "Please Stop," but any movement or resistance on my part called for further increase in medication. This would only serve to knock me out yet again.

The drugs would make me feel nauseated, out of control, and anxious. However, slowly I would pass out again. It was miserable. One session of the scab picking would take hours. I know because they would come and get me right after the children on my ward would eat lunch, and I would be returned right close to dinner, being served with the same children on the same ward. Last, I calculated that is close to four or five hours. I was not eating at this point in my recovery.

Each time, I would act out and start begging them to quit all the picking and probing. One or the other of the nurses would make a lame response like, "The grafting has to be policed and kept as clean as possible, Cynthia." As if I understood what the word *policed* meant. I have never forgotten that word, *policed*.

I felt so helpless and out of control. No matter how hard I kicked and squirmed and fought, they would not stop. The only peace I got was when I lost consciousness temporarily. Thank God.

After they finished picking off all the scabs they could remove, they would move me into this oversized stainless steel tub with Jacuzzi jets shooting the saltwater around violently—same receptive cycle.

I would begin in with all the shouting, kicking, and struggling. "No, no!" I would scream, but nonetheless they were going to put me down in that stinging salt bath.

Each time that they would try to lower me down into the vicious warm water, they were driven to inject me with more morphine just to be able to force me down in the tub, despise took over in my heart. I can recall the violent feeling that would take me over each time I had to go through this horrific event. They were going to place me in the water no matter what I said. Thankfully, a mixture of the morphine and the shock of such a horrendous painful procedure would cause me to pass out.

I thought that I was getting better, but that was not the case.

CHAPTER TWO

Say Your Goodbyes

THIS PARTICULAR DAY, MY MOM was following my grandma as they both entered, walking down the long Burn Ward walkway. My grandma was so sad. My mom, whom I do not recall visiting but twice, was just physically there. The rest of her was checked out. My mom and my grandma never saw eye to eye on anything. On the rare occasions that they were in the same room, there was always a notable friction. On this morning, though, I sensed that something was different. Grandma's blue eyes were not smiling. Mom was so quiet.

The doctor came in to the room; I was still in my crib with the netting off. He pulled my grandma and my mom to the side; sensing that Grandma was the one in authority, he spoke to her quietly.

They seemed to be just out of my hearing range, yet I struggled to see what it was that he was saying to cause such sad looks on their faces. Finally, after what seemed like forever, they slowly approached my crib as they continued to talk. I will never forget what I heard.

He solemnly said, "I am so sorry to tell you this. We have given it our best work. The staph infection has taken over her body. Nothing short of a miracle will save her."

My grandmother tried so hard to stifle her sob, but it still slipped out.

"You really should say your goodbyes to her. She probably won't make it through the night."

With this, the doctor left the room.

I will never forget this day. I kept waiting for my grandma to say something. I was certain she would. My mom quickly excused herself. She went home or whatever she did all day while I sat in the hospital. MIA as usual. I think she must have been asked to come that day, by the doctors, in order to receive the news. Time ticked by, but she just went on with the rest of the day as if nothing had been said, like she had not just heard the news that I was dying. She carried on, keeping her busy routine as usual.

The day moved on like any other typical day. Standard. Repetitive. My grandma remained; she always was the one I could rely on.

The doctors had told my grandma that I had contracted a staph infection and that no amount of surgeries or salt baths could help me.

I remember hearing, "She isn't doing well … Chances are that she is not going to make it through the night … I can't believe she's still alive," and other comments such as these on a daily basis. Their comments were always negative. They would discuss things right in front of me, as if I was not even there. I suppose that since I was drugged up on morphine, they figured I was too young to understand. I understood perfectly. I was going to die.

One doctor even said in one of these conversations, "It would probably be better for her if she were to just die. The repercussions of living in these scars would be almost unbearable."

Later in life I came to understand these were actually curses that had been placed on me, unknowingly by the people saying them. Once I realized the stronghold the words that had been so naively been spoken over me, had upon my life, God moved me to fast, pray, and to seek for a breakthrough. In 2014, God broke the satanic stronghold that these words had over my life. What a difference a few days of prayer, fasting, and deliverance can make in a person's life.

My grandma continued to visit me each and every day. I do not think a day went by that she did not visit.

I still spent many long days existing down inside that cage of a crib. The top of the crib was covered in white messed netting, like what you would see on a volleyball court. I detested that crib. Where did they think I was going to go anyhow? These were the thoughts in my now five-year-old mind. The caged crib would cause me additional apprehension, anxiety, and constant feelings of entrapment, as I grew older. It was not until I was in my midforties that God would disclose to me that this was one of the core root issues that were connected to this daunting anxiety that continually hovered over me. God took me through a series of deliverances, and this was just one more He added to the mix.

It was several months in to my hospital stay that I began to feel desperately lonely. A loneliness that would haunt me for fifty years. A deep-seated loneliness. I became scared, hard, angry, and accusatory. All these feelings were in my head. I never expressed verbally how I really "felt" about being burned. The topic was never up for debate. I would look down on my bandages or on the times when the doctors and nurses would unbandage me and leave me naked so they could examine me, and I would start feeling ill. The smell gagged me. The sight of the burns made me feel so very ugly. I would see the look on the doctors' and nurses' faces as they glared down at my small little being. So pathetic. I took those thoughts that I perceived they were thinking, and I internalized them. It would be the way I was to feel about myself for many years to come: all the way deep down in my soul. They would be feelings I would need to swim through in order to find peace. Though those feelings turned to shame and tried to destroy me, I was more determined than ever to be rid of them—and to instead be an overcomer.

Jesus and the Five Lil' Angels Dancing

I woke up from an evening sleep; it was late into the night. I awoke to see Jesus and five little angels dancing around my bed. Like an unseen air was gently and gracefully moving them around the bed. Their feet were not touching the ground. Jesus was on the left side of my bed and was leading what seemed to be a pack of angels. I began to count them—one, two; there were a total of five angels, similar to my height at the time, and they were following in a dance pattern that was so soothing, there was no reason to be scared. These five lil' angels were each holding one another's hands; as with the first angel, she was holding on to Jesus's hand. They were following Jesus in a rhythmical skip, like a skipping dancing move. As they methodically flowed around the bed moving in a pattern that only heaven could understand. I could not help but notice how carefree and happy they all seemed. Jesus never looked at me, nor did any of the angels. Jesus was wearing a long sheet like a drape, as were the five little angels, similar to a long flowing pajama gown. Each had what looked like a rose ribbon belt-looking thing and one around their foreheads. The roses were dark burgundy layered tightly upon the sashes. Jesus only had one on his forehead—all in the same coloring. The roses had an even deeper-dark-purple burgundy in the rim of the roses. All this was very detailed. As they skipped around my bed, they formed a circular motion. I could not help but notice how elegantly they all seemed skimming across the floor. Their gowns were so very long, and yet they were not bothered one bit at how very long they were. Not a care in the world. Wow what a wonderful way to be. Oh, how I wanted to be out of the pain I was so deeply in. I thought about it for a second or two, and the thought crossed my mind, I wanted to be with them. Without any verbal communication, I could hear this voice. It translated a thought to me, one that would change my life on this earth forever. It seemed as if nothing hindered them from going about their angelic mission, to come and visit me, and to get me to make up my mind to whether I wanted to live or die. This voice impressed upon me that it would rather I decide to live; however, if I wanted to die and go to be with Jesus, that was okay too. It was as if I translated back to the voice, that I was not sure I could hold up to the accountability of living in this scarred-up body. Again, this voice impressed upon me that it was my choice. This voice spoke clearly and said in me, "You will have the strength to withstand the people of this world." Jesus was holding on to the first lil' angel's hand, to form a completed line dancing around and around near my bed. It was at that point that I decided that I was going to choose to live or give it my best shot. Slowly, Jesus escorted them off their heavenly platform.

At five years old, I knew enough to know that I was going to live. Now living with these ugly scars would prove to be a much more difficult ordeal. Little did I know that God's will for me to live far surpassed my own desire to live. Little did I know how bitter my heart would become or how hate would try its best to entirely consume me.

Having no idea that burns on one's body are not acceptable by society, or by rude people, I was not prepared for what life had in store for me. All I knew in that moment was that I was alive, breathing, and that I was going to survive another day.

It was like little curses being spoken over me again and again. I struggled through this in life until I finally received deliverance from the unknowing curses in my early fifties.

Like a wave that came smashing down upon me that wonderful angelic day, it would be only just the beginning of a fight for my mental sanity and my spiritual deliverance. From hollow family tree generational curses, generational strongholds and addictions to negative dark emotions, it was a lot for one child to bear.

Out came the two white Styrofoam cups. One was filled with small cut pieces of watermelon and the other with cantaloupe. Because of all the bandages, I could not feed myself very well, so Grandma fed me the juicy ripe fruit piece by piece. As usual, I had no appetite because of all the medicines and being fed intravenously for so long. I began to have a real love for fruit. Fruit represented the depth of love my grandma had for me. Nurturing. Warmth. Hope.

Each day, my grandma would come and visit. As she would approach my bed, she would always whistle; it definitely was not whistling Dixie, it was more of an off-key and constant whistle that she would do merely to alert me that it was she on the way to my bed. At that point, in my hospital stay, anyone approaching my area would bring up instant fear of the unknown. Though that may seem insignificant, the memory of that whistle is something that brings me an instant invited chuckle and a joy to this day.

Each day since the ominous news from the doctor, she would end her visit by saying, "I love you, Cindy. I'll see you tomorrow." Sometimes, she would even wink. I knew my grandma loved me, I could feel it. Who would say that they would be seeing me tomorrow … if I was going to die?

As the years went by, I would use the love I could feel coming from my grandma as a gauge to measure with, any amount of love coming from other people. In order for me to allow others into my circle of love, they would have to measure up to the love-gauge that had been instilled in me from the love of my grandma. This measuring tape of love would prove to help protect me from any false hope others would try to give me by telling me that they loved me.

Existence after Salt Baths

Amazingly, after Jesus and the lil' angels visited me, I was getting more and more well. The nurses would come to my bed twice a day to come and prick my small finger for blood, smearing it on one of their glass slides. I noticed before too long that the nurse would return to test my blood, and there was a smile that accompanied her face, which I had not previously seen. My blood count was finally rising. During this time, the old surgical nurses and doctors who had performed all the debris-removal torture started one by one popping their head into my curtain in order to witness my miraculous recovery. They would always appear so overjoyed to see that the girl they thought was doomed was finally healing. Overcoming I was.

After much travail, many weeks of torment, excruciating pain, and debilitating fear, I was finally on my way to healing. It amazes me that the side of my body, as concaved and deteriorated as it was, kept trying to heal. Do not let me fool you; the trauma was not over. I was still all wrapped in those ugly green dressings. I still had to have those dressings changed. I was still on heavy pain meds. Still getting my daily pinpricks for blood counts etc., still not allowed to get out of the loathsome cage of a crib and walk around. Besides the watermelon and cantaloupe that my grandmother brought with her, I had not had any desire to eat much of anything of value. I relied on liquid vitamins. At least it was no longer constant turmoil.

I was beginning to see a way out of this torment that was my burnt body. I could just act as if none of it was there. I could act as if I was just living out a really bad movie, telling myself that this horrific event was not real and definitely did not happen to little ol' me. I could just forget that it ever happened at all. I began to pretend that these burns just were not there. In my mind, I began to fantasize that I had a normal unscarred body. This seemed at the time to make it easier for me to swallow; the ugliness of the scars were just too unbearable for me to accept. I would try and convince myself that the entire event never even happened. I began living in my mind, the only place that seemed safe for me to feel.

While on the Burn Ward, to the right side of me, on the opposite side of the room, I had the displeasure of meeting a punk male kid. From the looks of things, he had been there awhile, and he had very few visitors. He had old used syringes, minus the actual needle. Trying to aggravate me, he would threaten me with these syringes. He would tell me he was going to come over to my bed and give me a shot. I would get so scared. I was receiving some sort of shot several times a day, and I would be very nervous and anxious every time the nurses would give them to me. They would administer them to me in my left upper arm, one of the only areas of my upper body that was burn free. I am certain these shots were painkillers and antibiotics. The burns were still healing, and I was still living in an awful lot of pain. This older boy thought he would get his thrills by pretending he had any power at all to come over and give me a shot. I can only imagine that he quite possibly had bullying issues that he had to deal with, as he grew older, you think?

As the days would pass by, I was beginning to finally get clearer thoughts. I was coming out from under the fog of the heavily injected morphine. I realized I had not seen my mom and dad almost the entire time I was in the hospital. I could recall my mom having been there two times, and she had not returned since the bad news from the doctor. My dad only visited once. My grandma was not a fan of either of them. She had told my dad to never return.

I do not remember before the age of three feeling this horrible animosity inside of me toward my mom. Recently, my aunt has confirmed to me that both she and my grandmother raised me at this time of my life. She explained to me that when I was born, my mom told my aunt that she could name me, and so she did. After my birth, when it came time to leave the hospital, my aunt and my grandmother took me home with them to live. My grandma was not satisfied with the way my mom had been taking care of my older sister thus far, so why should she trust her to make any changes? She announced aggressively that she would be taking me home from the hospital, and so it was. My mom was not bothered by this arrangement. It actually was more convenient for her. One less mouth to feed. I was told years later once my grandma passed away, of course, that I was breastfed as an infant. Really? This was far before breast pumps. Why add such a huge whopping lie on top of an already destructive life story? There was no breastfeeding going on here. The lies people tell themselves so that they can live with themselves. Lies lies lies. Despicable.

My mom and dad were living in a house that they had built. My dad was always a hard worker, constantly working to make more money to provide for his family. He was deeply in love with my mother, and he kept trying with all his might to do the right thing in their lives. He lacked the skills though. The problem was that they wanted the things of this world more than they wanted God in their lives. As far back as I can remember, both my parents smoked and drank on a daily basis. It seemed to only increase the rest of my childhood days. Consequently, I never bonded with either my mom or dad; instead, I bonded with my grandma and aunt.

My parents began being the life of the party. They ended up partying just about every night. Amazingly, on Sunday they would attend church and even taught Sunday school. The problem being, you cannot mix the two. If you put a little mud in the water, you get contaminated muddy water. Fact.

CHAPTER THREE

Miserable Homecoming

IT WAS A GLOOMY DAY, as if the clouds wanted to rain but they could not. My mom had come to bring me home from the hospital. My grandma was also there on that very petrifying overcast day. I drove home in a car with my mom. Along with her was a strange woman I had never seen before. She was a beautiful soft-spoken and kind woman who would be my new nanny. My grandma had hired her to help with my recovery as well as to help with all the household responsibilities. The ride home was supposed to be a happy one; however, it was very frightening. I felt very uncomfortable sitting in the car. No matter how I tried to adjust my bandaged body, I could feel even the slightest bump. I was nervous on the inside as well as on the outside. I was scared to death of my mom.

We pulled up to my house, the same house I had caught fire in. *Really*, I thought, *do I really have to go back into that house?* Fear was my friend since my grandma—who had become all I could rely on for months—did not ride home with me that day. I longed for her comfort. I just did not know what to expect. I had turned five in the hospital. While I do not recall much of it, I do remember that I did not want a birthday cake. I definitely did not want one with candles on it. My mom was young, and I do not think the reality of me being burnt was real to her. On the ride home from the hospital, she was more concerned about telling me that she was having a birthday party for me than she was about my comfort. She kept blabbing on and on. "This is going to be the best birthday party. All of your friends are coming over. There is going to be a piñata, and you are going to have fun," she commanded in a matter-of-fact tone. I could care less about any birthday, let alone a dumb party. I was more concerned about being seen by anyone. I was embarrassed to be seen with all these bandages still covering a large portion of my body. I longed for the solitude I had become accustomed to in the hospital. The last thing I wanted was to have friends around me. Celebrating a birthday was not on my bucket list.

The next-door neighbor was keeping an eye on my two siblings, and they were both there at the house when we arrived home. My older sister and my younger brother—a ray of sunshine on such a dark and cloudy day. Especially my brother, I loved him a lot; while I was not as close to my sister, I was close to my brother. I could only remember seeing the both of them one or two times since I had been burnt. Once I was transferred on to the Burn Ward, Mom brought them to see me outside the hospital room window. They were too young to enter the hospital. I suppose that once it was determined that I might survive, my grandma felt it was safe to bring them to see me. I was thankful for my grandma's discernment.

After my mom did not wake up the day I was burned, I did not feel safe being alone around my mom ever again—for the remainder of my life. I can only assume that the reason that I did not see my brother and sister is that my mom did not feel comfortable coming to the hospital after being intimidated by my very adamant grandma.

Explain This One, Mom

"Your dad is no longer going to be living with us," my mom said to me as I entered in at the front door of my old dark house. "He has moved out completely," she stated as a fact. Fear froze me on the inside. Disappointment blanketed me as she told me this part of the equation that she felt was so insignificant. Did she not know that he was my only hope I had left in this gloomy pit of a home? I just wanted to go hide under a rock. I remember feeling extremely uneasy that my dad was not going to be living with us anymore. Who was going to comfort and protect me? Obviously not her. How could I trust her?

All I wanted to do was go lie down and to be left alone. I hurt all over the place. I worried, did I smell? Depression had already begun to set in. My needs were not even a forethought; instead, there was going to be a party for me. I explained that I did not want to have a party. Nevertheless, there was a going to be one. I repeated again to her that I in no way wanted to have a party. I was shushed yet again. "Just get over it. The party is happening, and people are already coming over." I knew the niceness could not last too much longer.

I Said No Stinkin' Piñata, Lady

Within a short while after arriving home, there were friends of my mom showing up. Of course, they all had children. They flooded into our small home. The noise immediately began to bother me. Once all the company showed up, we were swiftly escorted to the backyard. There was a piñata dangling down from the wood lattice patio covering. I guess I was supposed to act excited, but I was not. What was she thinking? I did not participate in the hitting of the piñata. Duh. I really could not. My right arm was not in the best shape; it was very weak and was still healing from the last reconstructive grafting surgery.

My thought as a young girl was, what are these people thinking? Was the cake going to have candles on it? How long was I going to have to stand around and act all happy? And finally, when would this horrible nightmare end? Nobody even cared about what I needed or wanted. The only important thing was the outward appearance and trying to make our little family seem healthy and whole. What a big fat lie that was.

It did not take me long to realize that it was all about making my mom feel good. Out came the alcohol. Did she not learn from what had happened to me? I guess not! After all, she was a young parent, only sixteen when I was born, twenty-one at the time of this party. What could I have expected? The problem was these ugly defaming scars. What could I do so these scars would go away? Who cares about a stupid party anyhow, were my thoughts. What was there to celebrate anyway? I did my best to play the part.

About a half hour into the party, my grandma and my aunt showed up. Finally a trustworthy face, I thought. It did not take long for my grandma to be able to read the looks on my face and realize the torment that this party was causing for me. She went straight up to my mom to confront her on the relevance of having such an event when I was in no way in the proper mind-set to handle all this chaos. The argument escalated quickly and ended by my grandma and aunt leaving the party and me. The drinking escalated. The nightmare was not ending anytime soon. I was exhausted by the time the party was over.

Life of a Lie

Here is the thing. I was starting my life again living a lie. My scars happened to be in an area on my body to where I could hide the majority of them. I was placed in a position to where I felt I was to blame; at least this is how my mom made me feel. If I would have just gone by her rules and stayed out of her purse, then I would have never had the accident in the first place. Wow, what a responsibility to place on a four-year-old. I guess it was easier than her taking any blame. Denial was so much more convenient to grab on to—that and the beer bottle.

Hiding my scars and all the mischief and chaos they caused seemed to be the easiest way for me to exist in my home. I had decided to not share my experience with others, and that seemed just fine with my mom.

In making this decision, I was, in all reality, hiding who I really was. Instead, I made up who I wanted people to think I was. I thought I was not good enough for anyone to love me as I was. This is not good for a child's soul.

In the Way Again

Each crack of the skin, each outbreak and bursting open of a scab hurt severely. Something I was not allowed to complain or cry about, only "report it" to the nanny so that she could help "fix" the problem. Yes, I felt like I was just one big problem. I was in the way again.

Returning home from the hospital seemed exciting for about ten minutes. Then the truth set in of all the physical pain I was in. As I have been told, I was sent home from the hospital with a twenty-four-hour regiment of prescription painkillers. I do not ever remember being given any once I returned home. That is still an unanswered question that brings me much concern to this day.

Make no mistake, I was in pain. I still felt tired and weak all of the time with very little appetite. I did not want to get out of bed nor did I want to "play" with anyone or anything. My mom did not seem to want to understand this concept. While I understand that she was young and in full-blown denial mode, it still did not reduce the emotional and physical pain I was in.

My scars and graftings were still extremely sore; they continued to ooze and leak. They always smelled; but especially, not too long after my baths, they would begin to really exude a putrefying smell. While I am aware, my senses were on high alert, which should have been reasonably expected; they did smell disgustingly bad. I hated the entire ordeal that did not seem to be going away as each day passed.

I was a total miserable, edgy, angry, and an oozing, pus-filled secretion of a mess. What a disaster I was.

I was unwilling to confide in my mom since it had not proved to be successful in the past. Just the ride home from the hospital was evidence enough that she did not care what I wanted or how bad I felt. It was my life after all. I had absolutely no trust in her, something I never did obtain.

CHAPTER FOUR

The Divided Disconnect

WE WERE STILL LIVING IN the house with my mom that my parents had built together. The divorce was in the process, and we were bidding our time living in the house as it was being foreclosed upon. Through this time, my parents broke up and reunited many different times, never stopping the divorce proceedings. During all these difficulties, my mom became pregnant and then ended up miscarrying her fourth child. Soon after, she became pregnant for a fifth time; however, this did not seem to stop her from drinking and smoking and carrying on as if she was not.

My Inside World

I was still in my bandages, not as severely or changed as often. However, I was still experiencing periodic breaks in my graftings and scars. At this point, if there were a crack in the graftings, it would start bleeding. It seemed the longer the healing went on, when I did bump my side accidently, it would cause a real deep cut in the wound. This in turn would cause swelling and unbearable pain. The seepage was unreal and unusually painful.

I was still very thin, pale, and frail. My immune system was weak. I caught colds and got sore throat rather easily, which called for another trip to the doctor for antibiotics. That is just how they handled sickness in the '60s. Even though the doctor had placed me on prescription liquid vitamins, my health was not the best.

If I did carry on like the average child, I would become uncomfortable in my bandage coverings. I was already uncomfortable in my own body; adding sweaty moving bandages that would get looser and looser with each movement was not something I was prepared to want to physically or emotionally deal with. It would only cause me to "need" my mom's help. Something that seemed to put her into a rage at times. It was like, how dare you intrude on my life … again. Her looks said it all. This being the case, I chose to stay indoors more times than not. To the couch I would go and begin rocking.

If I did happen to go outside, and perhaps I would start sweating, it would not be too long before I would find myself back inside. I oftentimes would take another bath for the day and change into new fresh clothes. I learned to gauge the daily weather, and if it was too hot, I just did not go too long in the sun.

I had to monitor every situation just so. What a manipulative mess; I just wanted to be a kid, not a weather news reporter.

Repeat Offender—in the Bar Again

There were many late afternoons my mom would repeatedly return to the same bar, just located right down the street from our house. I recall on countless occasions in the evenings my mom lugging us three kids in the car and driving us all to—what was known in the sixties as—the Black Sheep Inn. It was an unhealthy routine that caused me great concern. Pulling up in front of the bar, she would stop the car and then place it in park and shut off the engine, turn to us three kids, and immediately command our attention with the look in her eye and the tone of her voice. We all knew the speech that was coming next. She would proceed sternly by saying, "Look at me" in a very mean tone of voice. "You had better keep eye contact and not flinch an inch," she would progress with her rant. She would just flat out tell us, "I am going in to the bar to have a few drinks." She would justify that further by saying, "I just need to relax for a few minutes, and I will be back in a few minutes," inferring that we were such a handful, that alcohol was needed to keep her sanity. She implied that our mere existence was the reason that she reached continually for the bottle. She would obnoxiously add, "Need I say that you had better be on your best behavior?" She would usually tack on a few additional intimidating and threatening guidelines as to how we were expected to behave while she was in the bar. She predictably would then throw in her regular horrifying ultimatums of punishments that were to follow if we were not quiet and on our best behavior while waiting in the dark cold car. They would range from, "Do you want to stand in a corner until your legs get numb?" to "Or stay in your room for an entire day?" What was not always stated but was inferred was a harsh smack in the head, which would accompany whatever punishment she felt was deserved if we dare interrupt her playtime.

After a few times of this same relapse behavior of being left in the car for who knows how long, one of us kids would say, once she was gone of course, "How would she even know if we were on our best behavior, she is not even here?" We would all three at one time or another express our disgust in her lack of caution for us while we were abandoned in the car. Unhealthy sibling bonding. We were all aware our mom had a problem with drinking too much alcohol—yes, even at our young age. It is astonishing how kids of alcoholics pick up on some of the simplest things. Our inward knower that we had on the inside kept us in tuned … that this was not the right way to treat kids. We may not have known the word "neglect," but we sure knew how it felt.

We Are Getting Cold out Here

Usually, a few minutes turned into an hour or even as long as two when she would frequent this bar. All I know is it was dark outside and I was scared and I could not stand getting cold. As I sat in the car with chills running through my still-healing body, my hate and distaste for an uncaring mom that I was stuck with would grow all the more. If she cared about me, she would know that these cold night drifts tortured my new body. She would have to have had a relationship where I was valued in order to know the details about me and my healing process. Of course, that was such taboo for her to talk about. Being stuck waiting in that car each time my mom would decide she "needed" a beer would only add to the unkind feelings of resentment I already carried for her.

I could not even begin to count how many drunk people I watched either going in to the bar or coming out from the bar. As I got older, I thought it was funny laughing at drunken people when I would see them out in public. I imagine this was the one warped way I dealt with my fears and anxieties.

I remember thinking how I wished I could go live at my dad's house. I justified in my mind that at least when we were visiting with him, and he would go to the bars, he would take me into the bar with him. He would set you up at a pool table and ask you if you wanted a soda or something to eat. Just the simple acknowledgement that I had feelings and needs lifted my spirits. He would robustly introduce all his kids in a proud and grandiose manner to all the people at the bar. It felt much better than being hidden in a freezing scary car. Though he was getting drunk too, I felt that I was not just an inconvenience, but that in some sick way, he was watching over me. None of it was right. As I got older, my thoughts were more like, "Who even takes a kid in a bar anyways?" However, it was my way of convincing myself that my dad at least loved me. Really? Messed-up scenarios.

The most tormenting part about waiting forever in a dark cold car was again the uncomfortable abrasive itchy, scratchy feeling my scars caused me as they rubbed against my shivering skin. Something, again, my mom did not want me to repeat over and over again. She would tell me that there was not a single thing that she could do to change it, so please quit complaining. I learned to just be quiet about it. Getting cold did not help either. It seemed to add to the numb feeling on the skin that I was already having difficulties grasping the concept of.

Instead, I was forced to be in the car with my two siblings, who seemed to be growing more and more aggressive by the day. Imagine that. Helpless feeling.

Far worse than my mom going into the bar and getting tossed as quickly as possible was when she would get in the car and try and drive us all home. Sometimes she would spontaneously change her mind and decide to drive several miles across town—windows rolled up, due to her sixties-style teased hair not wanting to be blown out of place. Cigarette after cigarette, and not being able to breathe, this would really create an anxiety in me that would seem to spiral out of control to a panic attack. Because I was not allowed to express any emotions—that would hinder her buzz, I was a mess trying to keep it all inside of me. I hated driving in a car with her. Period. You could not talk, or you would usually seem to get into some sort of trouble. You were talking either too loud or not talking nice enough, or who knows what lame excuse she would come up with, all because she could not stand kids—period. She was always promoting some new idea of a punishment. She would be all over the road. It is comical how a drunken person thinks that they are driving just fine! I always remember thinking if a police officer would just pull us over, then maybe she would quit driving drunk.

It was these acts of unloving kindness that made it fairly easy to realize I was not valued in my mom's eyes. That as well as the frequent comments she would make to me, such as, "Kids should be seen and not heard." Sometimes if she was in a real sarcastic mood, she would add on to that comment and say, "Sometimes I wished they weren't seen either." Those words would pierce deep into my soul. Wounds I took to heart for far too many years. She thought I did not understand it when she slyly would add the last part in, but I understood perfectly. At a very young age I was fully aware I was not wanted in her life. I would overhear her talking to one friend or the other, saying, "Not one of these kids was ever planned." How nice.

There were many times I felt that she quite possibly wished I had died the day I was burnt. Seems ruthless of me to say this, but my mom was all about how the exterior looked, particularly to men. I was burned, and that posed as an external problem. A problem that would cause people to stop on the roadside, campsite, or in the grocery store or just about anywhere and ask the same ol' wearisome question, "What happened to her?" My mom despised it whenever anyone would ask this question. I suppose it did not bring good but-terfly feelings to her stomach when this question would come barreling out of a perfect stranger's mouth. In addition, the fact that I was half of my dad's blood and looked a whole lot like him only seemed to make her all the more hateful toward me. Lonely.

Standing Dead Person

If I were not standing in a corner for lengthy minutes at a time, I would be on the couch rocking for hours. Yes, hours. I really hated standing in the corner. Interestingly enough, my mom did not make me stand in a corner if my grandma was anywhere around. This showed me that she was in some way aware of the extreme that she would take her punishments.

The most torturing part of standing in the corner was of course the pain of my scars. They continued to be itchy, prickly, and sweaty and would ooze. It would cause me to feel really panicky and temperamental. The feeling of being trapped is miserable. You were not to move an inch, and so if my scars itched, well oh well. This was not right. I knew I could not say a single word, or my time in the corner was elongated to oblivion. Feeling unloved. Sad.

It was not just your average "stand in the corner a few minutes" discipline. It would tarry for twenty, thirty, forty, or even sixty minutes. An average corner punishment entailed many different directives. You had to stand in the corner face to the wall, hands usually behind your back, feet lined up perfectly, including your toes practically touching the wall. There was absolutely no looking around. No noise, no talking, no jesting of any kind—until she told you that you could get out of the corner. You could not ask, "How much longer?" or "Can I go to the bathroom?" You just stood there quietly like a standing dead person. Many times my mom would put me in a corner for no good reason. Just the sound of my voice bothered her, or the fact that I was overhearing her inconsistencies in her storytelling with different friends. Sometimes, you were placed in the corner just for "sounding" too loud. Imagine that. It took me many years to figure out this tactic. Eventually, years later I learned to speak as quietly and monotone as possible, especially when in the house and particularly when my mom was nearby. And definitely on days when she had started drinking extra early. Usually when she had a friend stop over and they would begin shooting the breeze, it would become all too easy of an excuse to pop open the cap off an ol' beer bottle—and banish a kid or two to the corner. Lonely.

The way it seemed to work was this: if I asked a question, I would get punished for anything my mom could think of at that moment, even if it meant making things up. She would give me the evil eye and tell me, "Oh, you just think that you are so high and almighty. Believe me, you are no better than the others are." or "Stop being such an eavesdropper, you little prima donna, you need to learn to mind your own business. Maybe standing in the corner might teach you a lesson or two." These were the personal insults that she would spit out, which would always include a handful of vicious curse words. They would ricochet around in my head and echo back at me for hours. I could not seem to figure out why I deserved the punishments, and the verbal insults were definitely uncalled-for. What a mean person.

I had made up my mind when I came home from the hospital that I was going to keep an eye out for everyone and everything. If I could help it, no one was going to get hurt on my watch. Wow, what an awful mature decision for a five-year-old to shoulder.

When your mom shushes you off, while you are almost burning to death, a child tends to pay attention to everyone and everything around her—paying special attention to any words that came forth out of my mom's mouth.

The Unforgotten

The house we were living in finally finished the foreclosure process. Soon we moved to a townhome in a nearby city. This was supposed to be a fresh start with everything new so we could conveniently try to ignore the wicked past. Though the divorce was not final, my parents had finally called it quits. My mom was very full and pregnant at this time. The hired nanny was no longer living with our family. Soon after the move, my baby sister Sandy was born. Amazingly, my mom appeared to really love this baby. I say this because she seemed to actually touch and hold this baby. My dad insisted that this child was not his. Yes, he voiced his concerns, like everything else, very loudly. He did not care who heard him. He was an extremely outspoken man. He was very loud and boisterous, even if it was his own children who overheard his accusations. Though my dad insisted the fourth child was not his, the courts ordered him to pay child support for all of us children, including Sandy. My dad would come to pick us up for visitation; however, he never really acknowledged my baby sister, and therefore he never took her for any family visitations.

With my dad now out of the house, I would not see him and my mother together in the same room for many years to come. I had adopted the thought that their divorce was my fault. I felt because I had been burned, this was rightful cause for my dad to move out. Here I was coming out of the hospital, and my daddy was gone. Any stability I felt, besides from my grandma, came from being around my dad. That stability left when he removed himself from our home. They inevitably were bound for destruction. Nevertheless, as a small child, I assumed the blame needed to land on me.

What I had not assumed was that my dad had become completely hostile with my mom after I had caught on fire. He had blamed her. He began to fuel that hate with additional "things" my mom had done to hurt him. I began to accept his hate for my mom as well as my own hate for her, which turned into nothing but a massive hateful mess. This took me over forty years to sort through.

Even though my mom and dad had tried attending church on and off throughout the time they were married, they did not ever give up their old behaviors or old lifestyle, making it even more difficult for real change to take place. So while their old habits continued, it also made way for inviting additional bad habits and behaviors to join their party. My dad had begun hitting my mom. Once, he broke my mom's elbow. Another time, he hit her so hard in the head that he broke her eardrum. Not to mention, many times, he would just slap her in the face and punch her whenever he saw fit. He would curse at her to oblivion and call her, among other things, a two-bit whore. She would yell back cussing and accusing him of all sorts of infidelities himself. They were both guilty of lustful behaviors. My dad could become an even more physically violent man when he would drink. My mom was a promiscuous woman whether she drank or not. Drinking only accelerated her inappropriate behavior. She definitely became more seductive after she had downed several beers ... and of course, a doctor prescribed diet pills. Their drinking escalated as did their problems. Instead of giving up the alcohol, it was not too long before they both found reasons to quit going to church. My mom and dad knew of God and elected to turn their backs on him and boldly walk away. I say *boldly* because, through the years, I can recall hearing both my parents mock anyone whom they heard had turned their life over to God. They described them as being weak or shallow and just plain naive. For years they both made fun of anyone they knew of who served the Lord. The problem was that they had heard the good news of Jesus Christ, knew right from wrong, but they chose the world instead. They both had put their hands to the plow and almost immediately began looking back.

> And Jesus said unto him, "No man having
> put his hand to the plow, and looking back is fit
> for the kingdom of God." (Luke 9:62 KJV)

Almost immediately, their life went straight to the pits, and their children seemed to have paid the highest price. My mom and dad married young. My mom was thirteen, and my dad was nineteen. She had her first child at fourteen and had me at sixteen. My younger brother was born when I was two and a half. It was not too long before I took up the role of mother for my younger brother. These were the three kids that my blood mother and father had together.

My grandma did her homework. She was able to witness that though my mom had been given a blatant wakeup call when I was burned, she needed to straighten her act up and be more of an attentive mother. My mom chose to ignore this warning, losing any integrity she may have had left, and instead allowing the disease of alcoholism to lull away her overwhelming guilt. The price of losing any chance of being the mother her kids so badly needed was lost.

My grandma did not trust my mom to be responsible enough to care for her four grandchildren. My mom's drinking had proven to be quite heavy, to the point where she could not be counted on in an emergency, especially when she was passed out for the night. My grandpa had become a severe and chronic drunk. My grandma could see the similarities in their lack of ability to care for not only themselves but also anyone else. From looking at all points of the equation, my grandma decided it would probably be best to hire another live-in babysitter to make sure we were cared for day and night.

I felt so utterly disconnected from my whole family, but especially from my mom. I held on to a tremendous amount of disgust toward her for not waking up when I had been screaming my lungs out in agony. I blamed her for my scars. If she had woken up—like any good mother would have—when I first started begging her to help me, then possibly I would not have been so badly burnt. Why was she not there for me? Would I ever love her? Was I not important enough? My mom had disconnected from me as her child, and yet here I was living under the same roof as her. Something was very wrong with this picture. Maybe one day I could get to the bottom of it all.

I was still having to change my bandages daily, something I had become pretty good at. I tried to wear as loose of clothes as possible without looking silly. Any tight waistline fabric of elastic was extremely bothersome and irritating. The least touch, bang, or accidental hitting into anything only brought me more pain. Staying inside proved to be the safest method of survival.

My grandma was always modifying my clothing for me. She was extra aware of my uncomfortableness in my clothing and in my own skin.

Soon after Sandy was born, another tragedy struck our home.

CHAPTER FIVE

Dismissed Again

"MOMMA, THE BABY IS CRYING," I informed my mom as she stood in the driveway flirting with a friend's ex-husband. He had dropped off my sister, brother, and me from the park where we had been playing with his three kids earlier in the day. My brother and sister were running around playing in the lower part of the yard near where my mom had headed down to. I on the other hand was headed the opposite direction going straight back into the house as I was cold, something that happened to me quite easily after being burned.

"I'll be right there," she dismissively spat out of the side of her mouth as she flirtatiously leaned into the car smiling at the man.

I went back to my baby sister's five-inch–cracked-open door. She was in her crib tousling her small little body around as she continued crying and screaming at the top of her infant-sized lungs.

"It's okay, Sandy, I'll go try and get Momma again," I tried to soothe her with only my voice, knowing better than to enter her room.

Walking back out to the screen door a second time, I pleaded, "Momma, the baby is crying."

Looking annoyed, she shushed me and waved me away. "I said I will be there in a minute."

I trekked back over to the baby's room and peered in. She was not crying. She was lying there so unnaturally still. Something was not right.

Quickly I ran back out to the poverty-mentality screen door and yelled to my mom a final time, "Momma, the baby quit crying!"

Finally, I had gotten her attention. Up the stairs she fled. She had lodged herself between the crib and the mattress as she had been thrashing around screaming for help. She had suffocated. She was dead.

My mom began to scream and wail.

"Help! Somebody, help! She's not breathing!" she screamed.

My mom ran to the screen door of our upstairs townhome and began yelling out hysterically to anyone listening, "Somebody, helllpppp!"

Crying. Screaming. Chaos.

I stood there in horror. We were always warned to never ever pick the baby up. Should I have made an exception this time?

I had never seen my mom show so much love for someone, certainly not for me. I was not exactly sure why she hated me, but now it was going to add yet another stone in the coffin. This dread set in deep. "You are really in trouble now," I spoke to myself as my mom moved around the room screaming and pleading for her infant child to not be dead. I whispered under my breath, "Mom will never be able to love me now. You have really done it this time."

Hearing all of the screaming, my sister and brother came running in from the yard to see what was happening. They stood there in a haze not knowing what was expected of them. I went and stood by them, and we all huddled together. Who was she going to blame for this? Seemed like my mom always looked for someone to blame— never taking responsibility herself.

The police and the paramedics showed up, and it was a complete mad house. The attendant tried CPR, but it was too late. Sandy had died. They quickly removed my baby sister from the house. My mom was in hysteria. She kept screaming and hoping her infant daughter would come back to life. It was too late. Sandy had suffocated in her crib. She had squiggled and moved around so much, and she had lodged herself between the mattress and the crib sides until she got in such a position she could not breathe. I was freaking out both on the inside and out.

The police took my older sister, my baby brother, and me and had us sit down on the couch in the living room. They started by questioning my older sister. She told the officer she had not been in the house when all this happened. My brother was squirming around on the couch, only three years old, so he was of no real help to the officer. It was then that the officer looked at me and began questioning me with one question after another.

At the young age of five, I was the only one who had witnessed with my eyes what had happened leading up to my sister's death. I only knew to tell the truth, and so I proceeded to tell the officer what had happened. I told them how I had called my mom two times, and she would not come. When I finally yelled to her that the baby had stopped crying, she came barreling up the stairs from outside. The guilt was immense as I told the officers what had happened. I explained to the officers how if I had just picked her up, maybe she would still be alive. Through the guilt, I tried to get the officers to understand that I did not want to break the rules of the house and pick her up.

It was my fault, I thought. This was truly how I felt.

It was not too long before my grandma came. My mom was rightfully an emotional wreck. I felt so sorry for her. I felt so very powerless; there was not a thing I could do to console her, I was just a child. The next several weeks were utter depression around our home. My mom had been given a large bottle of pills from the doctor. Later in life she would confide in me that she contemplated taking this very bottle of pills to end her misery. When she reached over to grab them, they were not there. My grandma had come to the rescue yet again, and in some miraculous way, she had enough foreknowledge to remove them from my mom's presence.

It seemed as if my mom felt free to love her baby Sandy fully and deeply, that she was all hers. That she did not have to share her with anyone but herself since no man claimed to be her father. I have had the thought many times, since my sister's death, that whenever my mom would look at me or speak to me a certain way, she wished I were the child who had died. The burnt one. The one she was ashamed of, the one who brought back memories of some painful emotions every time she looked at me. The one who had conviction of right behavior yet was still a walking daily example of all her neglect.

Another Unseized Opportunity

After Sandy's death, my grandma hired yet another full-time nanny to care for us three remaining kids. This nanny was very mean. She did not hit us, but she screamed and threatened us daily. Her ways scared me.

We stayed in this townhome, where Sandy died, for only a little while longer, and then we moved again, back to the town we had previously left, to live in my grandma's house. Grandma and Grandpa had been renting it out while they rented a home closer to the beach. It just so happened that their renters had moved out. Grandma was gracious enough to let us move in to it even though my mom was not in good speaking terms (something that would never happen) with Grandma or Grandpa. Our full-time nanny was no longer with us by now. My grandma, for being so abusive to us children, fired her. One day, when I was five years old, she was busted, having me hang the clothes up on an outside clothesline.

The police investigated my mom for child abuse and neglect yet again. My grandparents, in their efforts to protect their remaining three grandchildren, were forced to put up a large chunk of money to fight to keep my mom from going to jail. The police were indicating that my mom was negligent in her parenting, and they planned to prove so in the court system. All the while, my grandma continued to lecture my mom in what, I am sure, my grandma thought was an encouraging manner. Grandma was warning her that she needed to try to give this parenting thing another shot in the arm. She needed to be more concerned with her kids and less focused on her partying, or she would most likely pay the ultimate consequence and loose custody of her kids—to an ex-husband she could not stand.

I am certain that my grandparents covered for my mom because my dad was waiting in the wings for her to mess up, yet again, so he could swoop in and gain custody of his kids. Because my dad had hit my mom on several occasions, my grandparents hated my dad and did not want him to get full custody of us kids. Being the choice between the worse of two evils, my grandma decided to get involved.

For the first time as an adult, my mom remained all on her own. No men, no nannies; well, for a while that was. She found employment at the local bowling alley, and she began working full-time on the night shift.

My sister and I changed schools again. It was school number two for me and school number three for my sister.

Weeks went by with a deep sadness hovering over the entire family and home. Life for my mom was horrific. I do not ever remember her crying so much and for such long periods. I felt so sorry for her, yet it appeared that she had completely disconnected from all three of us kids. A hate toward me had become rooted, and I could feel it. It did not feel good at all. I used to think that maybe I should have lied to the officers. How could a kid know to lie to an officer at such a young age of innocence?

If my older sister and I had felt that we needed to be independent before, we really felt it now. We got super good at getting ourselves up and ready for school. It was what was implied, yet not communicated. We would get up, get dressed, make our beds (before we dared leave our room), comb our hair, make our own breakfast—usually cold cereal with an occasional banana, brush our teeth, and pack our lunch for the day. The whole time my mom would be sleeping in her room. Thankfully, my sister knew how to tell time so that we were never late catching the school bus. We knew better. To have woken my mom up in the early morning would have irreversible consequences. Therefore, you just took care of yourselves. That is just what you do as a child of an alcoholic.

There were times when our teachers must have had a clue to something not being right. I remember one morning my sister and I took a huge paper bag left over from the grocery store and placed inside it a solitary banana. This was our lunch for the day. Crazy insanity.

After her shift would end, my mom usually hung out at the bowling alley and would party. She usually came home extremely intoxicated. I know because I could hear her enter the two-bedroom one-bath 732-square-foot house each night. She would work off and on as best she could. Still no nanny; instead, we had a surrogate babysitter who lived nine houses down on the same side of the street as we did. She watched us often.

I still had to daily bathe, rub the stinky and sticky lanolin oil on my burns, and then put on the netting covering, then my clothes. I was still consumed with hate because I had to live in these ugly scars. Those emotions hung close to my side, never leaving for any long periods.

I vowed that if my mom had another baby that I was going to make sure this one did not die. In my deepest knower, I knew that the life I was being forced to live was just not right. I blamed my mom, entirely.

On Saturdays, my sister and I would ask in advance if we could take the church bus to the same church my parents had attended at one time in their marriage. My mom was more than happy to get rid of us for a few hours on a Sunday morning, while she slept in. And so with that approval, my sister and I would get all ready by ourselves and stand outside on the sidewalk waiting to be picked up by the big periwinkle-blue church bus. Just watching it travel down our street would bring a sense of comfort, that I knew I would be safe for the next few hours. Little self-sufficient adults.

No New Habits in This House

Drinking and other numbing agents were a regular event in the house. My mom always seemed to have a cigarette in her hand and a glass bottle of beer in the other. I grew increasingly angry and disgusted with my mom's immature actions. Her mood swings grew increasingly less predictable.

I still felt so defiled in my body.

It did not take my mom too long and she was seeing a few different men at one time. She would bring one or the other home with her after her shift at the bowling alley was over. In they would enter the house giggling and talking rather loud and inappropriate. Would not be too long after entering the house I would hear the stereo begin to play. It would sound out on low volume, with some popular album my mom had purchased, yet not loud enough to cover up what it was that my mom was doing with these men she would randomly bring home. Overhearing the things happening made me dislike my mom even more. I could not figure out why she did not want to still be married to my dad. I did however think that at least they were not fighting as I used to overhear my dad and her doing late into the evenings. I now was hearing her have sex with men as opposed to her fighting with men. What a mess. Just saying.

Unnerving Expectations

When she would go to work, us kids would be left home alone and told that if there was an emergency that we could call the sitter who lived about nine houses away on the same side of the street. Behind her words was the message that it had better be a real emergency if we were to call on her. Those nights alone were very scary and lonely. The babysitter would come down to our house to fix us dinner and help to get us in our pajamas. Then she would set us up to watch television and then go home to her own family. It was unnerving. It definitely bred even more distress into me. My big sister was so brave. She had perfected keeping time, because she knew exactly when we were to get in bed. I am grateful for my older sister. She is a blessing.

I thought my grandma would come around and visit more often. The problem was my mom and my grandma just did not get along. The stress between them was ever increasing by the day. As my mom got older, she started talking up to my grandma. All the arguing drained Grandma eventually; she slowly backed off from visiting as much. I missed her.

My mom continued with all the drinking and started coming home later and later in the evenings. Still with several different men. I know because their voices were different. Little by little, it ended up narrowing down to just two different men. She would rotate one on a certain night and one on another night. I would think, who is going to be my next dad? I would lie in my dark bedroom and hear my mom and the two different strange men having sex. It made me feel disgusted with her. What had happened to my life? What was going to happen next?

Mind you, during all of this, I was still doing the daily procedure of bathing with prescription liquid cleansing soap, preparing my scars with generous portions of lanolin, draping, netting, and then clothing. My mom helped once in a while, but mostly I took care of myself. I could not stand her touching me or my body; it made me feel angry, and she could sense it, so she allowed me to care for myself as best I could.

Three Hours—too Far Away

At six years old, my mom married for the second time one of the two finalists in her barhopping, bowling alley, choice-picking adventures.

Our not-so-happy little family up and moved three hours away from my hometown. I was disheartened and discouraged moving so far away; this move took me farther away from my grandma and my real dad.

The new stepfather was extremely controlling, loud, and forceful, crafty, cunning, and yet sickeningly charming and abusive. Something was seriously off with this picture, which appeared to constantly be hanging crooked on our very dysfunctional hollow family tree wall.

He was a hard worker, one who understood follow-through. He had been in the US Army. My mom found this new man at one of the places she went to get drunk at, the bar or the bowling alley she befriended regularly. Perfect ... really what was she thinking?

CHAPTER SIX

Miserable Muddling Depression

Thou will keep him in perfect peace, whose
mind is stayed on thee, because he trusts in thee.
(Isaiah 26:3 KJV)

FROM AGE FOUR UNTIL I was fifty-six years old, I have suffered from
one form or another of oppression or depression. It would deepen
and then lessen then deepen and lessen, depending on my exterior
world surrounding me at the time.

I really enjoyed visits with my dad. The depression seemed to
lessen whenever he was around. He was always kind to me as a child.
When I say always, I mean always. He would seem to try to do things
with us kids that were fun and entertaining. While I am certain that
this depression was present when I was four, I would be negligent in
my story if I did not go back one step further.

The fighting between my parents was possibly what began a
long journey of looking for joy, love, peace, and some sort of sanity
in my life.

At a very young age, I was a compulsive counter. There was no
certain number I liked. I would change it up all the time. Most times,
it had to be an even count. I would count how many cups were in the
dish strainer. I would count how many shoes there were in a closet
or how many empty hangers were left hanging in the closet. I would
count how many windowpanes were in our windows. I would count
them over and over again. I would count to myself repetitively. Or I

would just count one, two, three, four, five, six … one, two, three, four, five, six … over and over and over until some sort of calm came over myself. If I did it aloud or too loudly, I would be reprimanded by my mother or new stepfather. So I learned to do it inside my head, where I lived most of the time anyhow. I do recall my real father saying to me on numerous occasions that I was a nervous child. I would guess so; my world around me was unstable for far too many years. My new counting friend.

My dad was a hard worker, and he made a good living from a young age. My mom enjoyed spending as much of his money as she could get her hands on. My mom was a fanatical clean freak perfectionist. What society would call nowadays an obsessive compulsive or OCD person. She expected us kids to live the same way. When I was asked to clean something, you had better do it right the first time, or you could expect to be critiqued about every portion of what it was you had done or not done correctly the first time and quite possibly punished when you were finished. She was never comfortable to just chill or hang around. Part of this behavior could have been attributed to her use of prescription diet pills. It was expected that we follow her rigid obsessive cleaning guidelines. She expected us to become her "mini-me's." I am certain this behavior only fueled my own obsessive behavior, which seemed to be growing by the day.

Being around my real dad seemed to soothe my compulsive behavior. He was relaxing to hang with, and he did not live nearly as clean. He was good at getting my mind off myself. He lived more in the moment—in the now. Instead of always trying to predict what would go wrong in the future. He was more of a positive role model for me to trust in.

Being inserted into this extreme-behavior home after living in a much calmer surrounding at birth to around age two and a half was very life-altering. My dad was twenty-one when I was born. Their relation was far from stable enough to be bringing me, their second child, into their world.

Though I do not have too many memories prior to this time, I do remember having a deep sense of love and comfort in my life. I do recall feeling a strong unbreakable bond with my grandma and my aunt. Then all of a sudden, my peace was robbed from me. Quite possibly had I lived in a disrupted home full-time as a newborn and never knew any difference, I may very well have adjusted to a disorderly life all along. Strange how that works, or for that matter does not work. Having been raised by my grandma and aunt in a very different environment and then being transferred over to a home where the adults would get so drunk they would pass out, I felt confused in my heart from then on in. Such confusion should never be acceptable for a child to have to suffer through.

I remember most often feeling unwanted, unloved, and in the way, when I was living with my mom. There was often fighting and arguing and a sense of unease daily in the home. While my dad was a carefree, silly jokester, and a friend to all who he encountered, my mom on the other hand was serious and strict and above all else extremely sensual with her body. This embarrassed me greatly. She sexually acted out in very untimely ways, especially when adding into the mix alcohol, prescription diet pills. Adding frequent groups of friends that she would invite over to the house to join in on the party would create a true recipe for yet another disaster. OCD behavior—onset.

At night, I would be sent to bed. As I lay in bed, I would hear the party that would be going on in the rest of the house. The noise and laughter and frequent arguments would go on late into the night. Getting out of bed was not an option. There would be no soothing words or comfort to help me to get to sleep. I knew all too well that interrupting them was not welcomed and that I would end up feeling even more scared and unwanted after my mom finished reprimanding me for disturbing her fun. So I would lie in the bed full of nervous fearful energy until I would finally drift off to sleep, hoping that I would not get woke up by their loud voices throughout the remainder of the nighttime. The only solace that I received was that my older sister was next to me in the room.

Frequently, after one of these gatherings, my mom and dad would end up in one of their vicious arguments, which would oftentimes wake me up. My dad would go storming out of the house. I remember fearing if this time maybe he would not come back. He usually would return later in the night or the next day, and the cycle would continue. My mom would crash out on the couch in order to avoid my dad in case he chose to return. I would often hear my mom bad-mouthing my dad when he was not around. She would be talking to one of her friends, or she would even be trying to convenience my sister or me of his loathsomeness.

I recall my mom being overly rude, harsh, and just flat out mean to me, as well as my siblings. There was a thick sense of being unwanted that was behind most words and looks that she would send my way. I certainly felt as if I was a bother to her. As it has been spoken by many a wise person, actions speak louder than words. I was a definite embarrassment. Knowing this fact brought me much hurt. I never could figure out why it was that my mom did not like me, but she did not. She seemed at times to try to like me, but the act would not last long, and then she would revert to her old ways. Hated for no reason.

A depression continued to lurk over me. I felt very uncomfortable living in my own home. I learned to cope through the depression, knowing that it was not going to go all the way away. I decided to just put it in my mental backpack and place it on the back burner of my life and to go about my day as best I could. I remember as young as four years old having seamlessly good strangers say to me, "Smile, honey." or "Put a smile on that pretty face of yours." I would get embarrassed that a perfect stranger could see through my face into my pain, and yet my own mother did not care enough to try to deal with her unhappy child.

My deep-seated loneliness and embedded fear had begun its course in my life. My dad was gone, and I was sad. He was such a comedian, so many of my memories about him bring laughter to the forefront of my mind even to this day. He would sing a song to get me to laugh. It went like this: "The old gray mare went poop on the sidewalk"—then he would add the sound effects of pooping—"the gray mare pooping." He was silly. It got me out of the zone, and that is what he was shooting for. He would ask you, "Did you have a bowel movement today?" Then he would seriously expect an answer. I thought it was so amusing. Odd personality.

Something happened when they divorced. A little switch went off on the inside of me that confirmed that I now must have no value whatsoever. What little I had, through my dad, was now leaving me. Depression was taking a deeper core in me.

My mom told me that I needed to accept the new stepfather. I never did. I did not like his demeanor or his cussing 24-7 foul mouth he so braggingly carried around for all to hear. I happen to believed that what a person speaks out of their mouth tells me a lot about what is going on, on the inside of their heart, their soul. Some have a sick diseased soul. He had both a corrupt heart and compromised soul, in my opinion.

Rhythmic Rocking

Early on, I would rock randomly. I would rock myself back and forth, back and forth on a couch or in a rocking chair. I do not remember rocking violently until I returned home from the hospital after being burnt. Once I returned home, the rocking only escalated. It was a way for me, in my small-undeveloped mind, to gain some sort of regulator switch in my very imperfect world that had quickly spun out of control. There would be so much chaos in my home, and it would make me feel nervous. I would obsess in my compulsive mind about how it was that I could change the ugly smelly scars that were all over my body. I hated being burnt. I hated living in the burns. I would sit on the corner of the couch rocking and dream about better days to come. I would rock and rock repeatedly as I hummed or counted to myself. If I sang aloud, I had to make sure it was not too showy, or I would get in trouble. Hours would pass, yes, hours, as I sat in this little corner of the world rocking back and forth, back and forth. No one interrupted me. No one stopped me. No one helped me. Someone, help me ... Please! Can you not see I need some help here?

I chose to stay in the house and rock versus going outside and taking the chance of getting hurt on my burns. My rocking would get on my sister's nerves. I could hear her complaining to my mom, "Mom, make her stop. Not again." Oh, how my poor sister hated my addiction of rocking.

65

My mom would say something to the effect of, "Oh, just let her rock. What is it hurting you?" or "She is crazy anyways, just ignore her, she cannot help herself."

Thus, I would rock away, in my own world, getting the only sense of peace my day would bring me. It was like a magnet that would draw me into the back-and-forth movement, instinctively, seemingly having no control to stop the addiction.

I would imagine different scenarios in my mind: When would my daddy return? When will my new stepfather stop being so foul and rude and sexually abusive to me? When will my mom stop what she is doing and just hold me tightly?

I truly felt orphaned. I felt betrayed, unlovable, and unimportant. Sometimes I would have, what I now know to be, anxiety come over me. I would jump up into the couch and begin to rock, and within minutes, calm would come over me. Built-in sedative.

The couch was my invisible friend. I would want to go to the couch and rock first thing in the morning on the weekends. However, my mom would insist on my daily chores being completed first. As I would be doing my chores, I would continually be thinking about the comfort that the couch would bring. The anticipation of the couch and all its warm fuzzy feelings of control of my inside pool of emotions was worth doing my chores right the first time, so I didn't have to repeat them a second or third time. My old best friends, my grandma, and my aunt had been lost, and the safe and secure feeling they brought into my life. I knew loss. I had lost a part of my body by having it burned off. I had lost my dad, who had always brought laughter. I had lost my ability to trust anyone. So much overwhelming loss. All of the above I would contemplate as I rocked. It was as though I thought that if I could rock long enough or hard enough, then maybe I could make all of this loss turn around to gain. Along with the rocking came all the neurotic counting. The only solace was that I would feel numb for a season, until the rocking would stop and I had to take my self-medicating life off pause and enter back into my unclear reality of a very unsafe world. It was a temporary fix for a permanent problem. On the weekends, I would rock for two to three hours at a time. Then take a break from rocking, eat lunch, and hopefully I was allowed to return back to the couch. Back and forth, back and forth.

My mom had a few good friends who all had several children. When her friends would come over to visit, it would get very chaotic in the house. It was not even a thought to interrupt her and her friends to dare ask for a drink of water or anything else. When all of the chaos would start, then off to the couch, I would go to rock away, separating myself from all of the hostile noise. Mom would tell me dismissively, "Go rock in your room." She even had my stepfather, who was a carpenter, take a regular kitchen table chair and turn it into a rocker on the bottom parts, and I would carefully slide the rocker into my bedroom and rock in there so as not to "bother" any of the company. When company was present, I was not allowed to sing when rocking—yes, I said *sing*. I had a rather good voice, and I loved to sing aloud. Especially at Christmastime when the hi-fi stereo would blast one of my favorite Christmas songs. This made a great recipe for my emotional peace of mind. Senseless rules.

If we were visiting at someone else's house, I was not allowed to rock on their couch at all. When there was noise, it meant that there would soon be trouble. I did not want to get into any trouble. If I happened to get into trouble, instead of dealing with the issue of who was at fault, my mom would blame all who were in her view. We would be shushed and sent to stand for an undetermined amount of time in some random corner. It was horrible punishment, one in which I never could understand. Sometimes my mom would be so engaged with talking with a friend about all her issues and problems; to take the time to "deal" with a child's dispute took too much time. She would assume you were at fault, and off to the corner she would send you! Anxiety attack.

Looking back at all of the rocking in my life is very painful for me. I often wonder why nothing was done to help me. I was crying out for help, and no one answered. I was trying so desperately to sedate myself, my own form of counseling since no one thought that I was in need of any. I felt so utterly abandoned, a feeling that I would have to eventually deal with as I got older. You can take a lot of things from a child, but when a parent who was actively in the picture is no longer in the picture or a close grandparent is too far away to visit but once or twice a year, you create a serious abandonment problem.

It is the parents' job to pay attention to the child. It is the parents' responsibility to raise the child, not just let the child exist day by day wavering in a deeply embedded loneliness. It is the parents' job to remain alert and pay close attention to the child's needs. My issues were evident, but ignored by my mom because to deal with issues would take up time out of her very important schedule. Oh, the Almighty Schedule.

I stopped most of the rocking in front of other people when I was around nine years old. Yes, nine. I realized I was too old to continue this habit, and my mom began forbidding it. It hurt my feelings each time I would overhear my mom call me crazy. That I was crazy. Who says that about their child? I did, however, continue rocking myself to sleep in bed every night, where no one could see; it seemed to help me to fall to sleep. It was not until my fifties, when my hip bone began to ache, that I finally stopped completely. Even as I am writing this book, the thought of wanting to rock still brings me comfort. Withdrawal.

Windows Please

As young as six years old, I recall suffering with extreme carsickness. When we would be driving in the car, I would experience an uncontrollable anxiety, and this would create in me a feeling of being carsick. I would tell my mom I was feeling nauseated. My mom's response was always a seemingly apathetic comment, "Just look out the window." This never seemed to help at all. The only thing that seemed to help was to just tune my mom out. Her words, her conversation, they all made me nervous. Her voice agitated me to no end. She was the cause of my nervous and anxious feelings. I never knew what to expect of her behavior, particularly in a car. I felt trapped being in her company in such a small area. I feared her presence. She would often make it a habit to be just on time. We were always running late in her mind.

My mom wore her hair fairly short and highly teased up and combed out real pretty, as was the custom in the sixties. Therefore, rolling the windows down and possibly messing up her hair was not up for discussion. There was not an air-conditioning option in our car either. That was back in the days where your average typical woman went in to the beauty salon and asked to have a weekly shampoo and set. The hairdresser would wash and set your hair. You would sit under a dryer for about thirty minutes. When your hair was dry, the hairdresser would take a rattail comb along with some good ol' aerosol hairspray, tease your hair to oblivion, and then comb it out all pretty and such. To think that you could catch a break and be able to roll a window down was a fantasy only made up in your head. To add more to the equation, she was also a chain-smoker; literally there was a cigarette lit up in her hand or hanging out of the car ashtray at all times. With all the windows rolled up, I would feel as if I was choking in a perpetual cloud of smoke. All of us kids were slammed into the car, gagging, as we would go driving down the road. You were not allowed to complain about the smoke choking you, or that was reason for punishment. You could be grounded to your room for the rest of the day, which was one of my mom's favorite indictments, to having to stand in a corner forever when she reached her destination. You just never knew what to expect. I learned to not say a thing about her foul-smelling cigarettes. Her goal was to get you to leave her alone.

I knew each time getting in a car with her she had probably been drinking or was on some sort of prescription drug. She admitted to using prescription diet pills for over ten years after my closest younger brother was born. I believe the anxiety was a direct link to this also. Someone, any one of us, would always get into some sort of trouble when we would be in the car with my mom. Every time, no kidding, never fail. My mom truly seemed to dislike parenting; of course, she was extremely young and impatient—her impatience never changed. I learned to always sit behind her as she drove. It became a habit of mine from a young age onward. I was not one to scream out, "Shotgun." No, I took the back seat silently and honorably. It saved me from being slapped as often because of this wise decision. Her arm could not reach behind the seat. I would hang on to the car door and its handle, as far to the left as humanly possible. In addition, it hurt my face when she would just lambast me with a full-force backhand of ammunition. It is hard for a driver to be smoking a cigarette and slap a child if you are positioned directly behind the driver's seat. I was a smart child, if you ask me. I learned young how to survive.

It seems as if some of the strictest punishments were dispensed out when any one of us kids would get in trouble while driving in a car with my mom. This was something I seriously wanted to try to avoid. When she was at a high point of anxiety, her punishments hit its peak.

I did not recover from carsickness until I was in my late thirties. Once God revealed to me the link, it was then I was able to allow Him to show me all the connections about how it affected me as a child. I went to Him in prayer and asked for Him to deliver me from any fears related to my past car endeavors. He did.

Chapter Seven

Adjusting to Two Drill Sergeants

MY MIND WAS SO UNSETTLED all of the time. Living with all these ugly scars was one thing; however, living with my mom was even harder to tolerate. It was almost like living in a constant thunderstorm. You never knew when she was going to strike. It was going to strike. Scary life. She was a very aggressive control freak. She would constantly repeat her rules for you to follow. How it was that she expected you to act, how quiet you were expected to speak, or if you were even allowed to speak at all. There were so many times in my childhood I was banned from talking. Do not get me wrong, I talked, I just really learned to limit what I said when my mom was around. I could be in the middle of talking just about anything, and if my mom got a wild hair up her nose, she would tell me to stop talking and that I was to remain silent until she told me I could talk again. Sometimes you were forbidden from talking for up to and sometimes exceeding a couple of hours. This was not some casual statement but an unashamed threat. You did not speak or else! This was another control tactic my mom practiced that caused me severe panic attacks—pulsating heartbeats and nervous interior outbursts. She controlled when and what you spoke. Being in close proximity of my mom was never a good thing; being in a car with her was self-deprecating. I feared her. If she disagreed with something that you said, then you were told to turn your head and look out the window and not to speak again until she told you different. This may seem so petty, but it was just about every time you rode in the car with her—to one child or the other. She never relented. It was as if she enjoyed correcting me—us. It seemed to help make her feel superior. Loads of times before she would discipline you with her words, she would spontaneously, and seemingly randomly, slap you in the face. I hated being slapped in the face. This is so shaming for anyone to endure. My face would sting.

I was seldom allowed to speak my opinion or viewpoint, so consequently I turned all my feelings inward. I was becoming a real mess. I felt defeated, unloved, ugly, and very afraid of life. Emotional ball of a mess.

My scars where never going away. They only seemed to be stretching as my body grew. However, I wondered, would this emotional abuse ever go away? The only positive progression that I saw was that I no longer had to be confined by all of the bandaging. I was finally able to advance the use of a single netlike covering that I placed over my chest, like a shirt, each day after I would bathe and generously lather my scars with lanolin. I wore this netting day after day for the longest time. This netting helped to keep the skin formed tightly so that the healing could continue. The scars had turned all sorts of ugly colors: from burgundy to purple to a dark matte brown; some parts were even triangles of white, as if it came from someone else's body skin. I recall thinking how much easier life would be if I had just died. Maybe I should have just died, I would tell myself, but how could I make that happen, I would ask myself. Eventually I would find something or someone to distract me from this thinking for a week or two. Children are very egocentrically focused; they feel that the entire world somehow revolves around just them. My mom was just a large kid herself. I had learned early on that the world definitely did *not* revolve around just me. In addition, if I forgot that fact, and possibly spoke out of turn, my mom was quick to remind me that it was not all about me.

I learned young that I was a child who was living with an addictive personality and an alcoholic parent. I tried to avoid being yelled at and corrected as much as was in my control. When my mom had no other adults in the room with her, she would say horribly mean demeaning comments to me. If I were to repeat them to another adult, she would call me a liar and state that I was just making things up. Who is another adult going to believe? I became good at waking up each morning and gauging what my mom's mood was for the day. It would change hour by hour, so you were forced to be on guard most all the time. A self-preserving trait any child of an alcoholic takes on. Depending on her mood, I could figure out how my day would be. I learned to try not to allow her mood to affect my mood. I am grateful God granted me intelligence and wisdom; He was definitely with me when I was a youngster. He never left my side. Most often on the weekends, I would hang out in my room. I would sit in my rocking chair, and I would rock in my rocker for hours on end. I would listen to Elvis Presley music. My real dad and stepmom had bought these albums for me. I would play them on the record player they had also bought me one Christmas. I would sing and sing, acting like my dad was listening, hoping he was proud of me. As I would sing, I would think of every situation that I could fix or make better. I was my own little adult on the inside. Those were some long lonely days. Oh, how I missed my dad and my grandma, who seemed to no longer be a large part of my life. I would go for months on end and not see her. I would go eight or nine months and not see my dad.

A New Little Brother

A few years into my mom's second marriage, she birthed another baby brother. He was adorable. He was my buddy. I loved him very much. My mom loved him too. I thought we were on a roll. Things might be looking up. Oh no, I was dreaming again.

After his birth, her drinking continued to escalate again. She never quit drinking while she was pregnant nor did she quit smoking cigarettes. This was not uncommon for an unsaved mom in the sixties.

Responsibilities Increase

More kids meant more responsibilities. My mom had her limit as to what she would do; everything else got shoved off onto us kids to do. Chores again.

By now, my sister and I would set the table for dinner, clear the table and wipe it down, wash and rinse the dishes, towel-dry them and put them away too! We inherited this chore clear back to when I was six years old and my sister was seven and a half. This was a job that was to be taken seriously with no giggling or goofing off. The dishes were expected to be done perfectly, or she would make us rewash all of them over again. Not just the ones that were dirty, but all the dishes that had been used in that meal would have to be rewashed. The sad part was that I do not recall a single time when my mom would come, examine the dishes and silverware, and not find something wrong with something. It did not seem to matter how hard we tried. I guess you could say she was just teaching us how to properly wash and dry and put away the dishes; however, it was in more of the critical harassing way in which she handled teaching us that I struggled with.

I came to expect that I would not please my mom or my stepfather. The two of them together were a sad team for parents. Certainly nothing to write Grandma about. They were neurotic, germophobes, pessimistic, illogical, irrational, self-absorbed, immature, and alcoholic adolescents trying to play their roles as young adults.

We were one sad sight for sore eyes. A family with a family tree that was extremely hollow. Hollow family tree.

My mom's continued use of prescription diet pills caused her to live on edge, and she would be consumed with overwhelming anxiety constantly. She acted as if she was in such control, where in fact she absolutely was *not*. She was so concerned with her figure; she would seldom eat anything of caloric significance. She saved her calories for her alcohol. As I became an adult and look back, I could see why she was so tense and overly sensitive all the time. Amphetamines, little or no food, and consistent alcohol drinking will do that to you. It definitely helps explain her extreme behavior toward us kids. My brother would do the simplest of mistakes, and out would come the belt. When I say that he would be whipped at four and a half years old, I mean beaten. I felt helpless not being able to help him. She would literally look for reasons to whip him as if she enjoyed it. Matter of fact, a sick-looking thrill would enter her eyes as she had found a much sought-after outlet for her pent-up rage. I spoke up one time begging my mom to quit hitting him. Well, that only got me punished. I felt so guilty each time she would take a belt to him. Please stop, Ms. Rageaholic.

Getting to know my stepfather was an interesting journey. He was an ex-military man, and he carried all the characteristics that followed; he was definitely OCD, ADD—you name it. He was a very rage-filled explosive person. He was constantly angry, corrective, rude, sarcastic, foul, and gossipy and a chauvinistic racist. He would talk behind my mom's back and to try to get me to see things or situations his way. That was completely inappropriate adult behavior. He believed in an extremely firm hand. I would watch how he would discipline my younger brother, and I knew that I did not want that wrath focused on me. It reinforced to me that I needed to walk the line and try not to make any waves, anything to keep from any further physical pain to my body.

He began molesting me a few months before my mom married him. He continued these gross sexual violations until I was eleven years old. Something I did not recall until I was thirty-six years old. My doctors called it repressed memory. Which when suppressed, acts as post-traumatic stress syndrome. My mind had already been toyed around with by my mom for so long, it didn't take much manipulation on his part to get me to "not say a word." I did not remember it until twenty-five years later!

We lived in a medium-income well-kept rental home in the heart of a very busy city. My mom and stepfather had goals and aspirations that they were trying hard to achieve. Us four kids being in the house seemed to just be an unwanted distraction. I was trying hard to just stay out of their way. I enjoyed school, and I pulled loads of As. Sometimes even straight As. School kept my mind entertained. I disliked being around all the other children; too many little people and a lack of trust for others was a remedy for social dysfunction.

It was evident that my mom was happiest while drinking her liquid friend—alcohol. She began making drinking buddies in her new neighborhood. I could care less for any of them. At seven and eight years old, I had made a few friends, but I was still most contented when I was alone in my room rocking and listening to my latest album that my dad and stepmom had bought me or going to school where neither parent could harm me. It just seemed to be far more soothing than dealing with all the family drama.

Living in my body was still an emotional chore for me; it consumed my core thoughts. I enjoyed helping care for my newest baby brother. He was a neat kid. What I could not understand was why my mom had another kid. She made it known that we were such a burden to her and that we should be lucky to even be breathing. Really? She definitely was not willing to stop or even cut back on her drinking. Escalation to the max.

What I did not understand was why she would not just let us go to live at our dad's house. At least I "felt" his love coming back at me. When we would visit him, all he would talk about was how much he wanted us to come live with him.

These years with my first stepfather were so sequestering for me. My mom had decided that she no longer needed to let us visit with our real dad as much as what was ordered by the courts. He had not been paying his child support payments on a regular basis. Therefore, she thought she had a right to take us away from our dad. Strange concept. I believe that a large part of this was that my new monster of a stepfather, who was actively sexually molesting my older sister and me, wanted to separate us as much as possible from our real dad. He would always beg me to call him "Daddy" in private. Though I would agree to do it when he was drunk and would beg, later I would always refer to him by his name. He was an absolute absurd person of a man.

A New Last Name in Town

There were a lot of head games that took place in this new city; changing our last name was only the beginning. As part of the mind-conditioning to accept him as our real father was the implementation that our last name would now be the same as his in this new town.

We were taken aside, and it was explained to us that he was going to be our new daddy now and we would have his last name. Once we moved, unbeknown to us, my dad was not told where we had gone to live for quite some time. At least two years. The way it was portrayed to us is that our real dad had lost interest in us. I knew better. I would ask over and over again for his address so that I could write him a letter. My mom reluctantly eventually gave it to me. I am not sure if she ever mailed those letters; however, it was my way of telling her to back off on all this other fake daddy stuff. I had a real dad, and it was going to stay that way.

My mom's ploys to separate us emotionally from our dad were not working. (Little did she know that the more she caused separation from my real dad, the more the pedophile stepfather was violating me and my sister). One such example is when my mom one time told us that my dad was going to pick us three kids up and take us to Disneyland. We got all excited and packed our overnight bags, went and sat on the front steps of our house; we waited and waited, and he never showed up. Then she swooped in, all condescending, and made the claim that he just did not come. She continued by saying, "What kind of a father does that, just not show up? I told you he did not care about you." That comment left me feeling completely hopeless. I would be better off dead, is what I thought.

Many years later, when I asked my dad about this circumstance, I discovered that he was unaware of what I was describing. That always bothered me that my mom would lie to that degree about such a serious issue. I will never understand hating my children to such a deep dark level that I would deliberately create a situation to harm them. Sick.

My mom was becoming a woman consumed with revenge. She would spitefully tell us hurtful stories about my father in order to make him look like an awful person. She despised the love that we had for each other. After a couple of years, we finally reunited with my dad.

Once reunited, we quickly forgot the loaded stories that my mom had spat out at us. I know he treated her lousily and violently, but I do not recall him ever once hitting me or my siblings as children. We saw for ourselves that my dad was nothing like the person she was describing to us. Instead, he was a very loving, generous, and funny dad. He was my friend and fellow comedian. He would teach us silly comical songs that he had made up. We thought he was a really cool dad. He would go out of his way to make sure that I knew that he loved me; repeatedly he'd tell me, while I was with him, how much he adored me. He would call me his beautiful child. My sister was just as beautiful. I am certain this is because he knew I felt ugly and all scarred up. It felt so incredible to hear those words; someone loved me. I mattered.

By age eight, I learned that in order to survive my mom as best as possible, I needed to think out each and every breath that I was going to breathe before I exhaled it. I was a very submissive obedient child. While some of my siblings were rebellious against my mom, I personally hated the way that it made me feel when my mom would degrade and insult me so much so, that I did whatever I could to avoid her insults. I learned to maneuver myself around her and her alcoholic ways. Nor did I like being hit with her hand or a belt. What could be so eternal that a parent would hit their child with a leather belt? I am not much for corporal punishment; it has to be for a real life-or-death serious reason that I would hit a child with a leather object.

I have three awesomely functional adult children, who each have several of their own children. Making me a grandma eleven times over again. I can count the times they were ever hit, and so can they.

By nine years old, I had a system for everything, from how to clean up after myself perfectly to how to keep my room just spotless. I went out of my way to help my mom to keep the house cleaned up in an attempt to get on her good side, if there was one. It would last a day or so, and she would go back to her old insulting ways. At times, it did appear she was seriously trying to love me; she just never could overcome the abhorrence she carried for me within her heart. However, I cherished all those times that I would watch her "try" to love me. Hoping and desiring that one day soon she would see that I was worth loving.

Tomato Soup, Cheese, Please

I had to endure watching my mom being miserably married for a second time. It was not gratifying.

One Saturday springtime afternoon, we were all sitting as a family together around in our bright-yellow dining room for lunch. My mom had made tomato soup and grilled cheese sandwiches. My older sister asked if she could add some cheese to her soup. My mom had no problem with that and said, "Yes."

My stepfather on the other hand said, "No."

My mom, ignoring his negative command, got up from the table to go and get the cheese from the fridge anyhow. She came back to the table and began cutting some cheese off the hub of cheese that she had fetched from the refrigerator. All of a sudden, my stepfather reached out and grabbed the oversized bowl of tomato soup that we had been serving our lunch out of and threw it as hard as he could into the air. It slammed against the ceiling, and tomato soup covered the whole dining room ceiling. Before you know it, the tomato soup was dripping down from the ceiling and all down the walls and all over all of us kids. My mom quickly dismissed us from the room. To our rooms we marched, scared and nervous as to what would happen next. The fighting began. They were both raging uncontrollably at each other. They screamed for about a half hour. Then all of a sudden, it all got really quiet. My stepfather had left the house. We remained in our rooms not knowing what to expect. He had went down the street a couple of houses to talk to a few of our neighbors. Before I knew what was happening, within that hour, we were all getting into the car and driving to Disneyland, neighbors too! The rest of that day was so awkward. My mom and stepfather went about the day as if we were one big happy family. All of us kids were in utter dismay as to who was going to clean up the tomato soup off the walls when we arrived back home? Definitely, that day, I walked on pins and needles so that things would not snap again, this time in public.

When we finally got back home in the early evening, we were told to go get our pajamas and brush our teeth and go directly to bed. You better believe that we brushed our teeth—we knew better.

My mom went into the dining room and began cleaning up the big mess that was now all dried up. I believe my stepfather even pitched in and assisted with the cleanup. We awoke in the morning to one bright clean kitchen. Weirdos.

It was a long time before any one of us kids asked to add embellishments anything to our food again. Well, except ketchup—we loved us some ketchup on our food, a habit we had inherited from our dad. It used to make our mom mad that we had picked up such a nasty foul habit as decorating our food in a liquid tomato. There must be something about those tomatoes. Ha ha ha.

There were often unspoken inferences being practiced in our home that were just waiting to rise up and cause additional chaos. Out in the open, my stepfather would constantly insult and criticize all of us, including my mom. Sometimes he would make vague comments about her weight, her looks, or her clothing choice. She was a gorgeous woman, and though we kids had a very limited wardrobe, it seemed to me that she was always dressed to the nines. Overhearing these comments he would make to my mom really offended and bothered me. I was still super self-conscious due to my burns, and when I would hear him insulting my beautiful mom, it would affect my own self-esteem, and it would become more and more damaged. The eating disorder began.

By ten years old, I was watching everything that went into my mouth. That is how anorexia starts; it starts in the mind first, with head trips of not measuring up to untrue body images of others. Voices that either are overheard or voices that are repeated in your mind by what you have watched or overseen others play out in your life. They tell you that you are fat and need to lose weight, and many other defaming words. A horrible disorder.

The arguing between my mom and stepdad began to escalate. The word *divorce* was quickly becoming as common as the list of cuss words that they called each other. It seemed that whichever side that I leaned to, whether my mom or my stepfather, I could not seem to win either way. They were in this sick cycle of dysfunction where they would almost compete to see who could be the meanest to the other.

The discipline also accelerated. I do not understand it, but somehow they began to compete in who was the best disciplinarian also. It was a sick relationship, only to worsen as each day passed by.

A Final New Baby Sister

At ten and a half years old, we moved to a new home that my stepfather had purchased for my mom in order to try to get her to stay with him. I had hopes that we could blend in this new area and new house, and no one would know what a hot mess my family was. I had hopes that he would stop touching me; that of course did not happen. Their fighting was reaching a serious peak of dysfunction.

My mom became pregnant for the sixth and final time. She birthed a beautiful baby sister. I adored her and protected her as much as I could from their abusive ways. I was like her second mom. I would change her diaper throughout the night and get her warm bottles too.

My mom began allowing us three kids to visit our dad again on a regular basis. We went back to our legal last name. Something we were told not to mention to our real dad. It was of course illegal. You cannot just randomly change your child's last name all because the stepfather wants to "feel" like he is the real dad. When he clearly is not. Dumb.

The fighting and insulting continued between my mom and my stepfather. They would scream and cuss, devouring each other with their words. It was the same cycle of addiction repeating itself. They would fight viciously, and then they would go into the honeymoon phase where they acted all in love—drinking, carousing, insulting, stressing, obsessing, overindulging, and living beyond their means. Then the rage would hit the fan, and the cycle would then repeat itself. Over and over, same cycle, different day. The honeymoon stage never lasted long. Seemingly, with no warning, they would be arguing again. Usually after one of their fights, my stepfather would go storming out of the house, squealing his tires out of the driveway. Only two hours later, he would show back up at the house carrying a six-pack wrapped in the usual sixties brown paper bag, a couple packs of cigarettes, and don't forget the Gallo wine. The house would be eerily quiet, everyone fearful of their tempers. Us kids knew that we had to be extra cautious if we did not want their anger to turn and spur out on to one of us. I most often would go to my room. The rocker was a permanent fixture in my room. If I played my cards right and gauged the atmosphere, then I could carefully sneak off into my room and start to rock, without being told, "No rocking." Like what did it matter to them anyways? Imbecile. Usually, if it was convenient to get me out of my mom's hair, she would relent. I knew enough to be ashamed of my rocking. I would hear comments of how crazy I was and how I was to be left alone. Each comment would stick into my heart like a dagger. Who says things like that about her daughter?

My stepfather began inviting one of his friends over almost every weekend. He was a quiet older man. He had sported some foul-smelling body odor and was constantly smoking a cigarette while holding an ever-present beer in his hand. He fit right in. My stepfather had four or five of these male friends that seemed to frequent our home far too often. Each time one of them was over, I would feel even more uncomfortable in my own home. I really disliked all of them, but this man in particular. He would lurk at me as I walked through the room, making my stomach roll in a very uncomfortable way. When these friends would come over, it would incite my stepfather to be even stricter, if possible. It was very humiliating. His demeaning behavior toward us was their entertainment for the day. Degrading comments and insults were the norm along with all the multiple cuss words. He would just dare you to respond in any such way so that he could show his authority by whipping you excessively with his belt or sending you to your room until dinnertime. He was an oppressive bully.

Speaking of dinnertime, it was torture. Dinner was habitually served promptly at five o'clock each day; by this time, both my mom and stepfather had already had a few drinks each, if not more. By dinnertime on a Saturday or Sunday, my stepfather's days off, they were plastered. Dinners were full of rules and discipline, correction, and insulting. The rules were as such that we would all sit in our designated seats. The adults would begin by serving themselves and then passing the dishes to the right, not the left, but only to the right. Only once everyone had been served could we ask permission to begin eating. If you needed a dish, of say vegetables, and it was sitting directly in front of you, then you could ask my stepfather by saying specific words such as, "May I please have some more corn?" No general terms were allowed, like saying, "Could you pass the meat?" This was not acceptable. Instead, "Please pass the meatloaf" was proper. My stepfather would answer you either "yes, you may" or "no, you may not." It was all so weird, like a sci-fi movie. If you dared to go for seconds and decided to reach for the dish, and that dish was, in his opinion, too far away from you, then he would firmly and swiftly stab your hand with his fork. My mom allowed it and never once spoke up to stop him. There goes that eating disorder I mentioned a few paragraphs ago.

In the mix of all this regimentation, my mom was constantly slipping comments in toward us girls about how many calories we were ingesting. Frequently, if you asked for seconds on anything, she would give you a big spill about eating too many calories and getting fat. She would elaborate on how many calories girls our age and height should eat. Making comments right there in front of everyone at the table such as, "When is the last time you got on the scale?" and "How much did you weigh?" It was extremely shaming! Just to give you an earful, by the sixth grade, I was 5'4" and 110 lbs., talk about bringing on a poor self-body image to a young woman. As if I did not already have one with my burns and all.

These unhealthy eating situations later added to an eating disorder I embraced gladly, I admit. I already had a very low self-image, and now I was being taught that if I got fat, then I was 100 percent off-limits unlovable.

Both my mom and my stepfather had no moral compass. They threw that out with their first-year frozen wedding cake. It was really embarrassing for me, especially when I would be out in the public, with either parent. Humiliation 101.

After watching my parents' behavior, I learned to carefully observe anyone I was considering for a friend. How did they treat the other kids in the class? What were they like when they spoke to other people? Their behavior to others would determine any future friendship with them. If they were kind, it would be only at this point I would possibly consider being their friend. I feared being treated badly by anyone else in my life. I hid my burns as best as possible. Hoping no one could or would get any eyeshot of them. I never discussed my "accident," as my mom would call it with anyone from my elementary class. I was super good at acting as if they didn't exist. However, I know they had to see something; pants were not allowed to be worn to school back then. My scars ran all the way down on the right side of my right leg, just inches from my kneecap. It's all just an illusion, I would tell myself.

Another Rocker, Anyone?

My baby brother was growing into a cute little boy. He was extra sensitive just like me. Before you know it, he began rocking just as I had. He probably watched me and just copied what I would do would be a good assumption; however, I do not think that was the issue. I think all the arguing and fighting scared him, and rocking was as soothing for him as it was for me.

Another Baby Sister

When I was ten years, old I was so pleased to have a little baby sister to come on the scene. One that I had the pleasure of taking care of or helping take care of. She was so sweet.

My mom and stepfather were now seeking some counseling for their dwindling marriage.

By this time, my emotions toward my mom were mostly just numb at this point; they would seem mutually so on my mom's side. It was just a matter of orders being given and not a mother-and-daughter relationship. From the outside looking in, it was obvious that my mom despised being a mother and the duties that it entailed. She acted as if I was just a nuisance that was in her way. This hurt me deeply.

I was a sickly child, frequently catching colds, pneumonia, ear infections, and sore throats. I had a weaker immune system due to the burns and all of the smoke that I had inhaled when I caught on fire. All the strong pain medications and high doses of antibiotics that I had to live on in order to survive played a big part in weakening my immune system. When I would complain to my mother that I did not feel good, my mom would actually get angry. She despised having to take care of me when I was not feeling well. It was always questioned—about whether or not I was really sick. Did I have a fever? Having a fever was somehow proof that I was sick. If I did not have a fever, it was determined I was lying and was not really sick. Sad.

On days when I was sick and had to stay home, my mom would be even more on edge than usual. I would do my best to stay in my room as much as possible. Or lie quietly on the couch and watch TV with a carefully lowered volume. Even so, I would do something wrong. She would be so anxious that anything that could possibly set her off would. Her anxiety would quickly turn to rage. Many times if no one else was around, I was the brunt of her rage.

I have always carried a burden for my mom. I would watch her actions and want so badly to yell to her, "Don't you see what you're doing is wrong? Wake up!" I had to stop emotionally stressing about her behaviors and just concentrate on establishing my own set of morals and beliefs. My mom had started to explore witchery and the powers of the mind in order, I can only assume, to bring her some sort of control in her own life. I disagreed strongly with this practice. It brought weirdness into our home. An even darker darkness. Imagine that.

Her alcoholism and daily drinking was increasing evermore. If I were to guess, I would elect to say that my mom could see that her life was spiraling out of control. She was severely unhappy in her second marriage, no wonder, since he liked little girls over grown women. Her desire for the escape of some sort of high was ever increasing, and the monetary expense of all of her vices was becoming an even heavier burden.

My older sister decided to *tell* on my stepfather. Counseling was at the request and demand of my mom and the cure-all to make this marriage work. I remained silent.

Early on in the counseling sessions, my mom received a phone call asking her if she knew if her husband would be making his next appointment since he had missed several before. This, along with discovering that he had been secretly sleeping with her hairdresser, was the final straw for my mom's marriage. What no one knew at the time was that my mom had been secretly dating the licensed psychologist and marriage counselor, who was also still married to his first wife and had eight kids. Messy.

The Midnight Knock

Let me introduce you to my new, soon-to-be-second stepfather. Then, in what seemed like no time, and a few nasty fights later, my first stepfather moved out and moved in with the hairdresser and his two little girls.

It was not any time before that hairdresser came knocking at our door late one evening. She was all bruised up, bloody, and crying. My mom was not sympathetic one bit. She wanted to know if he had ever beaten my mom up. With the door only open wide enough for a chain-lock to be stretched to maximum capacity, she abruptly answered, "No, never," and she slammed the door closed quickly.

I guess she did not stay in that relationship any time too long.

My mom got a job as a cocktail waitress, skimpy outfit and all. My job was to babysit in the evenings while she was at work. I was overjoyed to watch my younger siblings. I knew they would be tended to properly. He did some appalling things to me, and now it all stopped. Well, to my body, that is, but not in my head. This was the beginning of even worse sorrows to come.

Chapter Eight

Ill Behaviors

Keep in mind that I was not fully aware of how hurtful my ill behaviors were until years later. I am telling these stories in order that I might help someone who is looking for resolution in their life. They may have had similar types of behaviors and, therefore, can relate to the dysfunction in their own life. If you happen to be reading this story and are on the receiving end of some of my malicious behaviors, please forgive me.

By age ten, we always lived in neighborhoods we did not belong monetarily. Looking on the outside exterior of the homes, they were always well-groomed, windows shining, lawns manicured just right, and fences just perfectly aligned. On the inside of our home, though, were people living way above their means. Because they chose to live in the neighborhoods that they did not belong, money was always very tight. The first thing that would be cut was the needs of the children.

It was difficult for me most of the time. I constantly carried a chip on my shoulder. I never felt that I measured up to my friends. I was raised with minimal clothing, usually only two pairs of shoes, which you wore to play in or do chores, and the other was your newer pair for school. If they were not worn-out, you wore them until they wore out. One time I broke my right toe, and of course you cannot truly cast just a toe, or at least they did not cast me. My school shoes from the swelling of the toe split about two inches. However, the shoe itself was not worn-out—no new shoes for the rest of the school year. Seriously. My toe finally healed.

My dad would set us up when we would visit with him, for that I will always be grateful, making sure that for the time being we were well-dressed. He would have my stepmom take us shopping before we would return to my mom's house. It was such a kind gesture. Of course, my mom would criticize any kind gesture that came from him. I always seemed to take her criticism personal. It was hard not to. My dad showed his love through material provisions, a trait I would pick up as I grew older. In addition, I picked up his grandiose personality, which was not such a good trait in my opinion, unless of course you go into sales, which I did. It has taken me years to learn how to tame and calm this trait in myself.

In the new neighborhood, I was blessed to have made two new friends. I was so excited that I was allowed to go over to their houses. However, neither one of their parents ever allowed them to come in to the inside of my house. That fact never seemed to bother me much though because I was so thrilled to be away from home versus them coming to my home. Spending a majority of our time at their houses was a much-needed break. I feared that if they were to come to my house, then my stepfather might have made some sort of inappropriate comment or gesture toward them.

In the sixth grade, I had my little posse. At this point, there were about six of us who hung around together on a regular basis. I was the common link to all of them. It felt so comforting when I was around my tight group of friends. My homelife felt completely out of control, so I think that I compensated by making sure that I fit in at school.

Who did not fit in was my mom. She was working as a cocktail server, and her work outfit, which she had volunteered to make for all the female cocktail servers, was quite embarrassing for me. It was the late sixties, and hot pants and miniskirts were in style. Each late afternoon when my mom would get in the car to go to work, she would be wearing one of her not-so-appropriate outfits.

One of my friends' parents had driven by my house one day as my mom was just leaving for work. This encounter led to one of my close girlfriends asking me a shocking question.

I disagreed with her flamboyant behaviors that were now directly affecting my friendships, ones in which I had tried so hard to build.

Once, when I was in the fifth grade, one of these friends very seriously asked me, "Is your mom a prostitute?" I utterly contemplated the question and said no. Come to find out, it was assumed around the area that my mom was a prostitute, and that is why neither friend was allowed to come inside of my house.

My mom was a very attractive woman, and she was fully aware of her beauty. She was always dressed in very tight and provocative clothing. She enjoyed the attention that she received from men but especially enjoyed the thrill of making other women envious when she could catch their husband's eye pondering upon her. Sickening.

At home, my room was neat as a pin. It was expected of me. Period. All my toys were put in their proper place. All shoes belonged in a tightly woven little row in the bottom of the closet floor. Period. All my clothes were expected to be "hung up neatly," as my mom would say to me. I got it. There was never, I mean never, a sweater or jacket just lying around for some lazy reason. If so, then you could expect to be yelled at and possibly smacked upside the head a few times. We did have a coat rack at least, which stood right by the front door, and that was a blessing! I lived in a house and not a home, if you get my drift. Therefore, perfectionism came easily for me.

Getting ready for school was an ever-growing chore. You see, I had to get my brother ready for school now also. My mom had reverted to not getting up in the mornings, again. He was two school years behind me, and my sister was two school years ahead of me. By the fifth and sixth grade, my mom just about never got up in the mornings. Someone had to help my brother. I would pick out his clothes, style his hair, help him get his breakfast, and brush his teeth, five days a week. Most of it was against his will. I was bigger than he was, so if he was going to be known as my brother, then he was going to look good. Period, end of story.

Wavy hair ran in my dad's side of the family, so we three kids had some wave going on. On a typical school morning, I would completely wet my brother's head down in the bathroom sink. Holding him still between my legs, I would then take some Dippity-do or

VO5 and apply it. I would thoroughly comb it through his hair, then I would comb it straight back and push his hair at its natural growth line so I could place each wave perfectly about his head. It would stay that way the remainder of the day. Little did I know that at age nineteen, I would follow my grandma's example and go through cosmetology school to acquire my California state license. I guess I was a natural and did not know it yet.

I took neatness, prettiness, tidiness, and perfectionism as a sign that I was okay on the inside. Actually I was just at the beginning of creating a false sense of wholeness on the outside to cover up the incompleteness of self I was suffering with on the inside of me. I succeeded in becoming emotionally bankrupt until I hit bottom in my early forties. From my preteens to my midforties was a long road of reprise. Cycles of God showing me my un-Christian-like behavior, my denying it and having God show me yet again. He wanted me to submit and change my bad, family-of-origin learnt behavior.

Some behaviors were more obvious than others were.

While it is normal to bathe daily, it was essential for me. By the sixth grade, I had been through a lot. I was still suffering emotional and sexual abuse from my first stepfather. I had suffered inappropriate and abusive comments made to me frequently by my mom. On numerous occasions, she still would tell her friends that she thought I was crazy. I would overhear her talking to a few of her close friends about me. She would constantly tell people that she thought I was whatever. Really, then why didn't she take me to a counselor or something? One thing was for sure: I was definitely suffering from stroke deprivation. She never touched me in a positive way. It's as if she thought I had cooties and she could catch my burns. My mom just flat out did not like me—who I was or who I was becoming, so hugging me was completely out of the question. As if she was angry with me for burning myself. Strange coping concept.

She would allow my stepfather to both verbally and emotionally abuse me. My mom, on the other hand, would slap, hit, punch, kick, or swing at me, smack me in the head with an ol' rattail brush whenever she felt it was necessary. He carried this false sense of superiority that he was better than anyone and everyone around him and was not ashamed to let anyone within ear distance know about it. He was a very prejudiced man. Any person of any color other than Caucasian, he disliked for the most part.

I began trying to get away with bathing twice a day. This was not acceptable to my mom. However, she was not home in the evenings a lot of the time, so it was not hard to pull off. I liked the feeling of being clean. It just seemed natural to me to shower in the morning and then to bathe at night. Being sexually abused made me physically feel dirty; bathing seemed to take away some of that feeling, for a few hours at least.

Midpoint through my sixth-grade year, my mom and stepfather had talked and yelled about a divorce. It was not long past second semester that he finally moved out. My life was already tumultuous, so a couple of bathes a day was a way I could wash all the drama that my homelife had to offer away.

In addition to obsessively bathing, I began brushing my teeth neurotically. To this day, I still get agitated if my teeth do not feel clean. I've been known to brush them five to six times in a day. Less dentist trips.

I had a peculiar sense of humor, mixed with a touch of meanness, which seemed to be growing out of control. I would use my sense of humor to hurt people. This has been a challenge to overcome in my life. If I start feeling lousy on the inside, out would come the sarcasms against myself and others.

In the sixth grade, I hit a real groove in school. I felt right in my element with several friends and a bright head on my shoulders. There was one problem though; I would start laughing for no reason in class. A couple of my friends would start laughing, and I could not seem to stop myself from joining in. The teacher did not think it was so funny. After several warnings, I had a note sent home to my mom.

As I mentioned earlier, I never knew how my mom was going to react or respond to any given situation. This particular incident was different from any before.

My mom took me aside and explained to me, "You cannot be joining in with your girlfriends on these laughing fests. If you don't quit laughing in class and causing disruption, then not only are you going to be punished in school, but I am going to punish you at home also."

I tried to explain myself as best that I could as to why the laughing would begin, but no excuse was a good enough one.

My mom finally said, "Think about the day that John F. Kennedy was shot and killed, that should help you to stop on the join in."

Think about the president being shot and killed, really? That was a horrible thought to teach your child, but it worked. Strangely enough, from then on, when I would need to be worried about keeping a straight face, in order to not laugh, or for any other reason I would need to keep a straight face, I would just think of poor JFK. This peculiar advice would keep me out of lots of trouble for years on end. Sick.

Along about this time, I had taken on a perfectionism that would grow to hinder me all throughout life. To this day I still struggle with having to have things a certain way. I was becoming a fault-finder in just about everything I did.

When I would go to do my homework, I would write all the answers out on a piece of paper. If one letter was written that did not meet my standards for being neat or pretty enough, I would either take the paper and scrunch it up into a ball and throw it away or rip it into pieces, starting completely over again. Oftentimes it would take quite a few drafts—like ten to twelve drafts—in order to achieve my final sheet that met my approval. This is something that continued until the computer came to be part of my life.

I had been taught handwriting in the sixth grade. Boy, did I enjoy the artistic fashion in which I could write. My obsessive behavior was annoying, even to myself, and yet I continued. Perfectionism was my friend and closest enemy at times in my life. It gave me a sense of control in my out-of-control life.

Another example of my perfectionism was made obvious when I joined the junior Girl Scouts with some of my friends. If you were my friend and not in Girl Scouts, I wanted a good explanation as to why you did not want to join. Fridays after school was our normal Girl Scout meeting day. We would meet in one of the school classrooms for a few hours each week. It became a group thing to wear our uniforms to school on those days, as we did not really have time to go home, return to our meeting, and be on time. So uniforms it was on Fridays. I enjoyed it; it was one less day a week I had to worry about not fitting in.

The night before such a meeting was crazy. I went through a ritual of washing my uniform and ironing it to perfection each week. It had to be ironed perfectly, no pleat out of place, before I would put it on.

Somewhere in the mix of ironing my green Girl Scout uniform, I came up with the idea to start ironing my school clothes to perfection also. I would keep this habit of ironing my clothes before I wore them into my thirties. Who knows how many hours of my life were spent behind an ironing board. The perfectionism of each garment was so important to me. It was as if the way I was dressed determined my value and worth. I thought that if I looked clean and neat, no one would know what dirty thing had happened to me in my past.

Cookies, Anyone?

In addition to dealing with the uncomfortableness of hiding my burns, I was trying my best to fit in. I was trying extra hard and be accepted into a circle of friends who had all known one another since kindergarten. It took a while, but by the fifth grade, I felt that I had finally made it into the group. This came with, of course, many false fronts. It was a Friday. The Los Angeles school district was on strike, and the school was functioning purely with substitute teachers and aides that none of us kids were familiar with. There was a school fundraiser going on. The girls were standing behind a self-made counter selling four packs of cookies. My friends and I hatched a plan. We approached the counter as casually as possible and purchased one four-pack of cookies. While the young girl was collecting our money, we each grabbed as many packages of cookies as we could manage. Dashing to the back of the playground, we giggled all the way. Why we had decided to do such a thing, I am not sure, but I was definitely caught up right in the middle of it. The girls running the stand were screaming for someone to come and stop us. My heart racing, I ran as fast as my legs would carry me. I was so scared, and yet at the same time, I was having so much fun being part of this girl group.

We reached the edge of the playground where the sixth graders were playing kickball. Toss, toss, toss. We threw each package of cookies up and over the fence, laughing hysterically. Our plan was to be rid of the evidence and come back later to collect our bounty. For some odd reason, unbeknown to me, we never were even questioned or caught for that matter. After school, we gorged out on all the packages of cookies while laughing our heads off. Weirdo alert.

I was becoming somewhat of a bully. I could see myself changing, and yet I did not try to stop it at this time in my life. The release of acting out felt exhilarating.

My girlfriends seemed to have an access to a slew of random things that I did not: a package of gum in their very modern purse, a pair of knee-high Nancy Sinatra boots, or a Twiggy matte white lipstick. They were definitely dressed far finer than I was. The quality and variety of their clothes was something I would crave to obtain. I vowed to be enough of a success in life that I too could afford anything I desired.

To help myself to fit in, I began to steal quarters from my mom's change purse almost every weekday before school. The bartending my mom was doing in the evenings brought lots of spare change!

In the mornings, after I had gotten my baby brother and myself up and ready for school, I would sneak into my mom's bedroom, where she was still passed out from the night before. Careful to step silently, I would locate her purse with my eyes. Once it was spotted, I would assess the situation. Where was my mom on the bed? Did she appear to be in a deep sleep, or was she wrestling and moving around? If it seemed safe enough, I would attempt to take what I thought I deserved. Super carefully, I would unsnap my mom's change purse, attempting to remove four quarters at a time with as little noise as possible. I would put the first set of four quarters into my mouth between my teeth on one side, clamping them just as tightly as I could so they would not move or make any clanking noises to give me away. Once they were secure, I would grab four more quarters and proceed to place them on the other side of my mouth. If all of the remaining change in the purse was lying just right in her change purse, I would dip back in for a third time and put four more quarters into my left hand, squeezing super tightly. If I had three dollars' worth of change for the day, then I felt like victory had been achieved.

I would snap the change purse closed as quickly as I could without making any noise, constantly looking over at my mom to be certain she was not waking up, and placed it back snuggly into her purse.

What an adrenaline rush! Once I began backing up to leave the bedroom, I knew that success was just around the corner. I always walked backward so that if per chance she were to wake up, then I could play it off as if I was just then entering the room. Now all I had to do was get out of the room, close the door without a sound, and then I would be victorious. How victorious depended on the way the change had been sitting in the change purse. My goal was to steal at least two dollars each school day, which was the going rate to buy my school lunch like all of my friends each day. Any extra that I could pilfer would be used to give away to anyone who was not "privileged" enough to have lunch money as I did that day. Each time I was able to give money to someone "less fortunate," then I felt like I fit more into the well-to-do crowd that was my group of friends. In reality, I was just getting rid of any of the evidence to be able to point a finger at me for being the thief. What a big fat false front I was portraying to myself.

I became hypersensitive to making sure that all my angles were covered. In addition, I had begun a very sick game to see just how far I could push things. What could I get away with? I knew how much my mom drank when she got home each night. I also knew that it was not unusual for her to hang out at the bar and have a few drinks after her shift ended. I knew that if I stole money early in the morning before she got up to count her tips she had made from bartending the night before, then she would have no clue that it had been stolen. I felt that she owed me things that I was lacking, basic things like lunch money. We would have had money for the material things that

I saw all my friends have if she did not blow all her money night after night on her alcohol.

Well into my thirties, I dealt with why I had felt the need to steal from my mom. I am grateful that God has had grace on me for my bad behavior. I am also grateful that I never became a thief for a living. I became rather good at it. I stole from my mom's change purse up until the end of my mom's second marriage, which put me in a new school and a new town. I only stopped because it became too difficult to get away with it anymore. I always felt that she owed me something, and stealing was my way of paying myself back from what was being taken from me. Love and time, the two things I was not receiving and that she fell short of giving to me.

It would be unreasonably easy to say that I never stole from anyone again, and equally untrue. When I was twelve years old, and at the local grocery store with one of my friends, I stole a pair of nylons while my friend stole a pack of gum. We were both caught. The store manager called both our parents. My mom listened to what the manager had to say and then informed him that she was in the middle of cooking dinner, so he would just have to tell me to walk directly home.

That was one very long walk home. I was not sure of what to expect from my mom. Had I finally been exposed? What was she going to do? As I approached the back door to the house, I took a deep breath of relief; my second stepfather was home, so her rage would be somewhat in check at least. My mom was about halfway through making dinner and about halfway to being drunk.

She looked at me and stated, "You are not a thief. Don't ever lower yourself to being a thief." Turning her back to me, she said, "Now help me get the table set for dinner." That was the end of the discussion. I thought to myself, what are you talking about, not being a thief, you are a thief, you stole away my childhood by staying as drunk as possible my entire life!

Chapter Nine

Deep Longing

I STILL CARRIED A DEEP longing to understand the God that I was introduced to at a young age. In my neighborhood, I noticed a church down at the end of the road from where I lived. I asked my mom if I could go to the church. She only had one question, "Is it Protestant?" I had no clue. That did not stop me from answering without a blink, "Of course it is." So for the next two years, my older sister and I attended this church off and on. I am certain that God's word was deposited into my spirit, even if I was not yet born-again.

I felt safe in this church, around all these godly people. I believe that I was called of God at a very young age. His protective hand was upon me. It just took me many years to understand His drawing in my life.

Just because my mom and dad chose to turn away from God does not mean that God turned away from them. Certainly, it did not mean that God no longer cared about me. I believe that God heard my mom's and dad's prayers, just as He had heard my grandma's prayers through the years that she had been raised in a Christian home. Just because they chose to rebel against the mighty hand of God, it did not remove His hand from them. We are not that powerful. We are only as powerful as the Word of God is present in our lives. The further we walk away from God, the less powerful we become as spiritual beings. That is a fact.

I thank God for my younger days when He would draw me into church. I believe God was watching after me then just as He still does now, as I am a full-grown adult. By God drawing me into His sanctuary, the hope for me as a child was that maybe my mom could remember how much better our life had been compared to how out of control it had spiraled.

My sister and I both sang in the church choir and participated in church play. My mom and my stepfather came, though they were very facetious the entire time. The play could not end quickly enough so they could return to their home and their alcohol. Talk about being out of their element.

At my stepfather's suggestion, my mom had gotten involved in Girl Scouts of America when I was seven years old. Both my sister and I were somewhat still involved up until the divorce. He also strongly encouraged my mom to get involved in an all-girls softball team when I was nine and ten. My mom, for the first time, was a part of my life in the public eye. She treated me fairly nice in front of others; however, because of all of the emotional insults that she had made toward me up until that point in my life, I could not receive her good behavior as love. In my heart, I knew that she was just "reacting" to how she knew she was supposed to treat her daughter. I never felt that she loved me on her own free will, without there being something in it for her. The way that she treated us when not on display versus the way she treated us when others were around proved to me that she had some conviction about how to be a good loving parent.

The game that she played was so Jekyll and Hyde. We would be in the room with say my grandma or my aunt, and she would be on her best behavior. This meant that we needed to be playing our part too, that all was good. Then when they would leave, the inevitable would and did occur. The ultimate hurt. She would revert to being unconcerned, uncaring, short-tempered, and insulting. She would use unnecessary physical force just for the kick of it. Disgusting.

I grew up believing that my mom enjoyed hitting her kids. It was an adrenaline rush for her when she would use a belt on my baby brother. I helplessly sat by and witnessed beating after beating. I do believe that my mom had conviction about abusing her children, yet she never seemed to yield to that conviction. I personally believe that my mom was entirely too young to be parenting five children. She never had the temperament to be a parent. All five of us kids were afraid of her for many years to come. Bullying was her lifetime companion.

All that I really needed was a hug. My mom was not a hugger of her children, not at least when I lived in her home. She did not like her children to touch her. She was afraid we might mess up her hairdo or put a wrinkle in her clothes. I definitely suffered from stroke deprecation growing up. My mom just did not touch me, unless of course I was being slapped across the face or upside the head. There were no casual kisses or affectionate squeezes, ever. Not that I can recall. I in return, I become very standoffish toward her. It was obvious that I did not approve of her. The immeasurable gap between us was huge. I felt safe with the gap imposed; if she did not have access to me, then she could not hurt me. My mom had her favorite kids, and I did not make the cut.

My grandmother and my mom had grown even further apart. We could see my grandma and grandpa a few times a year in that time of my life, usually for sure at Christmastime and at least once or twice in the summertime. They would drive up the West Coast to see us all. I loved seeing my grandma. Not so much my grandpa; he had become a super bad whiskey alcoholic. He would visit with grandma every time they came; however, he most often was passed out on the living room couch. Grandma would be humiliated by his behaviors. Ashamed.

My grandma and grandpa had both become alcoholics, but my grandpa a severe alcoholic. Grandma never really seemed to be drunk, she just kept a slight buzz going on with her sip after sip. Grandpa had a bottle of whiskey and a glass that had a permanent home on the kitchen counter in whatever house he was. He frequently would go into the kitchen and fill the glass three-fourths full. In one harsh gulp, he would down the contents and then push the whiskey bottle back to its place until he next ventured into the kitchen, a few hours later. Grandma was not a whiskey drinker; starting at about two o'clock each day, she would start drinking, and that can of beer would be by her side until she crashed at night. She was also a chain-smoker; lung cancer is what finally took her life when I was twenty-five years old.

Despite the alcohol consumption, I cherished the times when my grandma would come to visit. She had a way of making me feel exceptional and loved. She always made chocolate fudge, oatmeal raisin cookies, and of course my favorite, chocolate chip cookies. This was a real treat for us since we did not really get many snacks. In my mom's opinion, the extra calories would do nothing but make us fat, plus the extra cost to purchase the ingredients to make the snacks could go toward something more important—alcohol. My grandma would allow us to eat, as much as we wanted to indulge in no matter what looks my mom would send our way. For the short time of her visits, we would remain under our grandma's safety net. No one was going to punish us while she was around. Grandma trumped Mom. Period.

She would always seem to find a private moment to ask me if I was doing okay. No, I was not doing okay, but I knew better than to answer with the truth. As soon as I would have told her how life really was at my house, she would have confronted my mother. I had no desire for an all-out war, which I would inevitably pay the price for by my mom once Grandma left to go back home. In ACA (Adult Children of Alcoholics), it is called the "no-talk rule." I had learned it well and had not even begun a program yet.

All the alcoholics in my life were control freaks. So many years spent numbing from reality with their alcohol had caused many issues in "my" family. Instead of yielding to God's will in their lives, they all chose their own paths away from God.

If an alcoholic does finally decide to give up the bottle, then shy of a miracle, they need to get quickly into some sort of support group such as AA (Alcoholics Anonymous). After a prolonged time with a pattern of bad, alcohol-induced, selfish choices, it is important to learn new healthy behavior and responses. If these new patterns are not learned, then the alcoholic will just become a "dry drunk"—no more alcohol but the same outbursts, the same outcomes, same addictive cycles using different vices, with no new responses.

When I was ten years old, my grandpa was offered the position of vice president of PSA Airlines, whom he had long worked for. He was one of the five people that had helped start that airline. Starting as an airplane mechanic, he had worked himself up to a suit and tie. The day that he was called into the office by his good friend and superior and was offered the job was a big crossroads for him. When offered the position, he quickly declined, confessing that in his suit jacket was a fifth of whiskey and that he had become completely dependent on it in order to get through the day and night. He knew that there was no way that he could complete the job that he was being ask to do. Surprised by this confession and the depth of his addiction, the company withdrew their offer and required him to seek some help. My grandpa went through a series of two or three different hospitalizations where he attempted to medically detox. His health was rapidly deteriorating, and his veins on the lower left part of his body had begun to collapse. Following his second attempt to rehabilitate, San Diego university medical hospital performed an experimental procedure where they put plastic in place of his veins; in exchange, he was to agree to an autopsy upon his death to see how well the veins had withstood. In 1972, he entered his final rehab at which point he stayed sober until a year before his death.

He finally was sober for the first time in my life. Though he was kinder to me, he still had one sore subject—my mom. He constantly berated and insulted her to me, calling her every name plausible. Though I may have agreed with the root of some of those comments, it was very hurtful to hear such venomous words spoken about her. The depth of his hostility was scary to me. I would not understand it fully for many years to come.

CHAPTER TEN

New Town, New Hope— another New Stepfather

I WAS YET TO FACE another hard challenge in my life. My mom was continuing the relationship with the marriage counselor who had helped her through her second divorce. Soon arrived a second step-father. He was never mean to me. I can count the words that he even spoke directly to me; they were very few. He had eight kids of his own, and he married my mom, who had five kids. Our plate was full. Our house was anything but quiet and peaceful. One good aspect of the marriage was that my mom's attention was divided even more, which meant less negative attention focused my way. I could blend more easily into the background, or should I say crowd, and not be noticed, a feeling that I had become all too comfortable with. Four or five children to a small bedroom was a bit much, but it was what it was.

I never really disliked this stepfather; I did however think that he was just using my mom as his adult built-in babysitter and a sex object. He needed someone to raise his kids, who ranged from two to sixteen years old. He was looking for someone to play the part of mother and wife for his family. What a choice he made choosing one of his patients for this part? Seriously?

One cool thing about my mom marrying the psychologist was that, for the most part, he did not treat his children verbally abusive, so when my mom would treat her own children badly or talk mean to them, it would cause her to stand out like an even bigger sore thumb. He was quick to analyze her and put her in the appropriate category. Because of this, when my new stepfather was home, my mom was an entirely different person. She was much nicer and would limit her mean comments to a minimum. She was always careful to not be overheard by her new husband, whom she insisted she was deeply in love with.

Let us just say that for good reason, I could not stand the two oldest boys. They were definitely favored out of his eight children. They were filled to overflowing with a bitter revulsion for my mother, their new stepmother. Besides each other, they treated everyone else with ill will, including their own six siblings. They came from a home where their mother had lost all control of their behavior. They lived on a warpath, insulting and demeaning any and every one they encountered, placing special attention on females whom they had a special distaste for. They nicknamed females dogs, and if they thought a girl was ugly or too fat, they would make a rough growl at them. They nicknamed all their siblings, including us stepsiblings. They called my older sister Hank, Tank the Pig. They were never corrected or stopped by neither my mom nor their father, my stepfather. The nickname that they favored most for me was Bubba Lips; yes, I have big lips. Boy, are they eating their words now, big lips are popular. My baby brother was called Bird, a nickname carried over from the first stepdad. In my opinion, they were a product of a much deeper problem even before they were introduced into my life. Analyze that. I did my best to ignore them and not speak to them the entire time they were in my life. Not good humans.

Murderous Junior High Days

The summer before the seventh grade, one of the girls at my new school heard that a large family had moved into the neighborhood. She and a group of her friends walked over to my house and introduced themselves to me. She encouraged me to walk over to her house on school mornings so that she could walk to school with me. I thank God for her in my life. I had no clue until school started that she was the most popular girl in school. I was a bit nervous about all the extra attention that came from having such a very popular friend, but things were looking up. This girl and I got along very well. She was from a broken home, and we seemed to get each other's broken-ness. Not to mention she had alcoholic parents—imagine that. Silent magnets.

Another girl lived in my cul-de-sac. She befriended me along with all my stepsisters during the first couple of days we moved into the new home. She became a very close and true friend. I entrusted her with my secret. I confided in her about my burns. She carried my secret all the way through school, never telling a soul. Now that is a true friend.

My new true friend told me a story one day about something one of our neighbors had done to her. Needless to say it was completely inappropriate. This neighbor had a little boy who I considered very bratty.

Being the loyal friend that I am, I decided to take a dollar out of my two-dollars-a-week allowance and buy an Ex-Lax chocolate bar. Yes, I said *Ex-Lax*; this is a laxative, if somehow you did not know. One day I lured this little bratty boy as he was wandering aimlessly in our neighborhood cul-de-sac, over in my front yard, and asked him if he wanted a bite of my chocolate bar. This was not difficult as he scrounged the neighborhood with little or no supervision. Of course, like any other six-year-old boy, he said yes. I broke a decent-size piece off, and he greedily ate it. I then offered him the rest of the bar, which he took and ate right up. The whole time I was able to keep a straight face, thinking about JFK, pretending I was just being friendly.

It was a Saturday morning, and his mom was getting ready to get groceries at the store, a good half hour away. The mom called him over, and he jumped right on into the back tan seat of the station wagon car. Away they went down the road.

A few hours later, they returned home from shopping, and they were not happy. The boy had proceeded to poop not just in his pants, liked I had hoped, but also all over himself and the back seat of their car. There was poop in every conceivable spot. The tan interior was not so pristine any longer.

The boy's mom had derived at a conclusion and came straight over to my house to tell my mom of the horrifying thing that I had done. Fortunately for me, my mom had a few drinks already that day. After dismissing the neighbor, she came to talk to me. Not knowing what my punishment would be, I became extremely nervous.

My mom proceeded to say to me with a forced straight JFK face, "You're lucky that I don't like those neighbors or their little bratty son, so ... do not ever do that again. It is very dangerous, you know." I was not aware it was dangerous. I only knew it would make him poop a lot. She then turned on her heels and left me there in the room. I just never knew what behavior she would punish and which she would let slide. Seemed like the things that really needed to be dealt with, she ignored a consequence. Dysfunctional.

No Problem with Direct Insults

I began insulting others just as I was being insulted at home. I could find something wrong with just about anyone that I chose too. I began criticizing complete strangers, becoming very rude in a public setting. I was even bold enough to insult a person directly to their face. If someone was, let us say, dirty and needed a bath, leave it to me to inform them.

I struggled with people who looked strange on the outside. I think it is sad that I was exhibiting so much hate to others for their looks, and here I was trying my best to cover up my own scars. With each insult that I placed on another person, my self-esteem would be falsely pumped up one more notch. Double standard. Confusion.

One day while my mom was sitting in the den with a handful of my stepsiblings and a few additional friends, she decided to pull out the old family photo album from when I was a kid. While she was casually flipping through the book, my heart stopped. I saw a picture that just appalled me. It was a snapshot of me in the salt baths—from the bad ol' days. A large stainless steel–looking tub standing all alone in this stainless room, all except the neatly tiled perfectly cleaned floors. This photo of me was inconspicuously placed in with the mix of all the other family photos. When my mom left the room to go refill her wineglass yet again, I quickly removed the photo from the album and angrily ripped it up into itty-bitty pieces and discarded it in the outside trashcan. How vile and humiliating. Why would anyone, let alone my own mother, have put such a personal despicable picture right there in the middle of this photo album? One that captures all these happy moments. One that you would show your friends. One that any stranger could view. I never did figure that one out. Heartbreaking memories exposed.

Betrayal Prohibited

My popular friend ended up having a crush on one of my older stepbrothers. I hated my two oldest stepbrothers. I made a vow and stuck to never speak to either of them again for the remainder of our parents' five-year marriage because of what they had done to me a few months prior to our parents' marriage. The younger stepbrother, who was three years older than me, had thrown me down on my own twin bed and raped me while the older stepbrother stood closely by watching and laughing and snickering and egging him on the entire time. Painful. Keeping the details to myself, I proceeded to tell my friend that he was a jerk and that he disrespected all females. That to like him, there had to be something wrong with her. I could not understand why she could not see him for what he really was. I let her know that clearly that if she entertained the idea of dating him or even liking him, then I would not remain her friend. She never ended up dating him, but her crush infuriated me. Betrayal 911.

The following year, this same girl was trying out for cheerleading, so I rallied against her for the open spot available on the team, purely so that she would not be chosen. I literally campaigned silently and behind her back through the whole freshman class so that the girl running against her would instead win. She was going to pay. Revenge is so evil; however, it became very comfortable to be vengeful. It was what I saw parented, and I repeated it. It was wrong.

New Posse

The eighth grade had come around, and I had built myself another posse again.

On Halloween that year, I wanted to have a costume desperately, but it was determined that it did not fit in "our" budget. Being the strong personality that I am, I talked all the girls in the group into painting their faces instead of wearing costumes. So that I would not be the odd man out. As I was finishing up trick-or-treating with my band of friends and had returned to my own neighborhood, a little boy had left his dad at the street side and was walking up on my grass to get some candy. He was wearing a bulky and awkward silver spray-painted box for a robot costume. I could tell that a lot of time and care had been put into creating his costume. Jealousy came smashing me right in the face, with it came the need to feel superior. I justified that I saw an easy target. As he was walking back down the grass, away from my house, I proceeded to knock him over onto the grass, stealing his pillowcase full of candy. My friends and I laughed hysterically as we ran away and sort of hid as fast as possible behind our family camping trailer. We remained there long enough for the dad to turn around, see what happened, and try to find the culprit. Sickly my heart was bouncing with this alarmingly crazy heartbeat, as if I had just achieved something good. Quickly thinking how best to not be caught and to not be discovered as the thieves, I took the candy and dumped it into my pillowcase and discarded the evidence of his container so as not to be accused. My friends and I were laughing and laughing all the way, as if I had just won the grand prize. I was becoming a bully meanie.

My behavior was getting out of control along with my disrespect for anyone who had what I wanted. Jealous intentions.

I Had a Little Secret

One day when I was in the bathroom throwing up after a family meal, I overheard my baby sister asking, "Where is Cindy at?" My mom casually yelled back to her, "She is in the bathroom throwing up." Crazy.

I came out of the bathroom expecting my mom to ground me to my room or some other similarly painful punishment. However, she did not say a single word to me, nor did she acknowledge me. She never addressed the incident until I was in my forties, and then she brought it up thinking it was normal behavior. What I started at thirteen had progressed to full-throttle bulimia by the time I was fourteen. By fourteen, I was throwing up daily. It came very easily for me. Purging offered me the much-desired feeling of control in my very out-of-control world. Throwing up is a sick delusion of a false truth. Once you throw up, you falsely tell yourself that you discarded all the bad that was in you. Food was the bad guy. It equated to fat, and fat was taught to me to be my enemy. It was implied that if I got fat, no one would like me, let alone could stand to look at me.

One day one of my hard-earned close girlfriends casually mentioned an easy way to lose weight. I grabbed on to it immediately. I was already very obsessive about brushing my teeth, so this throwing-up thing just gave me even more reason to brush more frequently. I never threw up at school; instead, I would just not eat. That as we all know can turn into anorexia, and that it did. I was up for trying anything to help myself feel better on the inside. My outsides were still so scarred up, and the burns did not seem to be shrinking, only to turn into a rainbow of colors.

It always amazed me that my mom never scolded me about throwing up or for not eating. It was extra important to my mom *how* her daughters looked. Who cares how they *felt*? In my mom's domain, it was more about the exterior by far. We lived in a very uppity area in Santa Barbara County, a place where a large family with thirteen children did not belong. We were far from matched up with most of our neighbors. All of us children, or at least the girls, were considerably underdressed compared to their competition in the town. Looks were very much so emphasized in my family. Us girls were expected to look good at all times. It was frequently said, "Hold your stomach in." or "Put your shoulders back, quit slouching, and stand up straight." If my stepfather was not around, my mom would often add to that corrective bossy comment by saying, "You look sloppy just like your father. You know he has bad posture, don't you?" You see, my mom was actually in love with her third husband and cared about what he thought of her, so she would put on an act when he was present. One of my mom's most favorite undermining self-esteem comments was, "Do you know how many calories are in that slice of bread?" I cannot count the number of times that I heard such disparaging remarks spoken to me. I am not a bread eater to this day.

Chapter Eleven

Newfound Fears

I HAD MANY FEARS AT a very young age. I took on a childhood that no youngster should have to withstand. I am not proud of the behaviors that I took on in order to cope. It is just how I handled not feeling loved.

My relationship with my grandma was not near as close as it had been in years past. I missed her company, her challenges, and even her bossy controlling ways. My grandma had a way of lifting me up with her comments. She believed in my success. She would tell me that I was smart and pretty, something that I do not recall hearing my mom ever say to me as a child. I was now living six hours away from her and desperately missed her comfort. She constantly was on my mind.

I was dreadfully uncomfortable in my body. I was so tired of having to make sure everything was always covered up. Seventh grade was right around the corner. While I was consumed with the uncomfortableness of living in my scars, for the time being, I was more concerned with being forced to dress and undress in front of my peers and classmates. Physical education class had become my greatest junior high fear. I had heard rumors that you were expected to take a shower every day when your forty-five-minute class was over. I had no idea how sneaky and manipulative I would have to become. There was absolutely no way that I was going to take my clothes off in front of all those girls. I was so terrified to the point I was losing sleep at nighttime. Insomnia.

I had a few weeks of summer left, and I spent them pondering on the upcoming physical education class that I dreaded taking. I had to come up with a plan. I decided that I needed to get a locker all the way to the far right corner closest to the front door of the gym entrance. I hoped that I could get PE first or second period so that my chances of success in receiving one of these remaining prized lockers was greater. My plan was that I could wait for everyone to get into the room, and then I could angle my body at forty-five degrees to the right. We were required to wear dresses at the school I attended. So therefore I had it figured that if I could slip off my nylons and slip my orange pinstriped polyester gym jumpsuit on underneath the dress, I would then remove my dress and pull the top part of the jumpsuit on, snapping it together at both shoulders. This was a pattern that I would need to repeat five days a week. Weary. I would constantly run the steps over in my head to reassure myself that I could do it. I even practiced a trial run in my bathroom at home in front of the mirror before school started that fall, making sure that nothing was showing. I was obsessed with doing it perfectly. Because the jumpsuit was sleeveless, I was forced to wear the white pullover sweatshirt I owned to cover up my top shoulder and arm area; if not, my scars would have been out for the world to see. I was determined to do whatever it took to keep my secret from getting out that I was not normal like everyone else in my school. I attended school on the West Coast and in an area that was very yuppie; I had reason for concern. Draining.

My fears were increasing day by day. Living the lie of who I was *not* seemed to not only be harming me, but the other choice was not even an option.

Many times in my life, people would catch a glimpse of my scars. I despised that split-second moment when I was revealed. Some people were nice about it, but a lot were very cruel. They would make a face while asking me, "What was that on your arm or leg?" As if it was some sort of contagious disease they were afraid they were going to catch. This was the question that I dreaded most. Inside I would be screaming, "What does it look like!" I could see the disgust on their face when they saw my secret. I had been exposed, and it made me so angry. Something was seriously wrong with me, and now they saw it too. I had no clue how to cope with the exposure. I only knew how to act when masked with deception. Being revealed exposed the cracks in the façade I was so desperately trying to live. I hated existing in my scars.

There was a second issue at hand. I was going to be attending a junior high on the military base. They had a strictly enforced dress code of dresses with sheer nude nylon hoses or knee socks. How was I going to hide my huge scar on my right leg? If someone found me out, they probably would not accept me anymore. These were not just thoughts; this was typical of how young girls treat one another in the upper-class town that I had landed myself in at this time in my life. I know I experienced it in the younger grades, and it only seemed to increase, as petty girls grew older.

When comments were made, and questions were asked, while I was at school, I would go home and tell my mom what had been said. Her typical response was, "Stop being so self-centered, self-conscious, and conceited, it is not that bad." Or she once said, "You're making a big deal about nothing, just get past it." Really? Nothing? Hello, have you seen my scars? She did not even acknowledge the reality of the situation and the trauma that I was facing. This I discovered is a very similar trait in alcoholics; it is called denial. D-e-n-i-a-l.

I was hiding my scars throughout my day when I was out in the public. To add more to the issue, my breast on the left was growing normal while the right side was completely flat due to the scar tissues' morphed formation that had molded over the entire chest area on the right side of my body. It was incredibly obvious that something was not right. To try to even out the appearance, I was stuffing my bra with more and more toilet paper to compensate for my ever-growing left-sided breast. Though toilet paper may seem soft, when you are wadding it up and having it rub on your scars throughout the entire day, getting sweaty and bunching up into little annoying balls, it was anything but comfortable. I was constantly having to go to the bathroom, self-consciously nervous that pieces would come out of my bra or that it would look lumpy, bumpy, and unnatural. Becoming quite the artist.

My chest was being rubbed red and raw, especially in my dreaded PE class where I had to run and move around a lot. You were expected to run a half mile two times a week and a mile and a third once a week. Besides the visible discomfort, the physical activity was very hard for me because when I was on fire, I inhaled a significant amount of smoke into my lungs. This caused me to have a lung that had shrunk enough that it affected me when I would run. I was always feeling short of breath, never quite understanding why, thinking that there was just something wrong with me that I could not keep up. When my heart rate would increase and I would have to breathe deeper and harder, it was very difficult. When I would complain to my mom, she would say to me, "Oh, stop whining, it will get easier when you get older." It was not getting any easier. It hurt for me to run, and yet she really did not care to hear about it. She saw me as just another complaining kid at this point in her life. She never even told me that my lung was damaged until I confronted her when I was nineteen years old. She later told me that she just did not want me to feel handicapped. What?

I truly hated life on planet earth. I hated the constant thoughts of how I might maneuver this or manipulate that in order to keep from being exposed. I hated having to look at my scars each and every day. I was not growing used to looking at them; that never did happen. My clothes were miserable. Anything that was fitted at all in the top part of my body was unbearable, yet I bore it. Life was emotionally tormenting and exhausting. I was drowning in anxiety—that and throwing up.

No Fatties Allowed

My mom was so obsessed with not having any fat children. I do not know if that was her real reason, or if in reality, she just did not want to buy more food than she had to, which would cost her additional money and would consequently take away from her budget for her alcohol. Absolutely, she had a budget for her alcohol.

I continued throwing up daily. The behaviors that you have to take on in order to keep this secret hidden are so obsessive, thought-provoking, and time-consuming; it fit right in with my life-style. One big denial hidden mess. I was good at it.

I remember coming home from school; my mom would be asleep, and I would carefully sneak into the kitchen and steal food. Yes, steal food. You see, if you did not ask to eat, and you, as my mom would put it, helped yourself, it was stealing in her eyes. This alone was not easy to get away with, as there were always at least six to twelve kids in the house at any given time. If it turned out that she was cooking spaghetti, then I had it made.

I would get out a serrated spoon and a plastic cup and strain the meat out of the sauce that was simmering on the stove as fast as I possibly could. I would quickly hide in the bathroom and feast on my cup of saucy meat.

My mom had a very strict rule about only having a "small snack" when we would come home from school, and you had to ask. Period. However, if she was not awake, because she had already gotten drunk once for the day and had passed out asleep, how were we to get food? I could never figure out all her rules. She constantly contradicted herself to make her rules fit her lifestyle for the time and the season.

She had her way of insulting me on my weight. I was not fat, keep that in mind, not even chubby, but my mom definitely had an issue with her kids eating too much. Consequently, I learned to sneak food and gorge on it when she was not looking or passed out. This was not that difficult because when I got home from school, she was usually taking her afternoon half-time nap before she got up to have yet another drink and start her second life when my stepfather got home. After mind-numbingly consuming the food, I would then go and throw it up in the bathroom. Not very healthy. My mom knew about it; as long as I did not mess up her clean bathroom in the process, then she never corrected me. Very sad is what I have to say about that situation.

Rebellion Was Rearing Its Ugly Head

In October of my seventh-grade year, a group of girls and I initiated a walkathon that ran from my bus stop to my junior high, approximately a five-mile walk. Each girl walking in the protest defiantly wore pants instead of our required dresses. We wore our pants all day long at school. During the school day, one of the eighth graders went up to the superintendent and stated that all of us protesters felt it was unfair that we had to wear dresses while the boys at the school were able to wear pants. She pointed out in her argument that the dresses just did not keep us warm enough. By the end of the school day, it was announced over the intercom that the dress code had officially been changed. We now were allowed to wear pants, though not jeans, to school. The whole classroom exploded in cheers. I was so elated! Finally, I would have some sort of relief. I could now cover up some more of my scars, and this would help me to be more at ease while I was at school, and I could stay warmer.

Though the dress code was now working in my favor, I still lived in fear of the daily never-ending taking a shower at the end of PE class. The coaches had offices that were set up above the gym locker room, lined with floor-length glass walls, where they could inspect into every crevice of the room, scrutinizing our every move. My school was located on a military base, and these teachers were like drill sergeants. Daily I would sneak, hide, and plot in order to avoid being called out for not taking the required shower.

I only ended up taking one shower during my entire two years of junior high, and that was a disaster. The only reason that I pretended to take a shower is that I thought that I had been spotted by one of the teachers.

I cannot help but think that if at any given point my mom had woken up and chose the path of righteousness, then God could have used her for greater things in this world. She could have had a perfect platform, in so many situations, to invoke change. Yet she chose her addiction, her denial, and her utter darkness.

When I later confronted her about why she did not help me with this horribly humiliating situation, she justified it by saying that she had told the coach that I was heavily scarred and that I would not be taking showers. I was infuriated. How dare she tell them that and not tell me. Did she even tell them, or was this yet another of her lies that she was making up in order to allow herself to cope with her failure as a parent? I had wasted so much of my time stressing about something that I was exempt from. How could she not tell me? With all the head trips that I stomached while I was in PE class, I ended up missing the natural ease of hanging out with my friends. I had separated myself for self-preservation's sake. Tormented again. Liar.

There were so many times that my mom would deliberately not do something in order to cause me harm. This was one of those times. Sad.

CHAPTER TWELVE

Visitations with My Dad

VISITATION WITH MY DAD HAD resumed and were anticipated with much excitement in my heart. My sister, brother, and I visited every summer for three months, one week at Christmas and one week at Easter too, until I left home at age sixteen. Visitations never included the actual day of the holiday. Ever. I loved visiting my dad and step-mom. I would long for the times when I could be around him. He was a cutup.

My dad tried his best. He would go out of his way to make sure we had the most fun summers ever. He would take us on vacation while we visited him. A real vacation, like a week at the Redwood Forest, Yellow Stone Park, or Twin Lakes. We loved it. The entire time we were with my dad, we just had to say, "Dad, can we have this or that?" "Get, get, get" is all that was on our minds. It was like living at Disneyland for a season. My dad would go out of his way to spend, spend, and spend on us three kids. This is the way that he was trying to show us his love for us.

My mom envied and yet hated my dad's success. He would set us up with an entire wardrobe as best as he could for each school year. This was for our well-being and not to get under my mom's skin, as much as she wanted to voice that it was. She understood the love that our dad had for us and would continually try to undermine that love to us, claiming that it did not exist. I knew that my dad loved me. I could see the love that he had for me in his eyes. Many times from a young age, my dad would repeat to me, "No matter what anyone

117

tells you, always know that I love you." That meant so much to me throughout my lifetime.

We would return home from summer vacation all ready for school, clothes and all. My mom despised it. She despised him, and she despised me.

My mom would heavily criticize any success my father achieved. She would call him a crock, a liar, a cheat—whatever came to her compulsive mind that particular day, she chose to be so hypercritical of him. I knew better. I watched how hard my dad worked when we would visit him. It's too bad she chose to hate him so deeply.

Still living in the scars. My left breast was a B cup while my right side still had not grown. It was as if I had a pancake up under my scarred-up skin. It would ache and throb at times, which was probably when it was trying to grow; it could not grow because it had nowhere to go. One day when I was at the fabric store, I saw a pad that was made to go inside of a bra. Wow! You mean I could use that and not have the ongoing hassle of all this toilet paper? So excited I begged my mom if she would please buy me one. She told me that if I wanted one of those pad thingies that I was trying to describe to her, then I would need to use my own money to pay for it. Deflated, anger rose up inside of me, and I thought to myself, *Really? How much did your gallon of Gallo cost you today? Is being drunk more important than my comfort?* I realized that yet again my mom did not care about me, neither did she care about the shame that I was suffering through. I was growing even bitterer with her self-absorbed life of acting as if she had no children that she was responsible for.

In order to fit in with all the kids and not look so lopsided, I continued stuffing my bra with wadded-up toilet paper. Summertime was right around the corner, and that meant the beach. Oh, how I dreaded it. One weekend my dad announced that we were going to spend the weekend at the bay. I had mixed feelings. I really wanted to go, but I did not want to get wet. When I would get wet, the toilet paper would soak up all the water. I would end up, as discreetly as possible, squeezing the water out of the toilet paper, with my hands best as I could and trying to reshape it to look like a normal breast or at least as close to the right side as possible. It was so humiliating.

The whole breast situation would be so all-consuming in my mind that what fun I could have been having would be lost. I did try to get up on the Jet Ski one time that weekend, and just as I had anticipated, I had to squeeze and reshape what toilet paper was remaining in my bathing suit top in order to make it look like it was "normal." Most of the toilet paper had escaped my bathing suit and was floating all too tellingly around where I swam. It was far from normal. It was so crushing and awkward. I could only hope that no one saw me. I am sure that they did. My dad never said a word as the toilet paper particles floated on top of the water. Embarrassing.

That night as we all sat around the dinner table, my dad decided that it was the time for him to bite the bullet and bring up the subject of my burns and how my breast was or was not developing. I was taken completely off guard. This was not discussed. Though I desperately wanted some answers, the dinner table in front of my step-mom and siblings was not the place I felt I could open up. Quickly I shut him down, pretending that everything was just fine. Doing whatever it would take to get the focus off me and my scars. Sadly, this subject never was breached again. Because my mom and dad barely spoke, my dad was ill-informed about most of my "breast not growing" issues.

Since my dad and mom never really had any conversation of any value until 1992, my dad was unaware of how my scars had healed.

I held a lot of bitterness and resentment toward my mom about this whole situation, which of course was never discussed. She knew that my one breast was growing and the other was not. I wondered, what did she think I was putting in my bra? Did she even care? If she cared, then why did she do nothing to help me out? It was a mess of a situation no matter how I looked at it.

After the traumatic experience with the toilet paper at the bay, I was determined that the breast pad could wait no longer. I babysat as much as possible and quickly purchased two A-size pads (they did not have a B-size one) from the fabric store, which I quickly seamed together to pass as my new breast. It also would move around and rub and aggravate and worsen the redness already on my skin, but at least it would not end up floating on top of the water somewhere.

Wrong Sort of Entertainment

By junior high, I had started smoking marijuana periodically. Having lived my life undiagnosed with severe depression, marijuana seemed to uplift and motivate me. I felt much happier while I was high. I would smoke sometimes before school began, but mostly I would smoke after school and on the weekends. My mom would bust me off and on, mostly off. When I did get caught, it brought minimal trouble. This definitely did not deter me from the intended task to emotionally try to feel better. It was not right, but I tried it for a season.

One time I got caught smoking cigarettes outside in the backyard. I was grounded to my room for thirty days. I smoked cigarettes in my room the entire time. You would have thought I should have gotten in far worse trouble for getting caught smoking pot, but no, it was the cigarettes I got in far more trouble for. Have you figured it out yet? If I kept smoking cigarettes, my mom, in her calculating brain, figured I would end up stealing them from her. This ultimately would end up costing her more money. She smoked over two packs of cigarettes a day. There was always a self-centered reason to her mad discipline. Madness.

At this point, there were already seven to eight children in the house smoking marijuana and stealing cigarettes. I guess that my having smoked marijuana was the least of her problems. It was yet another thing for the most part that my mom chose to ignore.

Chapter Thirteen

Dreaded Reconstructive Breast Surgery

I REMEMBER BEING TAKEN TO a plastic surgeon about my undeveloped right breast at age twelve. The doctor told my mom that he would like to see me back in about one year. A year had come and gone, and I began to wonder if I was going to be taken back to that plastic surgeon. Each time that I would ask my mom, she would put me off with one excuse or the other. The problem was that she did not know who was going to pay for it.

One day my mom had one of her close friends over to hang out. I was told to go to my room and leave them alone. While walking to my room, I heard my name mentioned. With the full knowledge that I would be severely punished for disobeying, I decided to hide out and listen to their conversation. My mom's friend was trying to get my mom to take me back in to the doctor to fix my breast that was not growing. My mom was dismissing her and telling her that it just was not feasible. I thank God to this day for the next sentence that came out of her friend's mouth, "Didn't the Shriners Crippled Children's help her in the past surgeries? Maybe they would be willing to help her again. Just give them a call." She encouraged my mom.

My father became a Shriner after they originally helped pay for the part of insurance that was not covered when I was first burned. He remained a member of the Shriners Club all the way up until his death, when I was fifty-five years old.

Amazingly a few days later, my mom contacted the Shriners Group, and they referred her to a specialist plastic surgeon in a close-by town that they were willing to work with. They agreed to cover most of the cost of the hospital stay. The plastic surgeon was graciously willing to wave his surgical fee also. His only stipulation was that I needed to come back in to his doctor's office in a year or so to see if the breast had grown. All the doctor wanted was this small favor? No problem. He was elated at my response. I said yes.

He admitted to me that this was going to be an experimental surgery, one he had never tackled before. The doctor was not sure whether the surgery would successfully work to allow my trapped breast to grow. All of this added to my anxiety about having my body cut open. Would it all be for nothing? He explained again to me that "we" may have waited too long because the other breast looked to be fully developed at this point. I was so scared.

It was an extremely emotional time for me. I was not close to my mom, yet she would be the one taking me to the hospital for my two-week stay. She would be the one who was going to come and visit me. What would we even talk about? We were like strangers living in two different worlds

Consequently, in the winter of 1971, at age thirteen, I went into the hospital to have corrective surgery and skin grafting done on my right breast. My breast was a C cup on the left side of my body, and my right breast was still flat and shaped like a badly morphed pancake. The skin grafting and plastic surgery that I had had at age five had left the right breast sort of cemented down with no way to expand. It caused me a lot of discomfort. The breast was trying to grow under the scar tissue. The throbbing and aching at this point was continuous. A subject that was off-limits to talk about.

Oh, how I looked forward to having the badly scarred breast cut into so that it could be released from the continual excruciating pain that I had been suffering from. This was one thing that the doctor did guarantee. Though he was sure that the pain would stop, he was not sure of how the breast would end up "looking" once he was done with the cutting.

The morning of the surgery had arrived, and I knew that I did not really have a choice; I had to take a chance. I was so uncertain. I prayed a silent prayer to God that if it was possible, could He please cause my breast to grow after surgery? It had been years since I had even prayed. Could God help me? Would God even care to hear me? The surgeon again mentioned in our final consultation that we may have waited too long to have the surgery, but that he felt in his calculation it might be worth a shot in the dark. This was no great surprise to me; my mom was always putting anything off that would cost her time and/or money. I believed it would grow; without a doubt, I was just sure it would grow. After all, I prayed and asked God to help it grow, right?

Thankfully, my favorite stepsister accompanied my mom and me to the hospital this morning, and this brought me so much immediate relief. I had grown extremely close with her. Her presence sure helped to smooth over the rugged emotional terrain in the room. I did not want to be alongside my mom as if we were some united front. That was just a lie. After all, I was a big thirteen-year-old now.

I was to stay there for two weeks. The doctor and his staff were very kind to me. I was extremely embarrassed and did not want anyone to know that I was burned, definitely not that I had a deformed breast and had to have corrective surgery to try to make it look somewhat normal. My mom had promised me that she would tell anyone who asked about me that I had to have some cysts removed. I did not know what a cyst was, but it sounded good to me. Boy, did I pray that she would keep that promise.

Thus, off to surgery I was wheeled, hooked up to all the necessary IVs. On came the anesthesia mask. They weren't black anymore, but they were still scary, large, and made you see black-and-white checkerboards right before passing out, praying in my head the whole way for safety and a successful surgery.

When I awoke that afternoon, I was extremely medicated, a feeling I knew all too well and despised. My mind was a muddy cloud. I felt completely out of control. I do not remember too much of the first week due to all of the pain medication being administered to me.

The doctor had made a half-moon incision underneath my right breast and had grafted skin from my left thigh. While I knew that I needed to take a chance with the reconstructive surgery, the fact that I now had a large eight-by-eight square patch cut off my left upper thigh was emotionally taxing. The last thing that I needed was yet another scar, which would eventually stretch and become larger, another part of my body to be ashamed of, another part to try to hide.

Bedridden and heavily medicated for my first week post-surgery, I was super impressed with my mom. She actually showed up at the hospital, from what I could discern in my fog, every day. During those visits, she would try her best to act the part of a loving mother, but it was too little too late. My heart was already hard. I just lay there playing along, allowing her charade not to penetrate. A few more years, and I could leave home and be away from her, was what I would convince myself that needed to happen.

The doctors and nurses would come in to change my bandages and to look at my progress. I loathed the smell. It was like a horrible wave of nausea as I remembered the reek of my festering burns. Horrific feelings washed over me causing me to feel completely helpless and out of control. The feelings would not seem to stop as they crashed over my mind minute by minute. The smell was all too familiar and daunting.

Once the bandages were removed, the doctor had one of his nurses hold a good-sized mirror in front of me so that I could see what had become of me after the surgery. My first responses were anger and fear. Anxiety maximized. What had I allowed the doctor to do to me? The doctor soothed me by explaining what had been done and why and how—and doing his best to calm me down. I slowly began to see through the anxiety and fear and glimpse the possible outcome. He was a very caring doctor. He took the time to cautiously guide me through my emotions each day with his expertly spoken words. Whereas my mother's words brought on more anxiety, the doctor's words soothed me. I was so overwhelmed with embarrassment, lying in the bed with my deepest shame fully exposed. So ugly. Cut up. Scarred again. I needed God's help but did not know enough to call out to Him for comfort. Once the doctor and nurses finally covered back up my scars and freshly cut-up breast, my anxiety seemed to subside. I was used to covering up. The doctor had explained that the nurses were going to rewrap me in a little different way for phase 2. When he spoke, all my worries seemed to have answers. The cut was severe and ugly. I could only hope that the breast would grow and not look too deformed.

The doctor promised to check back in on me the next day and expressed to me that I had done well through the surgery. He told me that I could probably go home in another week.

These two weeks were the longest time in my life that I had gone without bathing since my original burns had happened. I compulsively bathed two if not three times per day ever since my smelly burns. To be smelly was horrific. To not shower was extremely difficult for me. To not wash my hair was miserable; after all, I was a teenager now. I was grateful to have a bottle of Clairol Dry Shampoo that my mom recommended might come in handy.

The second week, I was finally able to get out of bed some and use the restroom versus the bedpan. However, no showers yet.

After the second week, I returned home. All I could do was wait and wait and wait to see if my breast would grow. Each day when I got dressed, I would inspect every aspect of my breast to see if it had grown the slightest bit.

January came around, and it was time to go back to school. I was still padding my bra with the original pad I had constructed, even though the doctor suggested that I not suppress the breast at all. I had worked too hard on my reputation, and I was not going to go to school looking all lopsided. When I put on my bra, those pads always went in to my right side, period. Though they slipped around and rubbed, they were better than the alternative rawness that the toilet paper had created. I became an expert at maneuvering in different fashions, in what I hoped looked like normal behavior, but in reality would result in adjusting my ill-fitted pad, which would try its best to squirm its way out of its designated area. Humiliating.

Within a few weeks of recovery, the scabbing began to set in. The smell of the healing wound was again familiar. It was at this point that I began to stuff, stuff, stuffing not only my bra but also my feelings and emotions. Undergoing this surgery had caused me to detach even more from my body. It took a good three more months of agonizing healing and way longer than that before there was significant growth.

Around June, my breast had finally reached around 75 percent of my goals; definitely nowhere close to being equal to my left side but with the underwire bra that the plastic surgeon highly recommended, it seemed to me to be less noticeable than before the surgery. With my pad in place, I felt for the first time that my disguise was complete.

I still had the tormenting questions being shot at me from random people at school. The questions I could answer, I did the best I could, while ignoring the ones that I could not. I was internalizing every ounce of it. With each question, my fear and anxiety of exposure would grow. The scars were very visible on my body, and kids are going to ask questions.

Disturbed Boyfriend

At the middle of my eighth-grade year, I met my first boyfriend. He was not a catch. While I was in the popular crowd, with quite a few friends, his friends were more interested in using his car, and so was I. A large group of my friends, maybe ten of us total, all went to the beach to party and hang out. He kissed me and, from then on, claimed me as his own. He immediately became obsessed with me. He called the next day, and he never stopped. He was quite bothersome. But he had a car, and a car meant freedom.

While he was nineteen and a senior in high school, I was thirteen and in the eighth grade. About the only thing that appealed to me was the fact that he had a car, and it meant that I could get out of my house more often.

To say that I had a healthy example of what a relationship should be would be a joke. Even so, I knew from the beginning that this was not right. I always had secret crushes but never even considered having a boyfriend because of all my hidden scarring. He on the other hand was so thrilled to have a girlfriend who was so popular and pretty (on the outside). He definitely did not come from the same social crowd that I was accustomed to. Snobby.

Starting the first week that we dated, he wanted me to write him a letter *every* school day and give it to my true friend so that she could give it to him each day at school. She was in ninth grade and attended the same school as him. He in turn would write me a letter that she would give back to me. While this may seem sweet and endearing, let me explain. These letters were his first step in trying to brainwash and control me. They needed to include no less than the following: what time I woke up, what I wore for the day, what I ate for breakfast, what color of eyeshadow I put on, what time I left for the bus, what happened in each and every classroom, and who I talked to and what about. I never had someone seem to care as much as he did. But on the other hand, I knew in my knower I was just using him for his access to his car. Seriously.

The first time that I missed writing him a letter was about two weeks into the so-called relationship. It was on a Friday, and I figured that I was going to see him in a few hours. He showed up at my house when school got out and was livid. He started accusing me of ignoring him. Asking me if I no longer wanted him as my boyfriend and letting me know that if that was the case, then I would be sorry. He was insinuating that he would blab his mouth about all my scarring. In a very sick way, he became my emotional caretaker who took the position of managing my thoughts.

Our relationship revolved around his sexually sick mind and all the things that he could dream up. I was just a vessel. During any interactions, I was lost in my body and stuck in my mind. I felt very violated, used, and degraded; and those were just the things that made him happy. The relationship was a spiraling out-of-control disaster that I always dreamed of getting out of and being rid of, but did not have the courage to do so. I guess we were both using each other, but did not know it or admit it until years later.

CHAPTER FOURTEEN

Liquid Journal

I DETESTED THE PRESENCE AND consumption of alcohol in my home, or anywhere for that matter. Every day my mom would go to the store and buy a gallon of Gallo wine. My stepfather would bring home a few six-packs of beer on his way home from work. Every day. In addition, they had two kegs of beer in the garage. They had thirteen kids between the two of them, and money was very snug. We kids were always dealing with only the bare minimum, and yet they bought their alcohol and consumed it daily. What I would have given for a new pair of pants that I did not have to babysit and save my money up to buy on my own. Teenage selfishness.

Each day, between her morning binge and her evening one, my mom would drink at least a gallon of wine. She did not see anything wrong with it. By the end of the night, there would be a half gallon of Gallo wine left and possibly a beer or two. This cycle remained up until I left home at sixteen. She would keep a fresh gallon and then the cold leftover half gallon from the night before. Sick ritual.

I got so frustrated at their alcoholism. Once when I was about fourteen, I got the wild idea to keep a journal writing down every ounce of alcohol that my mom and stepfather bought and brought into our home for a total of a thirty-day period. I felt so empowered documenting this liquid waste. When the thirty days was up, I took the letter-size piece of paper up and handed it to my mom and stepfather. They were sitting in the living room on a Sunday afternoon, and I just walked up to them and handed my mom the piece of paper. She said, "What is this?" I answered in my most brave voice, "This is a list of all of the alcohol that you and your husband have spent money on and drank in the last thirty days." I hoped to open up their eyes as to how much money was being flushed down the toilet just to give them a buzz. Whatever I had hoped to achieve did not happen. My mom flipped her lid, screaming and cussing me out. She was infuriated. Surprisingly after she told me to mind my own business and get out of her sight, that she could not stand to look at me, she did not ground me to my room. Maybe she had willfully forgotten. She instead ignored me for about a month. Literally. She did not look at me, talk to me, or even acknowledge that I existed. I found it to be quite peaceful. This was something that she would often do to me when I would challenge her on her rapidly debilitating morals.

Actually being ignored was one behavior I enjoyed at this point of being raised by my mom. It meant she would be minding her own business instead of trying to control every breathtaking aspect of my life. As I said earlier, I had little or no respect for my mom. I was the adult in the relationship for sure.

Keyette Girls Club

About a year and a half after I began smoking pot, I began to notice that my group of friends had shifted to what was commonly referred to as the Across the Street Gang. The kids who smoked pot and cigarettes would walk across the street from the school and indulge in any manner they saw fit. Because it was across the street and the school did not own that property, they never interceded. I did not care for the quality—or lack thereof—of the friends I had chosen. This crowd was scary and unpredictable. Midway through the ninth grade, I decided to change the group of friends that I was hanging around and stopped smoking pot. I immediately noticed that I could now pay attention so much more in class. I quit smoking cigarettes and marijuana for the next three years.

Midway through the ninth grade, I decided to run for Keyette Girls Club president. The president was elected by a majority vote, and I won. I had cleaned up my act.

Same Boyfriend, Same Problem

I still had the same boyfriend. He would visit from college about every third weekend. I carried on just fine while he was gone; it was when he was visiting that I suffered from loads of anxiety from his mind-control games. He was very scheming, short-tempered, and bossy. Yet I stayed with him. I was afraid to break up with him for fear that he would blab his mouth to all my friends about my scars; this could not happen. He always said that if I ever broke up with him that he would not want to go on living, that our love was forever and ever. He would force me to say I loved him and to repeat back to him that I could not live without him. That practice, I did not see at the time, is in itself a form of brainwashing. Scary.

My bulimia continued to accelerate along with much of the inappropriate acting-out behaviors.

By the end of my ninth-grade year, I had been dating the same boy for a year and a half. He fit right in with all the dysfunction that was my life. Most of my friends accepted him by now.

One day he came over to visit, and his first comment was that, "It looks like you have put on a few pounds. Your hips have gotten wider." Who does that? Who says that to someone? What was wrong with me that I allowed him to talk that way to me?

This comment was made boldly right in front of my mom, who by the look on her face did not think there was anything wrong with this behavior. He proceeded to go into my bathroom and get the family scale. He stated, "Get on it." My mom just watched the whole encounter never objecting. At this point in my life, I was five feet, six inches tall. I stepped onto the scale, and it read 130 pounds.

"Wow," my boyfriend said, feeling that his point was made. He let me know that I needed to lose weight. To make things more awkward, my mom agreed with him right there in my kitchen. She could always be counted on to knock me down a notch or two. I despised them both for deliberately trying to humiliate and shame me into an untruth. I was a beautiful girl, but you would not have known it that day. I grew to hate my mom even more for not standing up for me yet again. I was already throwing up on a regular basis at that point, and my mom knew of it. By having this knowledge, she was aware of how fragile I was about this subject, and she took the opportunity to damage me even further. Debilitating.

Leave it to me to having a super-controlling mom, to in turn choose a super-controlling boyfriend for myself. Go figure.

Not only was he controlling, he was obsessive, and I had become his new obsession.

Sex was on the forefront of his mind at all times, not normal healthy relations. He constantly wanted to push the boundaries to see what more he could get away with and what higher thrill he could reach. I was just a vehicle for his ungodly desires to be reached. With no self-esteem, I went along for the ride, the whole time thinking to myself what a pervert he was and how corrupt his mind was.

I wanted desperately to break off our relationship, but I was afraid. Several times, I almost got the nerve to, but I never followed through. I stayed as involved as possible with school, girls club, and anything else that would keep me busy enough to get away from him and to keep me far from being around my house.

By midtenth grade, my mom's third marriage was becoming noticeably weaker. They were both trying to function as alcoholics with not a whole lot of success as it turned out. Someone was always fighting, whether it was the parents, the parents and kids, or just the kids. The stepkids were constantly moving out and then moving back in. Gobs of times this happened possibly up to twenty different occasions. Oh, what glorious dysfunctional disruptions.

I was barely coping day to day. I had outgrown the lie that my mom cared one inch for me. I could see clearly now above the smoke screen of deception.

A Bit Confused

At seventeen, feeling my life was too far gone to fix, I decided to start smoking pot again. I continued smoking pot from that point on until I was saved at age twenty-two. During this time, I messed up a lot. I had started searching for some sort of peace, in all the wrong places. I was in way over my head with my worldly ways, and I desperately yearned for something new. I just did not know what it was that I needed in my life for change to occur.

I had married at sixteen—yes, to the same and only one boyfriend. Birthed two sons and was ready for the challenge of filing for a divorce. I just did not have the courage to leave or kick him out—yet.

Instead, we relocated back down the coast to live closer to my dad. He had found a very nice, newly built apartment. With my approval, my dad went out and rented it for my husband, my boys, and myself. My plan was to get a good job and then divorce him.

Little did I know that the man I was to fall deeply in love with would be living in the upstairs apartment! I was miserably married and sickened at that point by my current, unfaithful, adulterer, sexually and emotionally abusive husband, who was becoming even more abusive toward me by the day. I had merely married him in order to get out of my mom's house and to not be forced to move yet again as my mom's ever whim would hit her. Yet he thought I was in love with him; I was not. My husband did not get this part of the equation; he truly thought I loved him. Sadly, I did not have the courage to tell him that I was not in love with him. He was merely a stepping-stone that I used in order for me to get out of the miserable surroundings I was living in. Within three months, our marriage was headed to divorce court. He just did not know it yet. He was just as trapped as I was in our not-so-perfect marriage. He wanted out too. I was just the one who had the nerve to admit it.

I was so glad when God brought this new man into my life. He needed me as much as I needed him. He made me want to be a better person. His name was Dean. Dean was recently out of the Navy and decided to stay in San Diego when he got out. I thought he was adorable, I still do. This man on the outside appeared to respect people in general, which was something that my current husband did not show toward others.

With all the distasteful events that had happened to me by my first stepfather, stepbrothers, husband, and men in general, I took on a dislike for most all men. With the exception of my new second husband of thirty-seven years and my two sons, I would treat men badly.

If you were to ask me to, I could find something wrong with almost any man. Ignoring them was my first choice of disrespect.

Oh, and if I saw a man disrespecting a woman or child, I would go completely ballistic.

If I saw a woman treating her child badly, you would feel hard-pressed to get me to keep my mouth shut. Say I were to see a woman with her kids, and her kids had no shoes on, yet the mom had shoes on, you can bet I would let her know exactly what I thought.

If I saw a woman with her kid and she offhandedly hit her child in front of me, then I would tell her off, and then some. I was extremely opinionated in most everything in my life. I had become ubersensitive to any- and everyone in my presence. I had become very judgmental and hateful toward most people. I am sure that I was hard to live with. Sound familiar? I was becoming my mom all over again minus the alcohol. I did not like what I saw in myself, and I longed to be a better person. I craved feeling better on the inside. I needed change in my life; I just did not know how to go about achieving this change—yet.

Having a baby out of wedlock was very common in the late eighties. I knew that it was not right, but I was fearful to be married again. Despite my fears, two weeks after my first divorce was finalized, I married Dean. Shortly after marrying Dean, he was hired on with the local electric company. Being the hard worker he was raised up to be, he has moved up through the ranks quickly. What a blessing. God is good all the time.

Let me back up somewhat and go into further detail. You see, by the age of thirteen, I had my first and only high school boyfriend. He was nineteen years old and far too old for me. When I was in eighth grade, he was a senior. It was very dysfunctional and abusive. By age sixteen we were married, and I had two sons with him soon after. I was on birth control, and yet I still got pregnant. At age twenty-two, I met the man I am lovingly still married to thirty-seven years later. I left my first husband and married my second husband, and we ended up having a beautiful baby girl prior to being married.

By the eleventh grade, my two older stepbrothers, thank God, had finally moved out. I did not remain in the Keyette Club. All I wanted to do was find a way out of the home that I was living in. I could not take the constant criticism from my mom. I hated living under her roof as much as she hated having to see me each day living in her home.

The summer before the eleventh grade, our entire family returned home from a very stressful two-week beach camping trip. It was what we did every year; it is called a poor man's family vacation when you have a huge combined family of fifteen. No sooner did we get home and get our stuff unpacked and go into the kitchen to help assist making supper with my stepsisters, mom, and out of nowhere, my second stepfather walked in and announced to my mom that he no longer loved her and he wanted a divorce. He proceeded by explaining his cause for divorce. He elaborated that she was one of the meanest females he had ever met in his life and that he no longer could stand to look at her. Let alone be married to her. Keep in mind that both of them had, had an ample amount of alcohol consumed in them, and the evening was just getting started. They had argued the entire camping trip. What a long two weeks.

By this point, I knew that I had to get out of the house. I already babysit my three youngest siblings whenever I was told I had to. Conversation with my mom was very slim. Her alcoholism and prescription drug addiction were at the point where she embarrassed me anytime we had to be out in public. I wanted out, and I needed out as well. Their divorce was only a matter of time. Talk about pins and needles.

My boyfriend had been pressuring my mom, unbeknown to me, to allow him to marry me. My mom had told my boyfriend that if he could get a job making enough money, then he could in fact marry me. He had graduated early in the summer from a technical college, majoring in offset printing. He could not find a job where he thought the pay was sufficient.

One day, toward the end of summer, before my eleventh-grade year was going to begin, my boyfriend drove to a nearby city and enlisted himself in the Army. I was close to getting up the nerve to break it off from him and was completely unaware that he had been "negotiating" with my mom the terms to marry me, nor was I aware that he was going to join the Army. I was not happy at all. My all-about-me dreams were not going to happen. I had plans to go to college and become a high school home economics teacher. That was not going to happen.

Seemingly, out of the blue, he announces to me that my mom says that we can get married now. What? I basically acted happy even though I was miserable on the inside. I kept thinking to myself that if I remain at home, with all that is going on there, things would only become worse for me. My mom's addictions were escalating quickly at this point. She was already getting sloppy drunk passing out in the afternoon and then getting up yet again to repeat the pattern into the night.

In December of that same year, I found myself married at sixteen years old, hoping that I picked the best I could from the worse of two evils. I was feeling trapped and manipulated among other things. Here I was miserably married to my only boyfriend I had ever had, feeling more trapped than ever before. I was dumbfounded that he had spent two years of his life going through trade school learning a profession and that he just up and joined the military without a word to me. I felt like a shiny object that he was collecting instead of a partner in a relationship. I was a bystander watching my life happening to me without my permission. To this day, I am certain that in his inner knower, he had to have been reading some of my signals that I was not happy. I believe that was why he swooped in the way that he did. He knew that I thought at the time that anything would be better than the life I was living at home and that he was willing to exploit those feelings in order to obtain me. He knew he was about to lose me, and he could not allow that to happen. Obsession 101.

Quickly after we were married, I was whisked across the country to where he had been stationed, leaving my junior year of high school behind me at the end of the first semester.

I hated everything about living in this foreign state with my new husband. I was lonely, scared, fearful, angry, and just plain ol' messed up on the inside. I remained on the East Coast for three years. During this time, I went through two long pregnancies and had two amazingly handsome sons, I quickly graduated high school, and went through a cosmetology program where I received my cosmetology license. Those three years felt like they stretched on forever. I hated every second of living in a state I was unfamiliar with. It scared me living on the East Coast. The weather was super cold in the winter with loads and loads of snow and snowfall. The summers were bleak and sweltering hot. It seemed like worlds away from my California lifestyle and grossly different weather conditions.

I was so pleased when he was finally released from the Army, and we were able to move back to the West Coast, where I was from. I had a game plan that I frequently would work on with my cosmetology instructor, whom I had grown close. She was a true mother image to me. I was going to be able to get back home and could now finally divorce my husband. She was my confidant. She was aware of his controlling ways. She was fully aware of the sexual and emotional abuse that I was living in. She was my cheerleader. She helped me to see that I was living in a very controlling abusive relationship and that I needed to get me and my boys out and safe as soon as possible, before something even worse occurred.

Once I was settled back in my home turf, I scored a good job at a very upscale salon in a trendy growing new mall—as I had plotted with my instructor. I worked hard to excel at my trade, and soon I was bringing home more than my husband was. I wanted nothing more than to be out of this dysfunctional trap of a marriage. At this point, neither of us had any respect for each other, and we sure did not treat each other very well. I had a drive and goal that did not mesh well with how he saw life. We argued daily on our different viewpoints, which I despised doing in front of my kids.

When we would argue, my husband would frequently say to me, "You will never leave me. You are all burnt, and nobody is going to want you." I think that without going into too much detail, for my boys' sakes, you can get the idea of the type of man he was from this mere statement, and many others like it that he would use to hurt me and try to keep me emotionally and physically trapped.

I missed my grandma terribly. My grandma and grandpa had driven across the US to visit after my first son was born. I really cherished my visit with her. She encouraged me to complete going to cosmetology school. I heeded her advice; eight months pregnant, trudging along, I ended up graduating just three months before my husband got out of the Army. That visit from my grandparents provided me with just the right amount of courage that I needed in order to finish out my time on the East Coast, get back to the West Coast, and file for divorce.

CHAPTER FIFTEEN

Blue Eyes

ON DECEMBER 30, 1978, I finally got the nerve to tell my first husband that I wanted a divorce and that he needed to move out. I knew that I could afford to pay the rent for where I was living if I could get one of my newfound girlfriends to move in. I had no doubt that I could support my kids just fine and myself. He left reluctantly only to return very early the next morning sobbing, pleading, and moaning with me to stay married to him. That was not going to happen, if I had anything to say about it. Once I declined, the accusations began. "No one will ever want you with all of your burns," he spat at me. I felt so sad. I calmly told him to get out and that it was over. This was only the beginning of a tormenting two years to come.

The custody battle with my ex-husband over my two boys was brutal. I was very young and naive. He was still deeply emotionally infatuated and obsessed with me and made numerous outrageous claims in the divorce depositions, doing all that he could imagine so that he could gain custody of the boys in order to hopefully get me to come back to him. Finally, my lawyer told me that if we did not come to a resolution that the court was prepared to take the boys away from both of us and place them into the foster care system. I was terrified of that happening to them and not to mention intimidated. My life was spiraling out of control. I finally conceded to joint custody and allowed my ex-husband to retain parental custody of the boys. I had to stomach only having them in the summers and on rotating main holidays. The next four years were miserable. I sank into a bottomless depression. Just breathing became a task.

My ex would tell me that if I would just come back to him, then I could have my boys all that I wanted. I bounced back to him three more times, each time disgusted by him and yet so thrilled to see my boys. I had made some very poor decisions throughout this relationship, and it looked as if I was paying for every last one of them. Ultimately, I finalized the divorce. I made the choice that I could not live in that sick mess any longer. I loved my "blue eyes." There was a price for this freedom; and sadly, my boys paid the price for it. My heart longed for them each and every moment. Smiles were few and far between.

Spiritually Awoken

My fear of criticism, more times than not, has stopped me from doing many things in life. Perfectionism, in a very sick way, has become my friend. As a child, acting as a perfectionist actually seemed to bring me a sense of control and order on the inside.

Up until my early twenties, I depended on things in my life to be orderly, straight, organized, even, neat, and clean. Up until that age, it had worked for me, so why was it not working anymore?

At twenty-two years old, on June 17, 1980, at two o'clock in the afternoon, I asked Jesus Christ to be my Lord and Savior. Such a simple prayer it was that day, and yet it changed my entire life. I was watching my typical soap opera at home and was feeling extremely restless. Instead of leaving the TV on the same channel, which I always did at this time of day, I walked up to my TV and changed the channel. Of all channels to choose from, I chose the Christian channel CBN. I never sat down, I remained standing. I was glued to the TV listening to the speaker. He was asking the television audience if they were willing to give up their life, as they knew it, and trade it in for a new life in Christ? I answered the question that the preacher was posing. I spoke aloud, to the television, saying, "Yes, I want this Jesus." I would try anything to be truly happy. All of a sudden, I could hear myself repeating after the speaker. As I finished repeating the words, I could feel something had just happened to me. "Jesus, I need you!" I yelled. I finally got it. It was Jesus that I was lacking in my life. I needed Jesus; finally, I understood what it was that was missing within me.

You see, deep inside of me, from the time of my burns, I desired a pure, clear sense of direction for my life. I craved a goodness to be inside me from that young age. On the inside was the only place that I felt any sense of control. If I was good to others and treated them kindly, I noticed that I felt good on the inside. God had placed a moral compass inside of me at a very young age; though I took it into my own hands to seek justice, it was that moral compass that I would lean on into my twenties.

When I would do wrong as a child, I would have such a strong conviction to say that I was sorry or get the situation right so that my world seemed back in balance. If I could keep all my toys and dolls or whatever in order, then I could try to trick myself into feeling as if I felt good on the inside. It is amazing what denial will do for you when you do not have any other vice to rely on.

Somewhere around twenty-one years old, all chaos had broken out in my life. I could not seem to keep an order to things any longer on the inside of me. I was miserable emotionally. Miserable spiritually. I was a wreck. I needed help.

It was on that sunny summer day in 1980 when I asked Jesus to be my savior that I finally felt purely good on the inside. After repeating the prayer, which I now know was a salvation prayer, I became a new creature in Christ. I began to shake and cry. I felt so overpoweringly full of joy.

The speaker on the television was still talking. He said, "If you need someone to talk to, call this 8-0-0 number. Our prayer counselors are there to pray with you or just to listen to you if you need someone to talk with. Just pick up the phone and tell us about your experience." Boy, did I need someone I could talk with.

Still crying and shaking, I went to the phone on the wall and called the number on the screen. A woman named Ruth answered, "Thank you for calling the network. Who do I have the pleasure of speaking with?"

I gave her my name and told her what I had experienced. She explained to me what had just happened, quoting the scripture:

Except a man be born again, he cannot see
the kingdom of God. (John 3:3 KJV)

She explained how I was born once through my mother's canal and that now I had been born again through the spirit of God. It is amazing how the Holy Spirit works. Next, Ms. Ruth asked me if I wanted to receive the baptism of the Holy Spirit. Ironically, with no prior knowledge of what was going to happen, I said yes. Yes, I wanted this Holy Spirit she so faithfully offered for me to have. Come on, Holy Spirit, come on in.

She began to pray for me, "Lord Jesus, thank You for coming into this lady's life. I ask You now to baptize her in Your Holy Spirit." It was at that time that my body began to really shake, tremble, and sweat. Drops of sweat were running off my body. I began speaking in tongues. I was delivered from things I did not even know were oppressing me, baptized in the Holy Spirit right there in my own living room, over the phone with a divinely ordained, appointed, and anointed woman named Ruth interceding with and for me. It was awesomely dynamic.

When Dean came home from work that day, I was so excited. I quickly told him what I had experienced. Acting quite peculiar, he said, "Oh, don't worry, it will wear off." He went to church growing up, though he had never mentioned it to me, so he knew about religion, but he had never known of true conversion consisting of a relationship with Jesus Christ.

Shocked, I responded, "Well, I hope not." It never wore off. While he had been at work that day, I had gone through our apartment and got rid of any paraphernalia we had.

The inner voice of the Holy Spirit had told me to do this, so I obeyed. He was not pleased. For Dean, that meant that he just would stop talking for a few days; that I knew how to handle. I did not care if he was mad. I knew I was doing the right thing for my future—for our future. I was set free, delivered, and filled with God's Holy Spirit;

that is what was fresh on my mind. That was all that I needed for this day in my life. I never looked back!

This change in my life also put an end to my bulimia. The next day when I, by pattern, ate lunch and then retrieved to the bathroom to do my usual throwing up, the Holy Spirit spoke loud and clear in a sound I for some reason listened to and obeyed. It said, "Do not do that anymore. It is wrong and ungodly." I responded by saying, "Yes, sir, I hear You, God." I never deliberately threw up again. Praise God.

Living in the scars and the pain was extremely difficult. Instantaneously and immediately upon my salvation, God began doing a work in me, regarding my life and my childhood and my pain. Despite all the ugliness I felt on the inside of me, I kept pumping the Word of God from my oversized family Bible into my life, into my heart, and into my ears—daily. Constantly and on a regular basis, I found myself having to fight spiritual battle after spiritual battle, which would come at me from every angle. Though I received salvation on that miraculous day, I had a load of darkness in my past that had to be dealt with.

You see, there is good and there is bad in this world. There is right, and there is wrong. There is light, and there is darkness. There are angels, and there are demons. The angels fight for God and His people, and demons fight for the devil and darkness. This dark force wanted nothing more than to keep me constantly consumed in some sort of battle so that I could not have the freedom to breathe in the fresh air that God so wanted me to breathe in.

For several months after my salvation, I called Ms. Ruth in order to talk to her and gleam any spiritual advice that she had to offer to me in my life. If I did not understand a scripture or my salvation was attacked by others, I knew she was just a phone call away.

Praise God, I was invited to be involved in an awesome Bible study, where I was taught the Word of God, regularly. I learned the Word of God to such a degree that I began early on to use any godly insight that I had learnt to help me fight my battles. Quoting the Word of God aloud helped me fight and win many different victories in my life. I thank God daily for His infinite wisdom and His constant anointed hand that guides me.

My first five years of my salvation, God placed this group of people from the Bible study into my life, and He used these people to read the word with me. I learned quickly that I was *not* to give up and that God had a plan and a purpose for my life. I learned enough of the Word to know God must have marvelous plans for me, if the devil was continuously trying to stumble me with his darkness.

A Learnt Lesson

There is a way that seemeth right unto a man, but the end thereof are the ways of death. (Proverbs 14:12 KJV)

I learned years ago from a Bible teacher that if God tells me "no" or "not now," then God was either trying to protect me from something or to provide a better way, a better plan, or a different road that was far superior to walk than what I was currently walking. God has special plans for you that you may not see. I believe that most of the times when God redirects your path, it is because you have gone off course, and He is plucking you up and jump-starting you back onto the "God's will" road for your life and off the *worldly* road that you had drifted onto.

Despite all the muck and filth of my childhood, I also knew enough to know that God had brought me a new Christlike loving man into my life "for such a time as this" (Esther 4:14). I kept pressing on, looking forward, looking up, trusting the Word of God, never even willing to give in or give up, always believing, always hoping, and often thinking that one day I would have a "peace that passes all understanding" (Philippians 4:7). One day I would reobtain the custody of my sons. One day soon, I would tell myself. One day.

All that I had to do was to press on and believe—that, I did. Through Christ, I have been able to obtain an inner peace that this world could not even begin to match. My relationship with God trumps all others. Period. End of subject.

Just Being Who I Was

I had a hard time being who I was anytime I was around my mom after I became a Christian. Within days of my receiving Jesus Christ as my Lord and Savior, I called my mom on the phone and told her about my experience. There was such a huge drastic change in me that, for me, there was no mistaking that something amazing had happened. I was a completely different person. My mom responded by dismissing me and saying, "It won't last. You will see, it will wear off—it always wears off." Another curse God would have to bind. This was the second time that I had heard this "it won't last long" thing since my salvation. Undeterred, I was convinced that it had to be real.

I was crushed. I thought that she would want what I had. Well, she did not. Not only did she not want it, but also in a very sick way, she wanted me to lose what I had experienced. I could not understand why she did not want my Jesus. Why would a person not want to feel miraculously better? Her alcohol was her Jesus, so she thought. Sad.

Months later, I was traveling in the area, so I called to let my mom know that I was going to stop by her restaurant that she had recently opened. She casually told me to stop on by if I wanted to. I did stop in. The restaurant at that time was very crowded. I spoke quickly of my Jesus to her, so thrilled to share this joy with her that I was enjoying walking in. What was in her recognized what was now in me. Light versus dark, you know—one spirit knoweth another.

"Remove yourself from my presence right now! I do not want to ever hear you preach to me again!" she yelled way too loudly so that many of the customers looked over at us. "Leave my restaurant right now! Get out!" she loudly commanded. I was so mortified. Was I preaching at her? I just wanted to show her that there was a way out of this misery that we lived in each day. I wanted to share the astonishing joy I had found. My face full of tears and my head tucked down in embarrassment, I walked out of my mom's restaurant. Mean girl.

That day, when I left the restaurant, she succeeded in intimidating me. I avoided sharing my Jesus with her. I vowed to limit my, already seldom, visits with her to even less. I could not understand why my mom did not want better things for her daughter. I guess that when you do not love your daughter, then you do not want better things for her. Common denominator.

Years after the incident at the restaurant, I realized that my mom had been actively practicing witchcraft. She told me it herself. She very braggingly and darkly explained to me how she was not practicing "bad witchcraft" but that she was practicing "white witchcraft." Really! Oh, how the devil is a liar and a baffler. Though I had thought that her dabbling from years past was just a casual evil interest, I was to learn that she had become more engrossed in it over time. She had escalated to the point of using tarot cards and doing readings for others. This is not right. It is evil. I now understand that voice that spoke so loud and boldly that day she dismissed me so abruptly from her restaurant. She had become obsessed by her evil lifestyle, calling evil good. That is exactly how the devil works. Trickery.

When I had spoken to her in her restaurant, which was her territory, the satanic evil that possessed her spoke up to me, or the Christ in me. Now I got it. She had become one of the devil's own followers. Not good. Not good at all.

If I had previously thought that our relationship was strained, then I had no clue how traumatic it could really become. This was only the beginning of many more troubling conversations that I would encounter involving her. I wanted to just walk away from her entirely, and I did cut the ties on and off many different times throughout the years.

I felt compelled to try to help her, but she did not want to be helped. She seemed to enjoy being hateful, angry, resentful, rude, and mean toward others and me. Sound familiar?

Several years would go by before we spoke again. Evil had completely taken up residency in her. It became very rare to get a glimpse of the woman within who was not consumed with darkness. Criticism.

I now realize, years later when we would cross paths, that my mom was hardly ever present. At point in her life, she spent the majority of her time either high on alcohol, prescription drugs, marijuana, street drugs like cocaine, or all of the above mixed. It was very sad. What had happened to her to make her become this person? I constantly questioned her motives because they were so dark and debilitating to her and to all those around her.

At one point, I went out and bought her a Bible and had her name engraved on the cover. I thought that maybe if she could read some of the amazing words of God, then she would understand what I was experiencing and living. I carried the Bible with me until the next time that I saw her. When I gave the Bible to her, she looked me in the eyes and dismissively said, "Thanks, I will put it over on my bookshelf and let it collect dust with the rest of the Bibles that other people have given me." Talk about my stomach having a bomb go off inside of it. She is just so hateful that I do not see how this can ever change.

"Why?" I would ask God. "Why is she so bent on self-decaying? Why is she so unusually cruel? Most of all, God, why does she hate You, O Lord, so much?" Those questions have never been answered. As I grew in the Lord, I realized that my mother had become demon possessed. It is a very serious and sad situation. Messing around with drugs and alcohol with a mixture of witchcraft will quickly lead to possession of evil. Ultimate destruction. I pray for her when led.

Trying to repair the damage of my relationship with my mom was never going to happen as long as my mom continued down this path of self-destruction. I refused to compromise, even one inch, on my complete conversion to Christ. I was not going back to the dark world that Jesus had delivered me out from. The division remains to this day. Sad. Awkwardly sad.

Throughout the years, as God would lead me, I reached out to her hoping to show her the love of Jesus. My hope was that she would see the love of God shining within me. That she might sense what a dramatic difference God has made in every area of my life, but none of that seemed to matter to her. She still sees me as a "religious" person. I can only pray for her deliverance and salvation. I can only pray that God would keep my heart from becoming hard again toward her. God has delivered me from the deep-seated hatred that I had toward her, and I refuse to take it back on my shoulders. I have unclaimed it. She is in God's hands.

CHAPTER SIXTEEN

Grandma's Dying … No Crying

MY GRANDMA WAS A GREAT friend and confidant of mine. I could always feel her love. She was raised in the House of the Lord, but she chose to turn her back on Him at a young age. She married my grandpa, who was well on his way to becoming a very unhappy alcoholic. My mom always referred to him as a "couch drunk," and that is how I think of him to this day. My grandma, following his example, also became an alcoholic. She finally cut back her drinking to beer when my grandpa went to his final rehab, in 1972, when I was fourteen. She quit drinking as heavily, but she never worked a program or went back to church or put much effort toward finding out just why she had to drink every day, cuss, and act like a drunken sailor. She continued to have an occasional beer, never fully abstaining 100 percent from alcohol until a year before her death.

For the next two years, after I was saved, my relationship with my grandma flourished in so many ways. She loved my new husband; she truly thought we were suited for each other. She could see how having Jesus in my life had brought me so much contentment. However, she never ever allowed me to discuss Jesus in her presence. It was not allowed, so I never did.

I had shared the gospel with both my grandma and grandpa. They told me not to preach to them. I never did, I just led by example, which ended up paying off for me as well as for them as each one of them would come to the end of their lives.

My grandma and grandpa adored my daughter. Yes, I had my third child with my new husband. She is the love of my life. There is something about a little girl. She is the love of her daddy's life as well.

My grandma watched me grieve the loss of the full-custody arrangement of my two sons and watched how much I enjoyed each time they would come to visit. She acknowledged I was a good mother, and she was fully aware my ex-husband had lied to obtain custodial supervision of my sons. She never liked my ex-husband. She thought I was handling it just about as respectable as any mother could, considering I could not get an attorney who wanted the challenge of tackling a custody battle, one that had been recently finalized by the courts, that is. She knew me. She knew that I would not sit long on this decision without doing something positive to change it.

Meanwhile, our relationship grew with my grandma and grandpa. My husband's relationship grew between both her and my grandpa. My husband loved my grandparents just as if they were his own. It was beautiful to watch this relationship blossom into a solid healthy soul-tie.

My grandma was a "two and a half packs a day" cigarette smoker. One after another. She insisted on never quitting. She never did. She would die first.

I would clean her house once a week. My husband and I would mow their lawn weekly. She would have me clean her carpets every few months. She always insisted on paying me; there was no changing her mind. She was one of the most controlling people I have ever allowed to remain in my life. I do not care for controlling people; I instead like to be in control. None of which is healthy. Yet understandable considering how I was raised.

We would all go camping. My aunt would usually go with us too. My daughter really enjoyed these camping trips. We would have shrimp fries, tacos, and play dominoes. My grandma thoroughly enjoyed a routine. I enjoyed these times with her, and I am thankful to God for granting me this special time with her. Grandpa attended every event, but he was a man of few words, so you hardly even knew he was there.

Though we very seldom ever spoke of my burns, Grandma was one person I would speak with about them. She did answer many unanswered questions I had; all I had to do was ask them, and she would boldly answer them honestly. What was talked about was her utter disappointment in my mom's life and all her continued bad inappropriate decisions. All her multiple different boyfriends and partners seemed to upset her the most. She would say that she was just one big fat disappointment. This always made me feel uncomfortable, so I just never added anything to the subject whenever she would bring it up. It was brought up a lot.

She was my grandma, and I loved her no matter what. She was an awesome great-grandma too.

When I was twenty-four years old, I received a phone call from her. She called to inform me, "The family is getting together for a talk. I have something that I need to say to everyone." Therefore, that was that. When grandma told you to do something, you did it. What a long week.

What could she want to tell us all?

I was not prepared for what was about to happen.

Something told me that this was not going to be good news. Fear instantly sank in, and I did not have the courage to ask what the meeting was going to be about. About a week later, I arrived at my grandma's house with my husband and my daughter. On time—being late was not a viable option in her home. I was a bit shocked to see that my mom, my aunt, my older sister, my younger brother, and my grandpa were all there. Whew, what was going to happen?

Once we all had settled in her quant little eighty-square-foot living room, my grandma addressed us all in a very calm manner. She told all of us matter-of-factly, "I have terminal lung cancer." Just like that. Direct and to the point is how my grandma was, and she was not going to change now.

My stomach sank.

"I have seen a couple of doctors, and they all confirm that I am dying," she continued so abruptly and ever in control, never crying once, not even a tear.

My heart was beating so loud. I felt total devastation on the inside of me.

"I have about twelve months left to live, and I will refuse any treatment," she boldly exclaimed.

"If any of you want to cry about it, then you can just leave this room," she spoke in a demanding fashion.

Wow. What was I going to do without my grandma's support? She was my biggest fan. She was the one who knew me best?

I choked back the tears that were fighting a war to come pouring out. The room was so eerily quiet. We all just sat there too much in shock to speak a sound, glancing around at one another. Would anyone have the guts to speak up? Would anyone have the emotion to cry? And if so, what would anyone say?

She continued by saying, "I am going to hold my head up. I have lived a good life."

She took a long puff off her lite cigarette. Oh, how I hated that smell of her cigarettes in my hair.

"I will be in control when I die. I have already arranged everything with my doctor," she informed us boldly.

"Oh, and by the way, Cindy and Dean will be taking care of me. Is that okay, Cindy?"

What could I say? She is the one who took care of me when I was burnt; of course I would take care of her as she died of lung cancer. I responded by saying untearfully, "Of course I will, Grandma."

I think back on those words often. Really, does one really think that they are in control when they die? For God is the giver and the taker of life, no one else. Oh, how we limit the power of Almighty God.

> For God is the giver and taker of life.
> Deuteronomy (32:35 KJV)

Having had been an On Fire Christian for about two years of my life at this point, with my eyes wide open, I went into prayer mode. Praying in a tongue that sounded very wild and violent, I remained in a constant whisper. I guess you could say I was scared.

Grandma then went around the room, person by person releasing each one of us from any debt that we may have owed either her or my grandpa. I happened to owe her nothing of monetary value. I did however feel that I owed her my very existence of being alive! What an uncomfortable situation. I guess she wanted all of us to know that each one's debt was all satisfied, as to not have any additional family disputes. That was just like her, ironing out a problem before it became one.

She then said that she was open for questions. Again controlling what she would allow herself to expose. Crazy control. She proceeded to answer any one of us who had questions. I did not dare ask a single living thing. I was in a state of pause and process. She was my rock, my boss if I may. She was the one who could get through to my hardheadedness. She was so dear to me. Irreplaceable. God broke the mold the day she was born.

I thought to myself, how could my grandpa make it without her? He was totally dependent upon her. He literally did very little without her approval. I had a ton of concerns, none of which I chose to share in front of my dysfunctional family that day.

Slowly and cautiously, one by one, each of us left from the group gathered together at Grandma's house that day. The next nine months were some of the most carefully treaded ground that I had ever walked. Fortunately, she loved my daughter and sons because I spent the next nine months over at her home, sometimes for an entire day. I would cook breakfast, lunch, and dinner for her and Grandpa. The sicker she got, the less that she had the desire to eat. Nevertheless, I still put on the charade of a three-meals-a-day presentation, as if we were not all waiting for her to take her last breath. Eerie.

She knew that I would do anything for her. My relationship with God, though not a secret, was still not discussed or welcomed. I am certain that she could feel His presence in me and around me each day when I would show up to help her and Grandpa. I believe this is one reason she chose for me to care for her up to the very day she died. Up until the day, I drove her to the hospital to die. She had watched my life change right before her eyes; she knew whom it was that I called God. Jesus, my special Jesus.

I did the best that I could to keep on top of all the responsibility. I kept her home neat as a pin. I would do their laundry, run all their errands, and of course change her little white trash can that she had right by her side. The trash can would get full several times a day with tissues as she tried to clear her lungs of the blood that would work its way up her throat. Several times a day she would cough up large amounts of red clotty blood; it was painful for me to watch her dying. I learned to deal with it the same way that she dealt with the retched mess that I was when I was in the hospital. One day at a time.

One of my most cherished activities that I had with my grandma was baking in the kitchen with her perfecting our cookie recipes. I was always tweaking my recipe in order to make it more superior. One day she finally conceded and told me that my recipe was grander. I felt so accomplished that I was able to exceed her standard. She was an excellent baker herself, and therefore quite the stiff competition. The sicker she got, the less she could do. So I guess you could say I became the Last Baker Standing.

Weeks and months passed, and my grandma got progressively weaker. I would try to be as prayed up as I could possibly be before I would come over. It was difficult watching her waste away. However, it was my assignment, and I knew God had ordained me to do this task, and I planned on passing the test.

My grandma had made peace with the fact that she was dying. I could see in her eyes she had made peace with God. (Plus, I noticed she had pretty much quit all her foul mouth cussing. She had always been an advocate of cussing, and all of a sudden, after twenty-five years of hearing her foul mouth, she had stopped all of the nonsense babble.) I am sure of this; if she had not, I am certain she would have talked to me about it of all people. She never spoke about dying again after that first announcement. She never complained or cried that I saw or witnessed.

My grandpa would just sit helplessly in his chair in the living room and watch his television. Very few times I saw him tear up, which was actually uncommon for him to not do. He was quite the crier and had very little control over his emotions.

One day, nine months after her major announcement, I came over as usual, and my grandma very calmly stated to me, "It's time. I need to be driven to the hospital." The words, though expected, were heart-wrenching. I kept a straight face asking no questions and did as I was instructed. I drove her to the hospital one final time. What a very quiet ride that very sad lonely day. While I was heartbroken she was dying, I had a peace inside of me that she had gotten her heart right with God, for that I am thankful.

As we parked and walked up to the entrance of the hospital, my grandma had her one last cigarette. Wow, what an evil addiction. Sad. I truly dislike cigarette smoking. Nothing bothers me more than to see someone smoking in public. My attitude is, go smoke it in your own home, but do not infect my lungs with your ridiculous smelly habit. Can I get an amen?

My grandpa had just weeks before suffered a stroke and was just getting out from the hospital on the same day when she was going in to the hospital for the last time.

We arrived at the hospital midmorning, and Grandma died around seven thirty that same night. Obviously, my grandma was much more in tuned to her body than I realized.

Once my grandma died, things inside of me shifted. I had a renewed courage to speak up to my mom yet again. With my grandma dying, I had an anger well up inside me; somehow I was able to take that anger and turn it into faith, and I got the confidence, which turned to faith, and I spoke for the first time about my Jesus since she kicked me out of her restaurant years before. I thought to myself, *What is she going to do—hit me, kick me, make me stand in a corner?* The reality of life and death had hit me square in the face. I was not going to mess around with the facts as I lived them any longer. My relationship with my mom was severely strained, so for me to speak up to her could not possibly make it any worse. Amen.

I missed my grandma terribly. I had lost one of the key people in my life who I knew loved me. Though I missed her deeply, I had a sense of solemn peace because my grandma had years before shared with me that she had spent the first seventeen years of her life in church. She wanted me to know that despite all of her wayward ways that she knew of my Jesus. I was now completely confident that she had made her peace with God before she died.

Those Dancing Angels Again

Just days after the funeral, I went to my room to retire for the night. I was very weary from having to be around all the heathen family of origin relatives. I no sooner closed my eyes to doze off, and behold I was being visited by those five lil' angels and Jesus. They were dancing around my bed. The same way they had twenty years before.

I thought it was so interesting how they danced once for me prior to me getting better while in the hospital, when my grandma was looking after me; now they were dancing around me in the same rhythmic fashion just days after my grandma had died. Interesting.

Could it be that God was confirming to me that my grandma was okay and alive in Christ for eternity? Yes, I believe he was speaking to me loud and clear through the angels. I received that truth and rejoiced in its findings.

I finished watching the angels dance as Jesus slowly escorted them away, and I drifted fast to sleep.

Wow, how blessed was I that God cared enough to send me a sign from the heavens. Blessed, truly blessed I was.

God's Reward Is Always Plentiful

Within three months of my grandma's death, God elected to bless my husband and myself with our first home; and most importantly, He granted me full-time parental custody of my two boys! The seventh year—just as God had spoken to me years before, and I had hung on to that promise. It was a sad year and yet so rejoicing.

When I told my grandpa of this answer to my prayers, he was so happy for me he cried. He actually did not believe it until it all officially happened through the court system. He told me that my grandma would have been so proud of me for continuing to fight for my sons to live with me full-time. Grandpa was not the type to say complimentary words, but he made an exception this day. Those words were dearer to me than he ever could have known.

Once my grandma died, it came out from a relative that my grandma and grandpa had once, years before, been divorced for five years. They were married for five years and divorced for five years and then reunited and remained married for the next thirty-plus years until her death. I was absolutely astonished and confused to find out this foreign information. It was very hard for me to fathom. I asked my mom, and she confirmed that it was in fact the truth. She explained some of the story, but of course, in a family of dysfunction, you never get the whole truth. Knowing this fact helped me to understand some of my mom's dysfunctional behaviors toward her parents. Portions of truth.

My grandmother was by no means perfect. She was an overly bossy aggressive woman. On the flip side, she was extremely giving, kind, and loving. That was the side of her that I adored the most. I could live without the bossy part.

She was a politically correct grandma. Throughout the years, she would come and visit us, no matter where we were currently living or what man my mom was married to or living with at the time. She was a very devoted grandma, fair and impartial. I believe that because she fell severely short of motherhood, she wanted to make it up to her grandchildren; and that she did.

You see, my mom and dad married young. My mom was thirteen, and my dad was nineteen. My dad's mother signed the marriage certificate as if she were my mom's mother, and so the marriage began. Fraudulent.

I asked my grandma, when I was in my twenties, why she never contested the marriage. After all, what had taken place was a crime. She replied to me by saying that my mother was very out of control by age eleven. She thought that maybe if my mom was married, it would cause her to settle down. Well, obviously that did not work! Dysfunction breeds dysfunction, not wholeness, people.

My grandma and mom never really saw eye to eye on anything at all, all the days that I can ever remember. They disagreed on almost everything, down to how much mustard goes in a potato salad. It was a ridiculously immature relationship. It was as if, in a sick way, they both enjoyed disliking each other. Peculiar loathing.

Probably one of the best things that ever occurred in the favor of my mother was when my grandma died of terminal lung cancer. In a very sad way, it seemed to release my mom from the burden of faking yet another broken relationship.

My grandma was rebellious all the way to her deathbed. She was extremely dominant and outspoken to anyone she encountered. Nevertheless, I loved her dearly, and I always will.

Analogy of Psalm 23

Not long after my grandma died, I felt compelled to analyze Psalm 23. They chose to quote this chapter at her funeral. It has always intrigued me that my grandpa allowed it. He basically acted as if he were an atheist; though he never confessed this, his actions showed it.

> The Lord is my shepherd: the one who looks after me and goes before me and stands beside me.

> I shall not want: I shall not desire any lustful things this world has to offer.

> He maketh me: to comply to His ways of holiness. He makes known His ways to me. He lies me down in a green growing bed of His Holy Spirit. You shall breathe in wholesome oxygen that will strengthen you and stabilize your walk.

> He leadeth me: onto still water, into peace, out of chaos, and into a solemn calm in your life. Into a most grateful joy! He directs you down a path of your divine destiny. He will guide you.

> He restoreth me: He makes your wounded soul whole. He comforts me. God's power will surround you so much so that you have a genuine peace encompassing you.

He leadeth me: He will guide you 24-7, and that is a promise. He will teach you how to follow Him each step of the way. He will lead you down the righteous path, where He wants you to be, for His glory.

For thou art with me: God is with you every step of the way. He never leaves you. He stays with you when you're asleep and awake.

Thou preparest a table before me for my gain! Thou anointest my head with oil: The anointing that has been placed upon you has been there as you were conceived, and remains with you forever. Because you accepted the anointing from day one and continue to walk in it.

Thou preparest a table before me in the presence of your enemies: He will allow your enemies to see how beautifully blessed your life is, has been, and will be. So that they shall know that they have offended you, spoken evil against you, and done wrong acts to deliberately harm you. The table that is prepared for you is so your enemies can see just how lifted up you have been by God. They shall envy you but will never (in this earth) be able to reach up to the level of intimacy you have with God. They will never be able to gain back that in which they lost due to the fact that they spoke evil of you—for deliberate gain. God will raise you so high that their necks will get stiff looking up to where God has raised you too. Your suffering is never in vain! Never! God will fling wide the doors. Doors of blessing upon you so much you cannot even contain the blessings all to yourself.

He leadeth me in paths of righteousness: He will lead you down precise paths of enrichment and blessing on purpose, just to bless you, just to reward you on purpose, all so that God receives all the glory for everything.

Yea, though I walk through the valley of the shadow of death: Notice it says *through*, and His rod and His staff protect you by keeping a distance between you and evil. Nothing will harm you; you will have nothing to fear.

For thou art with me! His power and His angels comfort you.

Thy rod and staff comfort me: I will dwell in the house of the Lord forever.

Meeting My Joann

My neighbor asked me if she could have what I had. She was asking to be saved. In response, my husband and I had her repeat the sinners' prayer. When we were done, she said that she still wanted more. She was referring to the baptism of the Holy Spirit. I told her that if she wanted to, then she could come with me that night to the Bible study and that we would all lay hands on her and ask God to baptize her in the Holy Spirit. That night she received it. She danced round and round and round in a circle for the next hour and a half. She was sobbing, yielding, and speaking in her new prayer language. I had never experienced such a beautiful thing. Watching God deliver her and set her free was amazing. The Holy Spirit spoke to me and said, "I have given you a friend, one that you can see, touch, and talk to. You can trust her." Thirty-plus years later, this woman has remained my steadfast friend. We have laughed, cried, and shared our lives together. What a joy having her in my life. Blessing.

Looking back, I see how the Holy Spirit spoon-fed us both the Word of God. We could not have received the word and experiences, to the capacity that we needed, without that Bible study. I will be eternally grateful. Those folks sure knew how to discipline themselves to sit and read the Word of God and disciple us newly saved souls. I thank God for them often. Those three nights a week for five years packed full of God-breathed knowledge set me on a firm foundation in my faith and knowledge of who God is. They introduced the third person of the trinity, the Holy Spirit, to such a depth. They could not have known that I would go through such dark and lonely times where I would need to rely on the Holy Spirit to get me through, but God knew. God knows everything. He is perfect in all His ways.

We eventually left the Bible study, and God led us to a large nondenominational church. My friend came along with me. We are lifelong friends. She has been a friend of pure increase in my life. I love her deeply.

I read in scripture where Jesus says,

> And, behold, I send the promise of my Father upon you: tarry ye in the city of Jerusalem, until ye be clothed with power from on high. (Luke 24:49 KJV)

There comes a time in our salvation when we are to be carriers of the gospel. When we are young Christians, we graze and feed and feed some more. There comes a time when we have to give out those things that we have received in those deep, secret, and quiet times with God. He will prepare and provide a place for you to speak those manifestations of the Holy Spirit, secret valuable truths that only God would know, into another person's life. It is the letting go of these specifically revealed truths unto the body of Christ that God will reveal even more truths of His word to you. Those tidbits of knowledge that God has shown you in the spirit were only yours for the learning and not for the keeping. It is when you share them with the body of Christ that you grow deeper in God's love. You begin to trust God. It was in this growth process that I began to understand the level of trust I had in the Holy Spirit. I learned to share my secret times with others, when prompted and the anointing was upon me. It was in those moments that they could receive it best. The Holy Spirit is awesome like that. You can seek him as a friend, give Him out, and still He increases. Never lacking, He always fills up your cup. He not only fills you back up but He also fills up the person you shared Him with if they are willing to receive. What a beautiful God of increase I have as my friend. I will always cherish Him. Feed my sheep.

CHAPTER SEVENTEEN

Deathbed Conversions Do Happen

For thou hath not given us the spirit of fear;
but of power, and of love, and of a sound mind.
(2 Timothy 1:7 KJV)

THROUGH IT ALL, I THANK God for His divine power. A power that never stops working on my behalf, and yours too.

I am thankful that God embedded in me a trust for Him, one that constantly desires to pursue Him. I am thankful that God, on two separate occasions, sent Jesus and five lil' angels to dance around my bed. Both times, I was lying in bed, and God saw fit, by His marvelous grace, to reveal Jesus and His angels to me. Something that I could see with my eyes and hold on to with my memory. To bring me eventually to a place where I trusted Him to deliver me from the oppression of a lifelong battle with fear, unforgiveness, hatred, anxiety, and depression. See how all five of those go together? They are nothing but darkness sent by the devil to harm you and try to separate you from God.

I have spoken the good news of Christ to a fistful of people, one of which being my mom. I truly hope that before she leaves this life that she accepts Jesus as her Lord and Savior. For it is then I shall know that she has finally found peace. On what would be my last visit with my mom to date, before God showed me to make a separation and to cut the ties, I was able to share with her about her own father's salvation. Oh yes, I did, with God's help. A story that I would hold dear to my heart, not realizing I was to share it with my mom one day. God made the occasion as such that she was stuck traveling, driving in the car with me, my grandson, and with my husband, who was at the wheel. We all were driving to visit and eat at the restaurant that the film *Fried Green Tomatoes* in Juliette, Georgia, was shot at. Great movie by the way; if you have not seen, it is worth the viewing. Ha, it was a good long drive from Atlanta, Georgia, where we were living at the time.

I thought to myself that this is the perfect time to tell the wonderful story. I began by breaking down the story of a 1987 conversion of an old, tired, worn-out, sad, and wrinkled-up alcoholic grandpa who came to Jesus on his deathbed by way of God using me, his granddaughter. I proceeded by telling her about the almighty hand of the grace of God's Holy Spirit. She knew of how he had tried to commit suicide just days before his actual death and that he had been unsuccessful at achieving what he thought would be his last day on earth. What she did not know was my visit that I had with him, before he took his final breath. I continued telling my story of how my wonderful God spared him from dying just days before, just long enough for him to receive Jesus as his Lord and Savior.

I started my story by telling my mom how that the phone ringing awoke me at 2:00 a.m. on May 14, 1987, my birthday no less. I walked into the kitchen, groggy and dazed, to answer the phone on the wall—you know the old days, back before cell phones. It was my grandpa's doctor calling me from the hospital, which was located three hours away.

The voice on the phone said, "Can I please speak to Cynthia?"

I mumbled, "Speaking. How may I help you?"

"Do you have a grandfather named such and such?" the voice asked.

"I sure do," I replied.

"Well, I am his doctor here at the hospital, and he has been calling your name nonstop out loud for hours. He is disturbing the entire second floor. Worse than that is that he keeps popping the ventilator out of his mouth, which needs to remain in for him to stay alive. He has been warned that if he keeps popping it out of his mouth, then we here at the hospital will not keep putting it back in." Which of course they have to; he did not have a Do Not Resuscitate order. "It is getting so bad that the head nurse called me to come in and to try and calm your grandfather down," the doctor explained.

"Okay, and why are you calling me?" I asked.

"He is not doing so well. His lungs are filling up with fluids quicker than the machines can empty them out." (A side effect of ingesting carbon dioxide during his suicide attempt days earlier.) "Also, he is shaking his bed so loudly it is disrupting the entire floor," he added.

The doctor proceeded to explain, "When I got out of bed and came down here to reason with him, he stated that all he wants to do was to have one last talk with his granddaughter Cynthia. Is it possible for you to come here sometime soon, because we are not certain how much longer it will be before his lungs fill all the way up with fluids and he dies?"

After giving it some thought, I said, "I can be there shortly after I drop my three kids off at school in the morning. It would take me a few hours to get up to the hospital, but I will hurry."

"Okay, well, maybe if I let your grandpa know when you are coming, then I can get him to calm down some and stop upsetting everyone else on the floor, so they can get some rest," the doctor surmised.

I repeated to the doctor, "I will get there as fast as is possible."

There was going to be no more sleep for me that night. I called my good friend, the one who recently was saved and baptized in the Holy Spirit, who lived across the street; and she agreed to take her kids to school with me in the morning and then to make the drive up to Riverside County with me. We spent the ride up there talking about the power of God and what we hoped would take place in my grandpa's life. We prayed aloud for one another as we drove that long drive and for God to go before us, and for God to fill us with His power and holiness. I had the faith to believe that the reason my grandpa was calling for me to come and visit was that he knew that he was dying and he wanted to accept Jesus Christ as his Lord and Savior before he so rebelliously took his last breath.

We arrived at the hospital, not knowing what to expect after the phone call from the doctor, to find my grandpa lying calmly in his bed yet strapped down with restraints at every point of his body, a ventilator taped to his mouth. The only sign of distress were the big reindeer tears that were dropping from his eyes as he saw me walking up. He was always a big crier.

The look in his eyes was proof enough for me that my suspicions were correct; he was ready to repent and be born again.

I spoke quickly, not knowing when his last breathe might be, "Are you ready to die?" I asked him.

He shook his head no.

"Well, good, because without Christ, you will go to hell," I said bluntly, which is how my grandpa had always spoken, very bluntly. I proceeded, "Are you finally ready to accept Jesus Christ as your Lord and Savior?"

He nodded his head yes, huge uncontrollable tears still streaming down his cheeks.

I then said, "You should be grateful that you didn't die in your suicide attempt, don't you agree?" I wanted him to understand that he needed to repent for such a repulsive action.

He nodded his head yes.

I explained to him how the doctor had called me at two o'clock in the morning complaining about how hateful and disorderly he had been acting. I explained further how the doctor had said that my grandpa had been calling out my name. I then explained, "I drove up here to this hospital for one reason and one reason only, Grandpa, and that is to pray you into the kingdom of God. That is what you want, right?" I asked. Again he nodded his head yes. I explained to him how I was going to remove the ventilator from his lips, "It may be hard to breathe, but I need you to repeat after me, okay? This is what they call a sinner's prayer so that you can get all of your sins under the blood of the Lamb, accept Jesus as Lord, and stand in front of God once you pass over, with a clean slate. When we are done, I will put the ventilator back in your mouth. Are you ready?"

Grandpa nodded his head up and down very steadfastly. I reached over his chest, and I carefully removed the ventilator. Very quickly, I went through a sinner's prayer, Grandpa repeating right after me. With his mouth, he spoke almost in a whisper; his tone was covered over with such thick emotion, the tears never ceasing. My grandpa repeated the sinner's prayer after me. As soon as the prayer was finished, I cautiously replaced his ventilator back into his mouth, securing the edges of the tape that had weaseled themselves loose.

"Now, Grandpa, you can keep this ventilator in your mouth and have a chance to keep living, but if you pop it back out of your mouth, your flesh is going to die, but your spirit will go to heaven." I explained further, "They no longer are going to place the ventilator back into your mouth. It will be the final time." Looking deeply into his eyes, trying to gauge if he was comprehending the seriousness of what I was, step-by-step, explaining to him.

Tears still pouring down his face, he nodded his head up and down, yet again, yes. Yes, he understood.

Knowing in my knower he had made his mind up to die that day, I leaned over and kissed him devotedly on his cheek for what would be the last time. "Grandpa, I love you. I have to leave now. I will see you on the other side of heaven," I said as I walked out of his hospital room and down to my car. I cried in a victorious cry that day, all the way through the hospital and to my car. I did not care who saw me that bright and wonderful birthday day of mine. Yes, he had died on my birthday, one I shall not soon forget.

My new Christian friend, who would become a lifelong gift to me, was waiting prayerfully in the car. We started the three-hour-long drive back home. I explained to her about my time in the room with my grandpa, and we both rejoiced that he had finally given his life to Christ as best he understood him.

We arrived home that afternoon to a voice message left on my phone recorder. It was the doctor I had spoken to earlier that morning; he had left a very short message for me. He was informing me that my grandpa in fact had died. He had popped the ventilator out for the final time, and the attendees had not put it back in his mouth in time. His lungs had filled up with mucus, and he had lost his will to live.

As I finished telling my story of her father's salvation, I sat waiting in a thoughtful quietness.

My mom sat in the car silently after hearing me so adamantly describe her own father's last few hours on this earth. A few seconds went by, and my mom very rudely and sarcastically spoke, "Well, maybe I will call you if I ever need you to pray with me, if I ever get to the place where I need it." Wow.

My thoughts that day were very sorrowful. You see, we all need Jesus. That is why he died so that we might live an abundant life here on earth and life eternal as well. I say *might* because there will be some who will not want to receive Jesus as Lord and Savior; I hope she is not one of them.

The height, depth, and length God will go to, to win his sheep for his kingdom, through his love, has always impressed me. What a wonderful God. I am more than honored to be able to serve.

CHAPTER EIGHTEEN

My Desired Hope

MY HOPE IS THAT I have told my story, or parts thereof, as best as I can remember living it. Though it was extremely painful and sometimes seemingly unbearable at times, I found a way out! It may have taken me a whole lot longer than I would have liked; there are no shortcuts, but there are miracles. I felt it necessary to go into some particular details so that you the reader could get a glimpse into the depth of pain, neglect, and abuse that I lived through. My hope and desire is that I have showed that a way out of the pain does exist. It is not always as easy as one, two, and three. In my opinion, there are far too many self-help books out there that deal with the "steps" to take but do not address the emotional and spiritual damage that needs healing. God is present all the time. We need to acknowledge Him and seek Him constantly in the reading of His Word and through prayer, praise, and worship. When you are in a new relationship, you pursue that person. You go out of your way to get to know all about what makes them who they are. You try to please them. This is the type of desire that God has for us as His children. He craves that relationship with us. When you get to know God and build that type of relationship with Him, He will speak into your spirit. There is nothing that compares to the all-consuming love of the Father.

Child abuse is rotten. Psychological abuse is deadly. Both are usually well-hidden and full of shame. When you mix in alcoholism along with drug addiction, it can seem uncontrollable and brutal to overcome. Even a single act of child abuse can have life-altering consequences. It corrupts the God-given love within that child. Each time the child suffers added abuse, the amount of God's love that they feel is slowly being chipped away one splinter at a time.

For me, it came down to acknowledging that I needed help in the love department. At a young age, I realized that I was not loved or valued by my mom. Each time she would fail to protect me was only proof. When my mom would leave me in a car with my sister and my baby brother for hours while she "ran in real quickly" to the local bar, I was fully aware that I was not loved. When she drove home drunk driving all over the road, that is not love. Each time she would cuss at me calling me horrible names, that was not love. Each time she filled her grocery cart with wine and then told us kids there was not enough money for what we may have needed, I knew I was not loved. A bit of my heart was chiseled further and further away at each time. If I knew I was not loved, then I in turn had a hard time feeling worthy of God's true love for me. It became easier to act as if my mom was invisible. This seemed to keep me from feeling any sadder than I already felt. I had tried to love her anyway, but she was not interested in my godly pure love.

It was the lack of love from my mom that drove me to find out where the chain of love had been broken. It was brought to my attention, as I mentioned earlier, that I was not taken home from the hospital by my mom, nor raised by her for the first three years of my life. This can explain partly why there was no bond between my mom and me. In the past, when I tried to communicate to my mom that there was no love connection between her and I, she failed to mention this important factor to the very messed-up equation. I am grateful that I was able to have that bond—if not with my mom, then with my grandma and aunt.

> Moreover, if thy brother shall trespass against thee, go and tell him his fault between thee and him alone: if he shall hear thee, thou hast gained a brother. But if he will not hear thee, then take with thee one or two more, that in the mouth of two or three witnesses every word may be estab-

lished. And if he shall neglect to hear them, tell it unto the church: but if he neglect to hear the church, let him be unto thee as a heathen man and a publican. (Matthew 18:15–17 KJV)

As you have been reading, I am certain that there are those of you who could very well be saying, "Wow, she must really hate her mom." or "How could she write such horrible things about her mother?" Should this be anyone's question, I would answer like this to you: I do not hate my mom. I just want to make it clear that it is hard to love anyone that you do not respect. In my eyes, respect needs to be formed. When all boundaries have been denied, rightful borders, new healthy boundaries need to be redefined; this is a process and can take years in the developing process.

In my later years, I tried to be a friend to my mom. She would come visit me and act as if everything was fine, as she was drinking her liver out. Within a few days of her departure, I would receive a phone call or a visit from one of my siblings or from common friends. My mom had called one of them. The entire visit, which I thought had gone okay, would be distorted, exaggerated, and all out lied about in order to make me seem in the wrong or weird. She would take what is a fairly normal Christian family life, and she would mock how my family was living their life. As if something was oddly wrong with how we very normally followed patterns and strict avoidance of alcohol drinking, cigarette smoking, drug use, and foul language in our quaint family home. This would happen over and over again. It took me a long time to understand that the spirit that was in her was at war with the spirit that was in me and in my home, Jesus Christ.

There were a number of times when she would question my Christian values to my face. I would reply as best as I could. To not much avail. She would carry on and on about how she knew all about Christianity, yet she was nowhere near living a Christian life as I was. Yet she wanted to quiz me about my beliefs, and if I dared lift up the name of Jesus, this "thing" within her would flare up and get obnoxiously aggressive and want to start arguing about my life and how I was supposed to live it out. Really? Seriously? Not happening. Peculiar.

For example I was told by my mom that I was only—yes, only—in the hospital for six weeks. However, many years before I left the West Coast and moved to the South, my daughter and I went to the hospital where I stayed and received treatment. We went to the records department and spoke to an elderly women who was a supervisor in this department. We asked what the possibility of me getting my records from 1963 was. She somewhat chuckled and said, after trying to look up my name and the services rendered, that my records were in some file in some box in a hospital-ordained storage shed a few towns over. I asked if I could get copies of my records from them. It was at this point in the conversation that she became interested in me, my case; and she began asking me what I wanted my files for. I explained the age-long drawn-out story of how I was burned, what year I was burned, the severity of the burns, and how I had lived! She immediately perked up, and her eyes just about ready to tear up stated, "You are the Miracle Child!" She had heard stories about me all through the years about how I endured and had made it through and lived. She restated that that was the nickname they had given me, the Miracle Child. Talk about making someone's day. You could tell she was amazed I was standing and breathing right before her very eyes. She inquired as to why I wanted or needed my records. I explained I just wanted to know if I was in the hospital six weeks or six months, as a family member had once told me. She said with the injuries I sustained that it was more like six months and definitely not six weeks. With that information, she ended by saying that if my wish was to obtain my records, then because of all the complications, all the plastic surgeries performed, then I would need a court order to successfully obtain my medical records. I asked why, and she explained that the hospital would be leery of a lawsuit. I said to her, "Really?" What would I sue over? I am alive and kicking and happy. If it wasn't for those doctors, I would not be alive today. She shook her head and smiled hugely and then explained again that it would take a court order to receive those records. However, with that said, both my daughter and I had received the answer we were looking for. It was much longer than six weeks, just as I suspected. I had not been exaggerating how bad it really was all my life. Really? Pain minimized again.

About four years ago from this writing, God placed it in my spirit that I needed to sever the relationship with her. This has kept her from tale baring any current parts of my life. I needed to quit giving her access to my life. I needed to set boundaries and to no longer allow her into my life. The scriptures clearly speak volumes about coming against one of God's children.

> Touch not mine anointed, and do my prophets no harm. (1 Chronicles 16:22 KJV)
>
> But who so shall offend one of these little ones which believe in me, it were better for him that a millstone were hanged about his neck, and that he were drowned in the depth of the sea. Woe unto the world because of offences! For it must needs be that offences come; but woe to that man by whom the offence cometh! (Matthew 18:6–7 KJV)

I could quote several more.

The cycle of abuse needed to stop. I had the power and the right to stop it. As well as my husband wanted the connection cut. He was tired of seeing me hurt over and over again. While my mom was not able to curse at me, slap me, hit me, kick me, throw something at me, scream at me, or send me to my room for thirty days, she was still trying to keep the cycle of addiction going by, continuing to gossip about me to my friends and family members. When I would confront her about it, she would deny every bit of it.

My mom has always, very cunningly, kept a wedge between each of us siblings. The last five years prior to me cutting the ties, I was finally able to get enough courage to speak up to my mom that I no longer would listen to her degrade and insult my siblings. For me to have listened to the gossip was just as bad as if I were to spread it around myself. Gossip eats away at your very core of being while at the same time depositing little seeds of doubt and untruth. I stopped hitting the ball back. I walked down a different street. I was done.

> Therefore by their fruits you will know
> them. (Matthew 7:20 KJV)

My mom's fruits have always been rotten. They say that the proof is in the pudding, but I say that the proof is in the Word of God.

> A good tree cannot bear bad fruit, nor can
> a bad tree bear good fruit. (Matthew 7:18 KJV)

Should the fruits improve, I am sure that God will let me know. Until then I will stand on God's Word and obey His instructions.

Within six months, almost to the day, that I severed ties from my mom, God set me free from depression. I literally woke up one morning, and while lying in bed, I noticed something different; the dark cloud of depression was no longer there. Thank You, Jesus! I excitedly told my husband when he got home from work that day. His first response was to be a little leery, as most people would be. Time proved to him that it was true. God had set me free.

Is there a correlation? Yes, I believe so. In my obedience to separate, God finally answered my long and wearisome prayers. God delivered me from a deep, dark cloud of depression that had been hovering over me for years actually for most of my life. It has been over three years since the depression has left, and in Jesus's name, it does not have any permission to return!

> Though thy beginning was small, yet thy
> latter end should greatly increase. (Job 8:7 KJV)

Isaiah 61

Now I understand why the second day into my salvation God gave me this chapter. For years, I would read it repeatedly, but it was not until death hit close to home, when my father died, that I got it. I finally understood in the fullest.

God wanted me to share my story, to let God's people know that He will send someone to help those who are hurting. What about those who do not know Jesus? We have to be the only Bible that they may know. We have to reach out in love and express Christ to a lost and troubled world.

God spoke into my spirit another time while reading Isaiah 61. He said, "I am the grand prize. Share the grand prize with My sheep. There is so much joy to be found at the foot of God's throne."

God wants so much to release what is of Him that you have lost. Peace for your unrest, innocence for robbery of your purity, joy for your devastation, kindness for the unkindness, and love for your hate. God wants to deliver you from all your sorrows, bad memories, and destructive childhood, abuse, and neglect. He does not want you to live in it any longer. I have noticed that in the local church, these days, people do not have time for you, especially if you appear to be broken. Brokenness scares them, especially if they themselves are still in their own brokenness. Understandably.

We have so many broken leaders. How can the blind lead the blind? Let the wounded be delivered, and then they can see clearly to bring forth the word. Do yourselves a huge favor and get in a church where your leader/pastor is not wounded. I am not saying that they cannot be hurt, just not wounded. You often hear it spoken: get into a church where the entire Bible is being preached. I say get into a church where your leader is not broken from his past, yet is broken for Jesus Christ. Then they will automatically bring forth the Word of God because they will be walking in their destiny to remain in God's presence. In turn, they will carry His presence with them and share a portion of Him with you, the body of Christ.

This reminds me of the scripture when a man who is hungry goes and knocks at his neighbor's door. He tells the neighbor that he is hungry and asks if they have any bread. The neighbor says, "Yes, I have several loaves, but right now, I am really tired. Why don't you come back tomorrow?"

We would not do this. This is not God's character. If a man is hungry, our job as Christ's followers is to be giving. Feed them while the food is fresh. If you have a revelation or truth that God has given to you, it is not for you to hang on to selfishly. Instead, you should take a piece of the bread, of the truth, or of the spirit, and pass it around. If God places a person on your heart, then share your bread with them. You will know that it is God putting that person on your heart because it does not leave you. This is the Holy Spirit speaking to your heart. In turn, yield to the Holy Spirit by prayerfully reaching out to that person. This is how I learned to hear from, understand, and know the third part of the Godhead, the person of the Holy Spirit. It really was not until I began to yield to the call of the Holy Spirit upon my life that true divine deliverance took place in me. I have found that when God was teaching me to know the voice of the Holy Spirit, that those were some of my biggest gains and failures. I kept pursuing because I was desperate to know His voice. I knew that the Bible says that God speaks to His sheep through the voice of the Holy Spirit.

In John 10:27–30 of the four gospels, Jesus speaks, saying, "My sheep hear my voice, and I know them, and they follow me. And I give unto them eternal life; and they shall never perish; neither shall any man pluck them out of my hand. My Father, which gave them me, is greater than all; and NO MAN is able to pluck them out of my Fathers hand. I and my Father are one" (KJV).

Jesus spoke repeatedly about us being the sheep and Him being the shepherd. How His sheep need to hear His voice. I have found that the more time I spend reading over and over the four gospels, hearing the words that Jesus spoke and memorizing His sayings, the more in tune I become as I abide in His presence.

SECTION II

Keeping My Head Just Above the Vomit

Chapter Nineteen

Defective Outburst

BEING RAISED IN SUCH CHAOS and dysfunction, lacking God in our home, was very difficult for me. Throughout the years, I took on some odd, peculiar, and definitely cruel behaviors. I am not proud of them at all, but they must be told in order to give clarity on just how messed up and backward my thinking and coping mechanisms had become.

Well into my days of salvation and up into the past ten years, I have had coping mechanisms that were completely dysfunctional. Only recently have I been able to admit my ingrained and backward ways. Though it has been a slow change, I am becoming more socially functional—well, sort of. I am going to tell you about some real awkward things I did. I am not proud of any of them.

You may be reading this and wondering why I feel the way that I do, but I am here to tell you how miserably bad my upbringing was. I am not inflating it one bit; if anything, I am not telling it to the fullest. It took me years to overcome these different abuses. I was in denial for many years. It took me a long time to trust God, that He was going to deal with these different situations. It was up to Him to make these injustices in my life right, and not up to me.

Watching my mom and my first stepfather treat us children as if we were not important would prove to take a toll on my mind. When I grew up and left home, stumbling out into the world, I would encounter different situations where I would unknowingly begin to treat others as I was treated. This was not right.

If someone outwitted me, then I in turn would vow to pay him or her back.

If someone had the nerve to look at me in a way that I perceived was wrong, even just for too long, I would say something completely ungodly to him or her. I was replicating the same behavior that I had watched my mom do. This was not normal.

I began reacting to situations in an extremely sarcastic and rude domineer.

Kids would see my scars and make comments to me like, "Gross. What's on your leg? What happened to you?" They were mostly just reacting to seeing some very colorfully decorated scarring and grafting. I took it personal. Though they are not pretty to look at, they are my scars; they are a part of me. When someone dared to mention any of my disfigurements, I would go into defense mode, being cruel to whoever dared to mention it. I would find something about them that I thought was offensive and begin saying something cruel back at them. That usually hushed them up. It was not right, but as a kid, it was a tool I knew to use. It worked even if it was not right. I was in a total defense mode for years.

It was many years into my salvation before I was able to yield to the character defects that God wanted to deal with me about. It was a long process to retrain myself from the negative patterns and ways that I had taught myself to react to others' comments, opinions, and offensive remarks about my scars.

Don't Look at Me ...

I could not stand men looking at me, yet alone trying to flirt with me. It sickens me to no end. That is just not who I am.

If a man or a group of men looked too long or looked at my body in a wrong way or wrong places, I would call them names. Not cuss words but words like *stupid idiots*, *perverts*, etc. I would yell it to them, and I did not care who heard or overheard my screaming. I was rude, and it was not appropriate.

I have always dressed very modestly, so I did not see what they were looking at me to begin with. Not realizing for years that it had nothing to do with the issue.

I took any man looking at me as an insult. I assumed they had a girlfriend or wife at home, so why were they defiling themselves by lusting over me?

I could not stand it then, nor can I stand it now, when men try to flirt with me. If they even try, I am quick to cut them off emotionally.

While I can handle a one-on-one relationship with an adult male, such as one where I am behind the chair in my hairdressing days, I am still most comfortable with a female conversation. I do not know if this will ever change, and I am fine with this.

I have tamed down as I have gotten older, but this is an area that I am still placing before the Lord on a regular basis.

No Direct Insults

My life has been an ever-learning lesson.

When I was in my twenties, I got involved in playing softball in an A Division softball league. I was not too good when I first started out. Either you get good fast or you get dropped fast, so practice, practice, and practice I would go. I excelled very quickly at the sport.

One night I was playing in a rather competitive game, and the batter up had hit a single. As I was advancing to second base, the umpire behind the plate called me out.

It was dark out, and for the life of me, I could not figure out how the umpire could even see that far to call a close call and then to call me out. After all, there was another umpire whose job, I thought, was to make the outfield calls ... or so I thought.

I lost it. I looked up at the umpire and told him he made a dumb call. He immediately looked at me and said, "You are out of here. Get off the field, now."

I did not know at this very shallow time in my softball career that you were not allowed to make direct insults to the umpire. I learned that evening a big lesson.

I headed to the dugout when all of a sudden the umpire yelled again, saying, "I said off the field. Now. Matter of fact, get out of this park." *Really?* I thought, *He can tell me to leave the park too?* Apparently so.

My teammate that I was playing with that night spoke up, saying, "Yep, he can force you to leave the park, and you better listen too because he seems really serious. I will call you tomorrow."

Off the ballfield I went and out of the park that night.

My husband was humiliated with my behavior. He did not talk too much to me the next several days. Yet I still did not see what he was so upset about. I am a little slow sometimes.

I never did directly insult an umpire again in my ten-year stint in an amateur softball career.

The next day, my friend and I talked, or should I say she talked and I laughed. It was funny to me after the fact; she did not however think it was funny, only weird thinking on my behalf.

I embarrassed myself that night. I had some deep thinking to do. I began to evaluate the whys in which this situation made me respond the way I did to the umpire that evening. It had way more to do with the fact that he was a man in authority and less to do with me being called out at second base that night.

I am ashamed to admit it, but I have had many different kinds of outbursts throughout the years, even after receiving salvation. Finding the underlying cause of if it would prove to be long and difficult and tiresome on my soul.

Self-control was one of the fruits of the Spirit I had read about but had never really heard explained by any preacher, nor implemented for my own life until I was in my forties. Even after reading it in the Word of God, I still was completely unaware that I was greatly lacking in this area of my life. Especially when confronted with dealing with the male population.

Being Judgmental

Being judgmental of others was my weakest suit. If someone rubbed me the wrong way or would make me feel out of control in the slightest, I was quick to respond verbally about any given discomfort they were causing me to experience.

If I felt something they were doing was immoral, I too would give an opinion concerning the situation at hand. If they were wearing clothing that I thought was inappropriate, or too provocative, I was quick to speak up to a perfect stranger, not thinking it was wrong or judgmental. Another issue in my life that had brought me grief. A behavior I would constantly need to be improving upon. Judgy to an extreme—that was me.

No Questions Asked

I struggled with what was appropriate and what was not. I believe this is due to the way my mom dressed and acted especially in public as I was growing up.

The problem was it was not my business to judge how she would or would not be dressed. However, that did not seem to stop me from judging her verbally. The truth was that it embarrassed me.

My judgmental outbursts were spoken whether my husband or children were around or not. There were many times I would not speak out, but those are few and far between. It made no difference to me. I was going to clean up society one person at a time. I took matters in to my own mouth more times than not. "Lack of self-discipline" problem.

This is something over the years I have tried hard to curtail. A work in progress.

Way Too Many Times

Many times, I can look back and see how my outbursts were mean, derogatory, and completely preventable if I had only allowed the Lord to deal with me and my mouth early on in my salvation. This was not the case.

Far too many times, I would be driving in a car and spot a homeless man on the side of the road holding up some sort of a sign. This sign usually was telling all who would read it that they needed food or money. Sometimes it would be the same homeless person for months and months. I did not react each time I passed by them. However, I did respond multiple times to the same homeless person.

I would roll my window down and tell them, "Go get a job, and then you would have food to eat." If they were walking with a sign attached to them, I would yell out the window, "Hey, are you tired of walking? Well, run then!" I was just plain ol' mean. This behavior lasted at least up until and through my thirties. Sad, I know, but true. It is nothing that I am proud of.

What I had not considered until years later when all came crashing down on my life was that that person holding the sign quite possibly could not emotionally have held down a job for any significant amount of time. Of all people, I should have understood this. Compassion was not my strong suit when I was a younger Christian. Judgment was on the forefront plate of verbal and emotional execution.

This behavior I watched my dad exhibit. He would do the exact same thing, and I was wrongfully copying him. It was still wrong.

I have repented for these actions, and I try not to give into these thoughts any longer.

I tell you these behaviors hopefully to show you how mean and belligerent I had become. I was hard-hearted and full of rage. Ready to spur it out on whomever I thought got in my way. I believe this is in direct correlation to how I was raised. Disrespect for others.

It always amazes me how in spite of my bad uncorrected behaviors, God continued to bless me and my husband. Good thing God sees who we will become and not just our filthiness and ill behavior we are living in, in that moment. God sees deep inside us like no other.

Question Authority Constantly

For years, I would get speeding tickets and always think it was the cop's fault. Seriously. I thought that he needed to mind his own business.

My thoughts were along the lines of *My insurance is paid. My license is valid. My tires are not bald. My registration is current. Leave me alone. Go find someone else to harass.* Yes, I actually thought the cop was deliberately harassing me, never even giving it a thought that I was speeding over the speed limit, and it was his business to cite me. I thought the cop was just out to *get* me. Really?

This is some warped thinking if you ask me, now that I have fresh perspective years later. As if the cop does not already have enough to do on their shift as it is.

I believe it has to do with defying authority, and especially if it involved a male. In addition, I was not even going to consider doing the fake crying thingy a lot of women try and turn on with the cops.

Then when they would stop me and ask me a lame question like "Do you know how fast you were going?" My though was, *Well, it obviously was over the speed limit, or you would not have stopped me.* On the other hand, they would say, "Do you know why I stopped you?"

These were all dumb questions to me. My response was, "Here is my license and registration and proof of insurance. Now just write me the ticket." I refused to play nicely or try to talk the officer out of writing me a ticket. "Just write me the ticket," I would boldly tell the officer. I was in a hurry after all.

Now keep in mind I was an active licensed real estate agent for ten years, so I was on the road more than most drivers. It was my weary way of acting that needed changing.

My kids have informed me that they never quite knew if I was going to be arrested or not. No, I have never been arrested.

I have tamed down, or should I say slowed down nowadays. Ha ha.

No Neglect on My Watch

I have spoken up to many a moms in the grocery store or a mall for neglecting the needs of their children.

If it were cold outside, and I would spot a parent with a young child, one who could not fend for themselves, and the child was not warm enough or clothed properly with a sweater or a jacket, and the mom had a jacket on. Watch out. I would give that mom a piece of my mind. If the mom had shoes on and their child did not have a pair on, then I had a problem with it. Here I went off again spurring off at the tongue again. I guess I should have gone into the profession of child advocacy.

I would get agitated if I saw the mom put her needs in front of the child. It made me feel enraged on the inside, and I would burst at the seams holding on to my feelings. Sometimes I would hold it in and be doing okay. Then if I ran into her on another aisle, I would just bluntly lose it and go off on her. Not loudly, but very calmly and in a matter-of-fact tone, then I would just walk on as if nothing had just been said to her.

This is not a problem as much anymore. I have learned to try to mind my own business. Like I tell myself instead, "Cast the beam out of your own eye and do not worry about the splinter that is in thy neighbor's eye." I literally have to talk myself through it one word at a time. This seems to help me to get through any volatile situation when I am feeling weak on certain days.

Needless to say, my daughter has five children, and she always makes sure to adequately have them dressed and clothed for the season and the reason. My poor daughter, she loves me though. Cleanliness.

Or Else

I have been known on several occasions to spot someone stealing from a store. And I have gone up to them and told them that they had better put it back what it is that they tucked up under their shirt—or else. Or else I was going to report them to the store manager.

On the other hand, I have gone up to the store manager and reported to them if I had spotted someone stealing in a store. I guess I should have been an undercover cop too.

Yet I despised anyone having authority or control over me. I was a mess. However, I was God's mess, and He was willing to fix me; all I had to do was ask Him for help. It took me years to see that these outbursts were a much deeper internal problem than I even knew. Once I eventually handed the outbursting behaviors over to God and asked Him to fix all of my brokenness, He slowly began the healing process within me. Learning to submit was hard.

An End to the Aggressiveness

This would be one of the final times in my life that I would bring an end to the aggressiveness I showed in a public area. I was becoming weary of not yielding to the Holy Spirit's conviction. God's infinite grace.

One time this man and his two preteen daughters were standing in the checkout line at the department store. The man began belittling his daughters rather loudly. So much so that the two poor girls were completely embarrassed at his behavior and the attention it was drawing. I was just about done with my shopping, so I got a fire under me and proceeded to approach the line that he was standing in at quite a quick speed. As I approached the man, I did not slow down and proceeded to ram the man with my cart quite aggressively into his backside, lifting him up off his feet. Once he got his wits about himself, he turned around and looked at me giving all the signals that he desperately wanted to hit me. I kept a straight face and casually said, "Oh, excuse me, so sorry." My daughter who was at the store with me and had seen the entire incident slowly approached the line. She knew better than to crack a smile. It was one of those JFK times, and she knew it.

While it was not right for me to ram the cart into him, it did make me feel better. I justified it that at least I did not just walk by and watch the verbal abuse like everyone else seemed to be doing. I took action, though it was not my action to take. It took me a long time to walk in the fruits of the spirit—self-control.

Just a Few

These are just a few of my un-Christlike behaviors through the years. There were far too many to even write about. I tell them in hopes for that one who is reading can see that we all sin and fall short of the glory of God (Romans 3:23).

Possibly that you can take a glimpse into your own darkened corner and see that our behaviors and actions usually do link to the way we have been raised. On the other hand, they can also link to unfortunate situations we had been entangled with in our past. Truth.

Oftentimes the way we react to others is in direct correlation to these types of situations in our lives. It is when we allow God to reach down within our soul and, with God's, help fix or repair or replace that which is broken, we finally can reach some sort of solace in our lives. Consequently, our behavior will continue to improve over time and abound with new fresh experiences. Mine did, and I am thankful to God that they improved. Thankful.

CHAPTER TWENTY

Obsessive Behaviors

My obsessive behavior did not stop at mere people. When I moved to the country, I had the joy of buying six miniature horses. Much to the shock of the workers at the local country grocery store, I would make what would sometimes be a weekly visit to purchase bulk lettuce, apples, carrots, or any other produce that I could find that I thought they would get a joy from eating. I wanted to give them the variety that I never had as a child. I enjoyed watching the juices from the food drip from their mouths as they looked at me, in what I could only describe as a state of ecstasy. I believe I was healthily reliving out my childhood. Fun finally.

One time my daughter and I walked into our local Walmart to find a cart full of over a hundred discounted socks and tights for people to rummage through right near the entrance. The large sign that was attached to the front of the cart said, "Clearance Sale $." Wow. Jackpot. We started digging through the pile, elbow deep, pulling out one after another pair of treasures. Not long after I began, I had a thought: I want them all. I proceeded to pile all the socks that I had picked out of the discount cart right back in. Grabbing a hold of the handle on the cart, I maneuvered the discount cart straight over to the checkout line, large smile on my face and a feeling of euphoria coursing through my body. My daughter and I proceeded to grab handfuls of socks and pile them onto the counter. The cashier had a look of shock on her face. I guess I definitely gave her something to talk about for years to come. As far as the socks went, if I liked you, then you were getting some socks for at least the next year.

Spotless No Less, Got It!

While I was raising my kids, my house had to be spotless at all times. We were living in a two-story home, and bright-white walls were all the rage. I could not seem to get my three kids to keep their hands off my walls. Well, I had a solution for that: I proceeded to get a tub of joint compound and form a spikey modern artist pattern going down the entire wall that went up the vaulted staircase. Of course, I painted them all white and pristine. Problem solved, no more handprints.

While my kids were growing up, the main areas of my house were expected to be spotless, a rule that my kids learned the hard way. If something was left just lying around, it was not uncommon for me to pick it up and throw it away—in the trashcan outside, where they probably would not take the time to look. After a few times of this happening, the kids learned to take their stuff to their rooms.

One area that there is no doubt that I obsessed over while raising my kids was the amount of food in my house. It was not unusual for me to go to the grocery store with the kids and have multiple carts that we pushed. The kids would freely buy any and everything that they pleased, not just for them but also for the handful of friends each that seemed to congregate at my house when it was time to eat. Once the shopping was so extreme that my middle son took the receipt when we got home and tacked one end to the top of his wall. The receipt was so long that it trailed all the way down the length of the wall and then pooled up on the floor. Chuckle. Blessed.

Deal Closed

I went into real estate in the mid-eighties and did quite well in the profession. All those numbers and figures I could allow to twirl around in my head over and over again, went right along with my personality, ha ha ha. Count, count, count. When I would have a house that I had sold close escrow, it was very common for the kids and I, and their friends too if they were around, to go on a mall adventure. I say adventure because it was so much more than a trip to the mall. You had better wear your walking shoes because we would be spending the day there. The popular store at the time for teenage girls was Wet Seal. They always had a big wall display of about thirty different colors of jeans that they offered. Well, leave it to me; I was going to get my daughter a pair in every color, even if that meant going to multiple malls until the collection was complete. The biggest thrill I got was definitely when I could find an awesome sale. We would go from store to store buying up all the deals until the bags that we were carrying would be cutting off the circulation of our hands. Sometimes we would have to drag the bags down the mall to get to our car, only to load them up and turn around to go right back in and start up again where we left off.

Though my shopping was definitely obsessive, I also was a huge giver. My kids frequently would be told that they had to go into their closets and not to come back out until they could fill x number of trash bags full of clothes etc. They were instructed to not just give away stuff that they did not care for any longer but to include some things that would excite someone else when they received them. I always wanted my kids to know what it felt like to give to others without expecting anything back in return.

CHAPTER TWENTY-ONE

In the Red

IT WOULD BE NEGLIGENT FOR me to not talk about the deficit a child suffers when raised by alcoholic parents. For a child to be raised by alcoholics is extremely stressful to them. Not for the adult alcoholic, because they are half drunk most of the time.

In my case, both my parents became alcoholics very young and drank daily into their fifties. Alcohol, prescription and street drugs made for one awful combination. I never could figure out their personalities; they never stayed sober long enough for me to know who they were or were not becoming.

My father became a chronic alcoholic by the time he was twenty years old. He became a violent whiskey drunk when he was around forty years old. Being around him after seven o'clock at night was a known risk. Soon his life was an utter mess. He was in a lot of emotional pain. He tried to use alcohol to numb. He continued to run from his pain for many years. He had so many unresolved issues. He tried to overcome his pain, but never really succeeded to the fullest, until his last few years on planet earth. Sorrowful.

Giving his life to Christ certainly helped to lead him down the right trail; however, he was not always willing to surrender to the path of forgiveness. He tried to repair many breaches he had made. I will give him a lot of credit. For the skills he was working with and old outdated knowledge, he did pretty well. God is merciful. He was at peace with all of his children and his wife of forty years. Upon his passing, he was as whole as he wanted to be. Considering how the abuse of alcohol and prescription pills and how they had taken a toll on helping to destroy his health. He had done the best he could.

The day that I gave my life to Christ, I called my dad on the phone to share my good news. Though he was not mean as he could be, and had become by then, he was very sarcastic and rude. That day I asked God to return salvation to his house.

Both my parents had a bad experience with religion. Early in their marriage, they had turned to religion. They both helped in the children's Sunday school class, but as far as a change of lifestyle, that never really happened. That I can remember—no personal experience, no one-on-one with Jesus was ever really achieved.

A few days after I had initially called my dad to tell him of my experience, there was a knock at my front door. He came over in order to find out exactly what I thought had happened to me. I had nothing to lose. He seemed so interested in the change that had occurred within me. He could bear witness to the change. For starters, I was no longer smoking marijuana whenever I could get my hands on it.

My relationship with him at this point had become extremely rocky due to his alcoholism. I was afraid to be around him when he was drinking heavy. I laid it out on the line for him exactly how I had experienced it that awesome June 17 afternoon.

My dad, who was quite the conversationalist, was quiet in the early morning that day. If you wanted to catch my dad sober, it had to be in the early morning. He respectfully sat and listened to all of the details. My dad was fully aware of how deeply depressed I had become on a day-to-day basis. He knew how the loss of parental custody of my two sons had sent me into an even darker hole. For me to perk up and have such anointing behind my words as I told him of my life-altering experience, it really seemed to get his attention. Interested.

Without much feedback from my dad, yet feeling optimistic because he respected me enough to listen to my experience, it left me feeling high in my spirits when he left my house that day.

A few weeks passed, and my phone rang early on that Saturday morning. I had just woken up. I picked up my phone in my bedroom as my husband and I were still lying in our bed, to find that it was my dad on the other end of the line. He began talking strange: loud and repeating himself over and over. My husband was awake and could overhear the conversation that was taking place. My husband told me to just hang up, but I refused to give in to my dad's bullying tactics.

He was on an angry hungover rant about how much he despised and hated my mom. Mind you, it had been over fifteen years since they divorced from each other and began leading separate lives. He shouted at me, "You were never planned nor wanted. You were just sperm in a v———a." It did not hurt any less when he repeated that shocking statement three more times during the conversation, as he laughingly and hurtfully was trying to probe at me for some sort of a helpless reaction.

The ranting continued while I sat silently simmering on my end of the phone. He proceeded to tell me, "You are so worthless. I can never have respect for you if you are going to start taking this religious thing seriously." My heart became very pained as I cried quietly and listened. My husband repeated to me, "Just hang up." I still refused.

I sat there listening to him insulting me. He proceeded to explain to me why he knew Jesus never married. "Jesus was a homosexual. That is why he had twelve male disciples." I was so appalled that he was spouting such hurtful and slanderous words out of his mouth. It was disgusting. What a deplorable warped version of his interpretation of the gospel. I was sick to my stomach at this point, warding off any propensities of wanting to just all out start crying my guts out.

My husband kept whispering and gesturing to me, "Just hang up the phone."

Stubbornly I whispered back as my anger was intensifying, "No, he called me, so he can be the one to hang up." I remained on the phone and allowed him to continue.

The whole conversation was so sickening and one-sided. He flew as many insults at me as he could think up, and finally about an hour later, he hung up. I sat the phone down and began crying uncontrollably. I was so anguished inside by his words and behavior. This was the part of my dad that I did my best to avoid. My husband just held me and consoled me. That day my husband saw the mean man I had described to him that my dad was becoming. This phone call put a rift between my dad and me. I was hurting very deeply … why he had said the things he did. Why would he deliberately harm me? Why did he have the need to verbally attack and harm me? Painful. I despise alcohol. It ruins lives!

Keeping Your Vows

I vowed to God that day that I was going to fast until He confirmed to me that He would save my dad. Ten days later, in the middle of my dad's continuing dysfunction, the Holy Spirit spoke to me that He would save my dad. I was such a new Christian that I did not know that I probably did not need to wait those ten days to see a breakthrough with God. I probably needed the entire ten days for myself instead, to withstand the darkness that had been spoken over me and to help me to overcome the deep hurt my dad had inflicted upon me. Mean people.

I will pay my vows to the Lord now in the
presence of all His people. (Psalm 116:14 KJV)

In 1992, twelve years later, I received a phone call from my dad. He had been saved and delivered and began attending church. True change was evident within him. He was a very lost soul for many years, but God had a plan for his life, and salvation it was! I had not seen my dad oh so happy in so many years. Slowly and surely, God began moving deeply in areas of my dad's life, areas my dad had previously locked God out of. Yes, how we run the race matters, but what seriously matters is how we finish our race. My dad began to cry out to God, and that is what matters; he finished the race successfully. For this, I am extremely grateful. We had some pretty deep talks in the next several years. It was both healing for him as well as for me. Forgiveness goes a long way.

My dad passed away in 2013. Wow, what a spiritual wake-up call for me. I cried for six months straight. Every day. I was grieving like I had never known or experienced before. I always say that my dad's death helped heal my distressed soul. Miraculous how God does things.

I had never really grieved about anything in my life. Instead, I would go directly to anger mode, then I would go to my other friend—denial, always shutting down and remaining silent.

Now that he was gone for good, I was grieving the loss of not living with him in my home as a child, and now the loss of never getting to see him again on this earth. I had to grieve it all out. Once the grief finally lifted, I was a new person in the area of love. I could feel the full effects of love, as well as freely give love back out.

My dad ended up in his life on a road that he had not planned. As a young man, he had so many dreams and aspirations. Life had thrown him a curveball when he was nineteen; his father died of a sudden heart attack. I am not so sure my dad ever grieved his father's death out of his system. Then he ends up in an unwanted divorce, which brought him more loss and destruction. In the process, he married two other women. Yes, he was married to three women at one time. His mother, my grandmother, remarried a man she met who worked in the circus; this was for some reason very shaming to my father. He expected her to not remarry. When she did, he never accepted his stepfather. Later, his older sister died of tuberculosis. Because of her religious beliefs, she refused to have a blood transfusion. For that reason, my dad ultimately turned against religion altogether. He had mistakenly thought religion and relationship were one and the same. He learned differently when he received Christ in 1992. Amen, Jesus. He was left with an older brother of ten years in which he idolized. Not being rooted in the Word of God, he freaked out and lost any control he thought he had. He could not handle the loss of custody of his first three kids from his marriage to my mom. Nor could he handle the loss of my mom, whom he was deeply infatuated by. He sank deeper into his bottle of whiskey. Though he thought his whiskey was his greatest comrade and the answer to all his problems, it eventually turned on him. Alcohol has a way of doing that.

He eventually had a son with the second wife and three additional children with his third wife. The second marriage eventually was annulled; the first marriage to my mom was eventually after a long hard fight was finalized. The third marriage remained intact until his death. She was very loyal to him and helped him oh so much. My dad was very mentally unstable. Not mentally ill, just mentally unstable due to all the alcohol and substance abuse. I am grateful my stepmom hung in there concerning my dad. She loved him unconditionally, and he needed that in his life. She was dedicated to loving my dad even to a caretaking codependent fault. There is no doubt that God placed her in my dad's life in order to keep the road solid underneath his feet. She stuck by him through thick and thin. The whole time, she looked after her three kids and was the most amazing stepmother to me and my siblings, on the many occasions that we would get to come and see them. She was and is an awesome stepmom, and I will forever be grateful for the many times that she stepped up to the plate and became a pinch hitter of a mother for me in my life. She has gained my love and respect. I am proud of how she has continued to go forth and serve the Lord in her life. I am excited to see what is in store for her and me as we explore our friendship further. I pray many blessings befall her.

There is a saying that she used to repeat over and over to me through the years, which has always stuck to me, "We all have faults." I have always remembered it. Wow, is that ever the truth.

Chapter Twenty-Two

Deprivation Depression Deficit

I HAD INTERNALIZED, OR TURNED inward, all of the hate that I felt toward my mom and others. In not dealing with it, these dark, negative feelings had fed into the depression I was oppressed by.

Walking around in a depressed state is similar to walking around with a really bad stomach flu that does not want to ever leave you. It is a very heavy and ill feeling, one that almost makes you feel actually sick. There is nothing that you can do to control the monster that has a mind of its own. The heaviness of despair comes and goes quite unexpectedly. You at times feel so weak that you need to go and lie down in order to try to recuperate your energy. As soon as your energy levels are up some, you try to function yet again. This energy only appears in short spurts, and then you are down again. That is how depression works; it comes and goes. It presses into your mind and tries to get you to entertain certain thoughts, especially the ones rooted in untruth, and then it eases up. Depression tries to make you think that nobody cares, nobody really loves you, or that you will never amount to a single solitary thing.

I knew that I had to get past all these feelings and learn to love myself, regardless if the depression was going to leave or not. I had a family that needed me. I functioned, the best I knew how, caring for my husband and three children on a less-than-half-empty tank for many years.

I would read my Bible daily for as long of a period as I could. I had faith that one day God could and would set me free from this satanic dark spirit of oppressive depression. Yes, I believe that depression is a spirit. I know that I serve a God who does not want me oppressed by any evil thing. Therefore, though I suffered from the oppression of depression, I slowly was learning how to love myself. Knowing and believing one day God would and could deliver me.

Depression is anger turned inward. Anger is fueled by many collective ungodly obscure thoughts. Such as thoughts of revenge, resentment for past deliberate offences done against you, fear, failure, bitterness, strife, jealousy, envy, and hatred—just to name a few. All the things God tells us in His word not to partake in.

I had a journey to take, and I was driven and determined to swim my way through my horrific past and to find the underlying cause of these dark emotions. All the while, I was learning to love myself and treat myself well. My first day of deliverance was a beautiful landmark of deliverances in my life. Little did I know that there would be much more to come. I just needed to stay in the Word, listen, and obey the Holy Spirit; when any conviction came, yield, repent, and change so that I could learn to no longer negatively react to bad thoughts. Instead, that I could *act* as Christ would have me to act. This has been a long process to learn new behaviors, new habits, and new scripture-driven responses to my life.

I have made it through, and I am so thankful that God granted me the know-how through His Holy Spirit in order to get to the bottom of the vomit heap! Now when ungodly feelings come my way, I am quick to feel my way through the emotions and then repent and ask God for His help. It is much easier this way. Ignoring it does not make it disappear; calling it by name, calling it out for what it is, and then denouncing it or them—now that makes *it* leave. I refuse to walk in fear any longer.

Understanding Depression and Anxiety

While I am not a licensed doctor nor do I claim to be, I am an eighteen-year survivor of antidepressant usage. So I do know from firsthand knowledge what I am about to explain.

One thing I know for any person, child, or adult who has suffered trauma, abuse, neglect, violent acts, or problems is that to be whole, God requires you to *deal* with it.

Healing is a process. Most likely not a short process. Keep praying. Keep believing, and you shall receive your healing. That's what the Word of God states: to ask anything in Jesus's name, and ye shall receive.

Antidepressants and anti-anxiety medications are an awesome solution to a temporary problem.

If you have suffered a trauma, such as I did with my burns and much sexual abuse, you are definitely going to need some sort of therapy. Plus a doctor to help you through the experience so that you can be as emotionally stable as possible while dealing with all the pain. Oftentimes medication will be prescribed. Some people are able to go through this without medication, depending on how strong their mind is. God bless them. I however needed medication for a season. Some seasons are longer than others are; mine was much longer. I had several other horribly traumatic events occur in my life that added to my depression and anxiety, but the most traumatic was the burning of my body. The physical pain of my body on fire is one I cannot describe in human words, or to any human being that they might even begin to understand.

With regard to my physical body, I would have to lie there nude, cold and exposed while the doctors would daily pick away at the scabs that had formed. Yes, I was medicated on morphine and in and out of consciousness; however, I still had the experience of feeling violated while lying on the wide-open bed full of strange nurses and doctors. Bright lights blaring down at me. Them staring down at me so intently. The only solace I received was the warmth I felt from the heat of those high-beam heat-lamp lights provided.

My point is, where is the point of deliverance from the pain? There has to be some sort of deliverance for you to be able to continue on with a healthy life. Antidepressants seem to give you the nerve to begin digging through your pain and past. So that you can at least remain parked out, waiting for deliverance to at least somehow begin to take place in your life.

I recommend you try to find an educated counselor. One who is knowledgeable in their field. One who has swam through some issues themselves. Do not just try one counselor assuming that they can all do the same job; they all have diversities of expertise. Find one who is willing to listen and hear you out and to help with the validation of your pain so that you can eventually get out of the pain. They will need to help walk through the pain with you. Until you actually walk through and feel the pain. It is hard to truly identify the depth of the scaring in your heart, soul, and mind until you take this extremely vital step.

When your soul has been wounded, there is a chance of being healed. It does exist. A time where you, God, and possibly a trusted friend or partner can work and pray through the muck for a *soul* healing.

Unwanted Timing

I remember first being prescribed medication in 1994. I had become a very active real estate agent in San Diego County in Southern California. I was doing okay, or so I thought. I was doing all the things my counselor was advising me to do. What does that even mean? Okay, who is okay? We all have problems. Some just air their dirty laundry in the front yard instead of the backyard. I thought that up until that point, I had very carefully hidden my soiled clothing. On the other hand, had I really?

I had begun to suffer from severe anxiety, severe depression, and debilitating panic attacks. It had all begun to surface. My life was collapsing. I sought help from a different—what I hoped was from a more educated and knowledgeable—licensed psychologist.

I went from being a very prosperous real estate agent to suddenly having a difficult time following through with simple appointments. Any social event that I was supposed to attend would now bring me terrible fear. I was in my thirties and was selling a steady flow of houses. Still was married with my three children; you know, the complete white picket fence so many young women dream about obtaining. This wave of anxiety and depression was so untimely, so unwanted. It was ruining everything that I had worked so hard for. There were days when I did not want to get out of bed. I had always gotten up, taken a shower, and done my hair and makeup. I was losing interest in life itself.

I had three teenagers and a husband who had been traveling for his job. This made it easier for me to lie around and think. Think and think some more. I thought that if I could just "think" it all through, then I could put a bandage on it and get back to normal, and get back to work. This was not happening. So antidepressants it was.

One thing I have learned is that anytime you are feeling trapped, ensnared, or cornered, it is most often the devil. God is holy. He does not work in any type of manipulation. He is God.

Steps to Deliverance

There are many avenues that God can take you down in order to receive your deliverance. Everyone's path is slightly different; here are just a few examples of possibilities you can try to apply to your own situation and life.

Personal Prayer Session

Number One: You can enter into a daily regular prayer session, similar to a counseling session. One-on-one with you and the Holy Spirit, the great healing comforter.

Set aside a few hours of private time: you, your Bible, a pen, and notebook and some praise music playing in the background. Begin your time with prayer and praise to God. Ask for forgiveness for your sins. You want everything under the blood so that you do not give Satan any footholds. Begin writing or journaling things down that the Holy Spirit guides you to write. This is a way to get the *junk out* of you. Follow this with prayer, praise, and thanksgiving worship and of course the reading of the Bible aloud. I like to read the words of Jesus, therein lies loads of power to overcome.

For me, as I continue into praise and offer adoration up to God, He will sometimes bring a bad violation to the forefront of my mind.

I then ask God, if I am still carrying any part of this violation within me, that He would set me free from any ungodly ties or pain that I am carrying around in my life.

You can pray like this: "I surrender the violation that was done to me, over to You, and ask for a miraculous healing of any pain it is placing on me." As the Holy Spirit reveals to you the different emotions of pain that you have suffered, begin calling them out and binding them from attacking you ever again. Ask God to cast them as far as the east is from the west, in Jesus's name.

For example, when a soon-to-be stepbrother, fourteen-year-old teenage boy, raped me at age twelve—as his sixteen-year-old brother watched it—brought me much shame, low self-esteem, pain, and embarrassment to my female parts being exposed. It also brought an added nauseating feeling toward men and a need to discredit, belittle, and insult men in any and every situation available to me. As God brings forth these feelings, thoughts, and emotions while you are in your prayer mode, ask Him for help. Name them one by one as they come to you and surrender them to God. Tell God that He can have each and every one of them.

As I do this exercise, I notice God's presence begin to increase in the room and upon me. If the trauma was quite severe, like it was for me, your body might begin to feel weak or begin to shake or tremble. Allow yourself to surrender to God and the Holy Spirit's presence. Allow Him to deliver your body, mind, and spirit from whatever it may be that you are needing. You will notice as you do this each time, you can go deeper and deeper into the memories, feelings, emotions, and temperament that has you in bondage too. *Always* do this in the name of Jesus.

For example, the next time you enter into prayer and praise, admit to God that you still are having thoughts, feelings, emotions, and/or reactions to others regarding the violations you were subjected to. Name what you are now feeling. What is it? Jealousy of other women who never had to endure your violations, who are not embarrassed of their bodies, who do not feel ashamed of how they look in public. Admit all these different emotions and feelings to God in prayer, and plead the covering in the blood of the Lamb. Ask

God to remove the old yucky emotions and replace them with new, fresh, godly, and clean emotions of purity, sureness, wholeness, and cleanliness. He will do it if you just ask Him to do it.

Sometimes you have to repeat it a few times. This is more for you than anything else.

Pray again:

> I release all ungodly feelings connected to or related to this _____ (whatever it is: rape, molestation, abuse, body scarring, offense, etc.).
> In addition, I receive all good to replace this bad. In Jesus's name.

I always pray in Jesus's name, because therein lies the power.

Eventually, you will find as you are walking through life that you will become a happier, more joyful, and content person.

If even deeper feelings come back up again, and they most likely will, since the devil wants that territory back he once had. Then you have to enter into prayer again and press through and get to the bottom of the still-attached violation—until you cut it completely out from your life and past memories. Amen.

You may need one or two people to enter into prayer with you for strength to fight this last bit of what it is that has you hostage and in bondage. Yes, you are in bondage if you are being controlled by the past violations that are oppressing your mind. God did not send Jesus to pay for our sins because life was going to be all peaches and cream. He sent Jesus so that through His victory of rising from the dead, we too could have victory and healing in every single solitary area of our lives.

Chapter Twenty-Three

Receiving Your Gift

When I came to Jesus, and began serving Him, God blessed me for my blind obedience. I knew not of Him, and yet I wanted all of Him. As I went about my life for years, I could not feel love, but I could read about it in His holy word. Oh, how I wanted that love. I was filled with a lot of hatred, anger, and bitterness; and yet still I was trying to be obedient to the Lord. For this, He rewarded me. God rewards those who diligently seek Him. While I struggled to walk in obedience, God placed a hedge about me, cushioning me each day as I went out into a world filled with scary people. For your obedience, God will begin to move mountains that no one else can move. He will open doors that no one else can open. God will deliver you if you seek Him. God always looks upon the heart of man. Something no one else can see or do.

Little by little, through much travail, fasting, and tears, God won all of me. There became more of God and less of me. He must increase, I must decrease. He reached down within the depths of my darkened soul and healed my innermost being. He made me complete when no one else could do so. No therapist, no counselor, no husband, no friend, no preacher, no one but God could complete me. God is faithful.

Because of my former shame, the shame that was keeping me locked up with the power of fear, He gave me the power to be an overcomer through His righteousness. I am an overcomer for Christ. I beat all odds!

Get Contagious—it Works

After I was first saved, I continuously shared my new experiences and joys I was having with Jesus to my husband; and within a month, after I was saved, he was saved also. He too received deliverance and acknowledged his salvation publically. While I am certain this is not always the case, it was the case for me. I was fine with that. I was amazed how God brought us salvation so close together. Allowing the power and love of Jesus to shine through me and reflect onto him, he will tell you, you had a huge impact on him, accepting Jesus Christ as his Lord and Savior. He saw a change in me, and he wanted what I had for himself. For this, I will always be grateful. Impeccable timing.

God always knows how much we can and cannot handle. I needed my husband to share in all the increases God had for us together as a couple. God answers prayers.

The next thirty years would be rugged terrain, but we went through it together. From home Bible study three nights a week for five years to dealing with total dysfunction in our habits created by our family of origin lifestyles. Regardless, we went through it together side by side.

Through it all, the past would constantly try to place a thorn in one or the other of our sides. We knew each other's hearts and that God had drawn us together, which helped us to never stop loving each other. There were some very deep valleys in my life, but Dean remained stable. He became my rock. I could go to him and ask him to pray for me or just to hold me and not say a word, and he would stand firm silently. When we lost parental custody of my two boys from my first marriage, Dean held me many, many tearful nights. I took the loss very hard. I did not understand what God was doing, but I knew there had to be a plan. Through it all, I prayed and loved my sons deeply. Losing parental custody did not take away the love I had for my sons—if anything, it only deepened it.

There have been a few times in my life when I have encountered other women who had also lost parental custody of their child/children. I was able to use my testimony as a tool for the glory of

God in order to encourage them to keep praying and seeking and to never give up hope in trusting God, in the midst of it all. God is the pilot, and you are just the passenger. When you realize your position in your relationship with the Lord is when things will really begin to happen for the good in your life.

Be Grateful for What You Have

Through the years, I have consulted a few different plastic surgeons, just to see if there was anything they could do to modify the appearance of my right breast or my scars.

One of the plastic surgeons, after looking at my scars, said that whoever had done my surgery in 1963 must have had an anointing upon his hands. Yes, he said that. He continued by saying, "They did not have the knowledge or ability that would have been required back in 1963 for the outcome that I had received." This surgeon added that he would not even consider attempting a surgery on me. He felt any further surgery would only cause further damage and scarring and that I should be grateful and just carry on as usual. Whew.

Being as stubborn as I was, I saw a second plastic surgeon, and he did not use the word *anointed*; however, he did say close to the same thing as the first surgeon. I finally left it well enough alone. It is what it is.

Therefore, at age thirty-five, I determined that it was what it was. On a bad day, the very worst thing that I could do is to get dressed in front of a mirror. I have learned to gauge my days and respond accordingly. Most days, that means no mirrors below the shoulders. My husband Dean has always just accepted me for who and how I am. Man, I want to be more like that. His "little firecracker" is what he calls me! So glad he loves me.

I must truly say that we have seen increases each year as we have kept our hands to the plow. Many of our married friends have wavered in their walk with Christ and ended up divorced, and that has been sad to watch. As for us, we chose to stand strong. We could not allow the opinion of others to detour us off the trail God had so gracefully placed us upon. No matter how enticing our friends may have tried to make it look to us, we kept tilling forward in the name of Jesus and for His glory, even at the loss of several sets of friends. Sad, I know.

As God would reveal different areas of pain in our lives, we would refuse to cower; but instead we ran at it with a purpose of overcoming through Christ. However, we may not have always dealt with the issues in the right manner; through it all, we would go to God to help us to cope and to grow. We have learned that there are some things that you cannot change, but you can learn through Christ how to bear them. Blessed is the man who learns to bear what he cannot change.

Salvation Message

Nothing ever really satisfied me until God called me unto Himself. I had no peace until I found the prince of peace. I could do nothing to be happy. The only thing that satisfied me was when God would speak my name and tell me that He would move in me and in my situation. He would speak this into my life often. Nothing else mattered; nothing else filled the deep dark hole that my childhood had left in me. It was only God's presence in my daily walk that would fill in the giant cracks of my soul. I began to press in to daily prayer from the point of my salvation. The Holy Spirit had gotten a hold of me, and I just wanted to dwell where He was. I desired to be obedient for what it was that God wanted for me in my life. I have determined through experience that salvation in Jesus is the only way to happily live on this planet. No matter what! That it is not just God, as you understand Him, it's God through Jesus Christ that leads to eternal life; and life on planet earth then becomes worth living. "Pay it forward" is the plan.

Healing the Tar-Infested Soul

"Give me a heart given to no compromise." God spoke these words to me when my dad passed away. To look at my life, you would think that I had lived a life like that; however, if you were to look deeper into my soul, the way only God can do, it was filled with dark black tar. At least that is how God showed it to me while in prayer under the anointing of the Holy Spirit one afternoon.

Once He showed me the darkness in my soul, the only choice I had was to cry out for deliverance. For only God can take all of my chaos and put in back into perfect ordained order.

I thought that I had forgiven my enemies. I thought that I had forgiven those who had spitefully spoken evil against me. I thought I had forgiven those in my life who had used me. I began praying for anyone that I could think of who might fit into one of these categories in my life. I repented until I could feel the forgiveness that I was extending to them set me free. This was not a short process. One very long afternoon. Forgiveness and release.

As days and weeks went by, and certain people would cross my mind, if I had any bad thoughts that accompanied my feelings, then I would release them to God and ask God's forgiveness for allowing my mind to take up any space and time with those bad judgments.

I continue this pattern to this day. After all, the Bible tells me to love those who curse me and deliberately speak spiteful and deceitful words against me.

> But I say unto you, Love your enemies,
> bless them that curse you, do good to them that
> hate you, and pray for them which despitefully
> use you, and persecute you. (Matthew 5:44 KJV)

I could sense a difference in how I was beginning to feel down in my deepest innermost part of my being. My soul was released, and I was really beginning to experience divine deliverance. As the years went by, I began to run to God much quicker than in the past. My relationship with God was able to increase even deeper than ever before. To levels I had only hoped for and dreamed about.

You see, God loves everybody, even your enemies. God is a God of love and healing. He wants to be your everything, your true love, your best friend, your refuge in times of trouble, and your king in times of increase.

It was my time for increase. While my relationship had always been tight with God, when I released my enemies over to God, He gave me the oil of joy for mourning.

Isaiah 61:3

God spoke to me to mourn no more. That He was my joy. My relationship with God became even more of a deep loving friendship. My bestie.

When we have held our past hostage, then deliverance must take place. I learned to release my past and call upon His name. I learned to allow my soul to rest in Him. I learned I was being a doer of the Word and not just a hearer of the Word. Cool.

But be ye doers of the word, and not hearers
only, deceiving your own selves. (James 1:22 KJV)

CHAPTER TWENTY-FOUR

Calling

For Many Are Called but Few Are Chosen

I REALIZE THAT I HAVE been called to hear God's voice. Wow. God chose me. He loves me. What an awesome God I serve. Such a beautiful God, that I would be His child and called His own. That He would know me by name. He knows exactly how many hairs are on my head. He fills every crack in my life up with His liquid love. When He looks at me, He smiles. That is what repentance and forgiveness brings me: a God who knows me far better than I know myself, a God who loves me at all times—24-7. Sweetness. Pureness God is. Satan desired to take my life, but God had a different plan. His plan. His will, not darkness's will. I was chosen by God. This is something I understood at a very young age: when He allowed me to live and not die in the hospital in 1963. By God's miraculous provision, He chose to heal me, and He allowed me to continue breathing on planet earth. He gave me a special anointing to spread the gospel and feed His sheep. There is an anointing that comes along with giving your testimony and telling your story. Man, did I have a story. God sending His son Jesus and five lil' angels to dance around my bed at the precise perilous time in my life; now that seems to me to be called chosen. I feel that I am blessed far greater than I ever would have been if I had lived a simple Cinderella life. Grateful mercies.

> Ye have not chosen me, but I have chosen you, and ordained you, that ye should go and bring forth fruit, and that your fruit should remain: that whatsoever ye shall ask of the Father in my name, he may give you. (John 15:16 KJV)

Living for me meant becoming something different from what would have been—had I never been burned. It seems obvious to me that God changed the direction of my path while allowing a fire to consume my body 70 percent, leaving 40 percent scarred for life. I could dwell in my misery, as I did for a while, or I could choose to set precedence in the Body of Christ. I chose the latter. Amen.

Be Chosen

I began at a young age understanding that there was some sort of presence around me—leading me, protecting me, guiding me, sending me, starting me, stopping me, and gently convicting me. I was not entirely sure what to call this presence, but I knew it was with me, and I am extremely thankful for it. Holy Spirit and a great grandmother who prayed religiously for her offspring—come to find out. That presence is the Holy Spirit.

It is as if God had written a script just for me. It may sound arrogant, but it really is just confidence and a secure sureness. I am sure that God had a plan for my life. Many times growing up, I questioned that plan. I no longer question His plan for my life. Finally. Scars it is.

It was not something that I could just go and talk about to my mom. She was preoccupied with her own issues and trying her best to cover it up with her use of alcohol. Neither did she want to discuss anything about God.

I grieved for her often.

Nevertheless, tucked away inside of me was the memory of how Jesus and His five lil' angels had danced around my bed, kept me assured that there was a plan in motion; I just needed to get on board with God's plan, God's will.

I believe that since God sent them, then He had a plan for me. It was in the dancing around my bed in the hospital that day that brought healing to me. Someone was praying for me. I am not sure who all they were, possibly a doctor or nurse or a visitor who was there seeing another patient, but my grandma was the most likely candidate. Maybe it was all just for her. Maybe it changed her for the greater good. Who knows? What I do know is that God allowed me to live because He had a plan for my life. Plans for an expected end. Hopeful.

> For I know the thoughts that I think toward you, saith the Lord, thoughts of peace, and not of evil, to give you an expected end. (Jeremiah 29:11 KJV)

Therefore, my journey and responsibility *was* and *is* to carry the presence of God with me wherever I go and to deposit as much of God as I can around our world. I must. I must obey God. Sounds like a tall order, but it is the order I have been called to.

I have in the past been accused of being too spiritual or thinking that I was more spiritual than others. You can never be too close to God. I have found that many people are not willing to do whatever is asked of them to do, in order to see God's will on this earth be fulfilled in their lives. That is not my problem, it is God's, and He will deal with it in the end as He may.

To give in to the enticing little parts of this world that draw us away from walking in pureness with God is *not* what I am about. Its price is too high. Eternal death, no thanks.

While no one is perfect, it should not be an excuse to find comfort in your sin. Your unwillingness to yield to God's still small voice will always come with a price to be paid.

Your greatest victory is in obedience, not in the disobedience. Choose to be chosen. It is the most awesome place to be.

> For many are called but few are chosen. (Matthew 22:14 KJV)

Making a New Best Friend—the Holy Spirit

Upon the baptism of the Holy Spirit, I had made a best friend for life. He was my comfort when I would be facing feelings and emotions that otherwise I would not have been able to face alone. I am thankful that shortly upon my salvation, within thirty minutes, God elected to baptize me in His precious Holy Spirit. I did not even know what the Holy Spirit was. I quickly learned.

Acknowledging my hatred was a huge step for me. Letting it go would take years. I had layer upon layer built up. Ignoring my hatred is something I was comfortable, sad to admit, doing ever since I was four years old. However, things were different now. I was a born-again Christian, baptized in God's Holy Spirit. I was spiritually accountable now.

Reading the Bible on a day-to-day basis. A habit that I quickly began craving each day was one good thing I learned to do. Something I highly recommend for all Christians to practice as often as possible in their lives.

I began reading in the New Testament, and I was learning so much new information each and every day. It was as if the Holy Spirit had a hold of my hand and we were walking and reading together.

There were days that the Holy Spirit was so present in the room that if anyone had entered the room that was an unbeliever, or even some believers, they really would not have known what was going on. My pain was real. My pain was deep. This is what it was going to take to root out my deeply embedded abusive past.

I challenged myself to read the entire New Testament. Having never read the Bible before, almost all the information was brand-new to me. Reading the Bible was so foreign to me and yet felt so right. I would read about the ways that I should act in order to be pleasing to God. Boy was I going to have to change. I would read about having no malice, bitterness, hatred, strife, revenge, envy, and jealousy—all of which I suffered from. I knew that I needed God to help me. From what I was reading, I could see that Jesus was all love and that I was all battered up on the inside. Repentance was on the forefront of my mind daily.

I would read the four gospels over and over again. I would read it out loud so that the word would sink into me. As I continued to do this, I noticed that I was slowly starting to *feel* better. Slowly, letting go of all of my pent-up and unhealthy emotions. Deep. Years of travail.

The Holy Spirit would break down the Bible scriptures one by one for me to understand. He would lead me to read certain scriptures, and as it was unfolding out of my mouth, the Holy Spirit would line it up so that I could identify with my life circumstances and situations.

You see, at the time that I received salvation, I was just closing out a two-year divorce and a miserable custody battle.

Yes, I had been married at sixteen, graduated high school, and moved across the country with my first husband and only boyfriend, who was serving in the military; had a son; graduated cosmetology academy; and birthed a second son. I moved back to where I was from and rightfully filed for a divorce. All of this was before the age of twenty-two. I had become pregnant with my third child and was going to be married to a man I had a big crush on. I call him Mr. Blue Eyes to this day. We were waiting for the divorce to be finalized so that we could be united in the eyes of God.

August 10 of 1980, my divorce was finalized. August 19, 1980, I was married to my second husband, best friend, and companion for life.

I had lost a very emotional unfair custody battle with my first husband. Of course he already knew that as he would win the battle, as he had said time and time again, that he would lie, cheat, and connive to keep these kids and to get me to come back to him again. He said I would be back because he knew how much I loved my sons and how I would not be able to stand to live without them. Deeper waves of depression set in. As I walked away and accepted the court's decision to only get visitation for ninety days every summer and every other Christmas holiday, I knew God one day would make a way for my sons to see the truth and want to come and live with their mom—me! That is another story in itself.

Nevertheless, I still married again, because I was for the first time in my life in love—and was also being loved back in return.

Though I was in a deep depression from the loss, I had suffered; I was in cloud nine with my new salvation, new husband, and my new baby girl. Tears of joy followed tears of sorrow. God's got this.

For now, I held on to Jesus, remaining in prayer as often as possible. I believe that God had sent me my new husband. Yes, even in my sin and destruction, God sent this man my way. God knows what we need, when we need it, and why we need it. He is holy.

God spoke to me back in June of that same year that I would regain custody in the seventh year. God fulfilled His promise, and in the seventh year too.

The scripture says that no man comes to the Father lest the Father draws him. Well, God drew me. God brought me true salvation. Not long after I was saved, Mr. Blue Eyes was saved too, as I told you earlier. How awesome is that!

My new beautiful blue-eyed daughter, Deana Joy, who help me write parts of my life story, brought me just that—joy. God used her to give me a new hope for my future. A future where there was a chance at being happy and feeling true joy and love. I have never regretted my decision to go forth with my life. What choice did I have? I pulled my bootstraps up, put both hands to the plow, and marched on obeying God just as He had called me to do. Fishers of men.

I continued reading the Bible daily and spending as much time as possible in prayer. I still desire more of God's word. When I was invited to read the Bible with a group of people, I was so excited.

In the Bible study, we read through the Word of God—twice. We started in Genesis, and we ended in Revelations five and a half years later. We would read and discuss, and read and discuss. Wow, did I ever need this, the Holy Spirit guiding me the whole way. I was learning and growing; I was even occasionally beginning to smile. I was so drawn to the word hour after hour. The Holy Spirit was beginning to reveal His magnitude and power in my life. My family of origin thought I was nuts, but they weren't?

I remained in this Bible study for a total of five years, reading the Bible completely through two times. I would take my three children with me each time. I thought it was good for them to hear the Word of God being read aloud. We would read well into the evenings; the children would eventually fall asleep. I experienced the laying on of hands toward others as well as receiving the laying on of hands for myself from others. Many deliverances would occur; it was very exciting watching the boldness in myself as well as in others.

Little did I know that the Holy Spirit was leading and guiding me the entire time. I really did not know enough about God or the Holy Spirit at this time in my life—to know that He was leading me. He was making sure that I was planted firmly by the rivers of waters in my life so that I could remain standing all these years later, thirty-seven in total as of this writing.

During the Bible studies, we would have long prayer meetings at the end of the reading. Regular attendees would bring newcomers, street people, the homeless, or strangers whom they had encountered throughout their week, people who would be in need of prayer and a warm cup of coffee. I experienced numerous encounters with the Holy Spirit in my life as well as in others' lives. I would experience salvations, baptisms in the Holy Spirit, and manifestations of the Holy Spirit.

These were the days of the hippies and the bikers. God would speak to me too fast, and I would obey. Many times after God would speak this to me, I would show up at the Bible study ready to be used of the Lord. Lo and behold, someone would have brought a guest, a drug-addicted hippie, a lonely street person, a drug-addicted diehard biker, etc.; it would inevitably be their night for deliverance. I was so delighted to step up and help volunteer to pray for them. I had learned the importance of remaining humble. Through much commitment, praise, and prayer, God—during these times—could use me in helping to assist in numerous of these salvations and deliverance moments. I grew even closer to God. He drew even closer to me. Learning to abide.

I have a deep love relationship with the Holy Spirit, the third part of the Godhead.

Resolving Who Is In Charge

I used to spend time pondering what my life could have been like if so many horrible things had not happened to me—if I never was burned, lost my innocence, had a loving and caring mother, lived in a functional and balanced home. You know all the simple things a child wants and desires.

Now I spend those moments marveling on how great my God is. I am so grateful that He was always there for me so that I could make it through. I thank Him that I lived a life, no matter how horrific, that caused me to seek His face to the depth that I have. God's presence, which I sought out in my darkest moments, is my most sacred possession. He is the light of my day, my dearest friend. He turned my torment into His victory. The scars that I have remind me that, against all odds, I have made it through. I have survived. I have conquered the ploys that the devil had placed upon my life to try and destroy me. What the devil meant for his evil destruction, God has turned around for His gain.

I used to say to myself, "Who raises their child that way? Who shows no love to their daughter? Who does that?" The answer is very sobering: lots of people do. Loads of ungodly, unsaved, worldly people do it every day in this world. For this reason, I will speak up and out on any rooftop God tells me to climb up on top of.

Therefore, it is time that people like me, who have survived such painful childhoods, speak up, speak out, and demand deliverance for God's people. In the name of Jesus.

Do You Crave the Calm?

I began early on in my salvation craving the calm that only God could give me. I have been blessed with the craving to desire peace in my soul. I get that not everyone has this same craving; nonetheless, I am not ashamed of the gospel that I so deeply desire. For it is my desire that God draws closest to me. Therefore, I set off the sail in my salvation and allowed God to be the only wind in my sail.

It was in the obedience of the submission to yielding my sail and my will over to God that I would feel oneness with the Father. When the sense of oneness came, I would submit my flesh to the Holy Spirit. This is where good and glorious things would happen for me.

It was as if my five senses were all heightened and a sixth sense, the Holy Spirit, ignited all around and within me. That sixth sense being in a place of a heavenly realm with my Jesus, oneness was found. The depth to which I could sense and feel Christ within me was enormously magnifying, and I would know things that I could not otherwise know. Things were healed that only God could heal. Things would be revealed that only God would have known to reveal.

When you are blessed with the knowledge that God has chosen for you to have, you must deposit it back out to where it is that He tells you to deposit it back out too. When God sows something within you, He does this so you can receive what it is He wants and needs for you to receive, so that in turn you can turn and sow it back out to His sheep. It is not for you to just hang on to. Obedience is key to God's presence in your life. Learn to obey. Feed His sheep.

It is in this time of deep prayer and worship and praise that things would be revealed in depth to me. As God was revealing, I would pray for whatever it was that God would reveal for me to pray about, or for whichever person He had revealed for me to pray for. That's the oneness with God that I am talking about. I am still in His presence, He is talking to my spirit, and I am responding in accordance to His will for my life.

Excelling in the gift of intercessory prayer comes into play at this point of oneness. God would speak a name of someone I know, and I would yield my spirit and flesh over to time in prayer with my spirit in complete obedient submission to God. It was a prayerful practice that I would learn very early on in my born-again life. You are feeding His sheep when you are in prayer for the brethren. I think that it was God's majestic way of beginning His healing in me that needed to be supernaturally healed. Emotional healing would take place each time I would submit to God, and in obedience, I would enter into a time of prayer for others; in addition, God would tend to my garden.

He would become my Abba Father, my papa, my daddy that I never had. Closeness to Him was evident. I was being awarded a spiritual daddy through my obedience to enter into an oneness with Him. It pleased God. He would become realness to me as if He were literally sitting beside me, or even deeper, like I was sitting on his lap.

This would happen to me often. I found that this time I was sharing with God could not be shared with just anyone. My best friend Joann and my daughter Deana Joy were the only two people I have ever been able to explain these experiences to. I have only shared a portion of these oneness experiences because the rest were for me and me alone.

Each time I would experience these one-on-one times with the Father, I would feel overwhelmed in a great way for hours or for the remainder of the day. God's presence would be all over me and wherever I went for that day: to the mailbox, to the hair salons, the grocery store, or wherever. I quickly learned to give out when God would tell me to give out. I wanted to please God, and in the deep desire came the same deep desire to obey God. In that, obedience came a desire to feel complete, nothing broken, but my own will. I longed to have more of God. The way for that to happen was to give what He had given me back out to whomever He would move upon me to speak to or give to or pray for.

I became God's, and God became mine, and no one could ever take this from me. I vowed to commit myself to even more time with the Father, all the days of my life, even if no one understood me or it. I understood my relationship with Jesus, and that is all that matters.

Entering into this arena of oneness with God is something I became very fond of. I longed to please God the Father.

Each time after my dollar-free session with God, I would notice that He had healed me in yet again another area. Areas I did not even realize needed healing until after the fact. Remarkable.

One thing that I have learned about myself is that I am an emotionally—oh, how would you say it ... I take things, situations, events, and circumstances in my life to heart. Whether they were good or bad, I would hold them close in my memory. Some I held so closely I actually suppressed them to survive, of which I am writing about in another book. It was in the suppressing that I survived five years of childhood molestations at the hands of my first stepfather. A suppression that would not surface until I was in my mid to late thirties. I believe the suppression saved me from something even worse that could have happened to me, that I quite possibly could not have handled at the time.

Oneness with God is an obtainable goal if you truly desire to keep pressing in and keep pressing on. It can happen for you too. God wants oneness with all who desire a deeper prayer life with Him. God loves to communicate with His sheep.

Making Amends

I have taken every reasonable effort to make amends with both my mom and my dad. My dad yielded, repented, and a wonderful relationship was formed. I hold a respect for my father, even though he has passed on.

I was able to make a few amends with my mom; however, she actively spreads untruths about me to family and friends, which impedes any relationship we could have. She lives in a cloud of denial when it comes to issues that I have either personally experienced or witnessed to be truth. One specific topic that we disagree on is the death of my baby sister Sandy when I was five. I was there, I experienced it too. I lost my baby sister. My mom is still grieving her loss and claims I was not present. Interesting fact: if I was not there, then how was it that the police who arrived on the scene interviewed me as to what I had witnessed upon her death? Lying never gets you very far. Painful.

Quite possibly the guilt of her neglectful hesitancy, which resulted in her death, is what makes her adamantly deny that I was not present in the house that day when I kept telling her that my baby sister was crying. When this subject is ever brought up in her presence, she becomes overcome with rage. I know the truth, and I am sticking to it. My heart breaks for the broken.

Trying to Mend Fences

One of my counselors once suggested that I invite my mom over to my house to have a detailed talk with her. I probed her for information concerning my abusive upbringing, just to see if she would finally admit to any part of it. Though she was not forthcoming in all aspects, I believe that she gave it as best of an effort as she could in her own dysfunctional way. Or at least as much as she wanted to be known by me.

Though I have repeatedly tried to reconcile my relationship with my mom over the years, you cannot make someone love you if they just do not love you. I hurt for far too many years, craving that love that a mother should have toward her daughter; but if it is not there, then it is just not there.

Instead of love, her response would contain direct and indirect insults. She would mock my Christianity. She continued making flagrant attempts to demean me to my family of origin, nucleus family and my longtime Christian friends. It was the attacking insults to my character that drew the final line in the sand for me. My mother-daughter relationship with her is no longer valid. I realized that anything she could do to try to discredit the truths that I had witnessed in my childhood was what her ultimate goal was to obtain. Hurtful.

After dealing with my mom's behavior my entire life, the Holy Spirit spoke to me to "cut the ties." I know this does not sit well with some of my family members or some of my friends; however, I know the voice of the Holy Spirit, and I know to obey any direct command He sends my way.

In response, I wrote her a letter and explained to her that I could no longer have her as an active part in my life. I thank God for the strength He imparted in me the day I was to write this letter. It was a sad day, but I had to be obedient. I was finally free from fighting a vicious war for her soul. God set me free that snowy cold day. There is something to be said about that step of obedience that God honors when we obey. I have never experienced such a solemn peace, where one would think there would be torment. Not everyone "is called" to sever their relationship with their birth mother; but for me, it is what God spoke for me to do. It was toxic. Kind of like when God spoke to Abram to go north; then, upon his obedience, he changed his name to Abraham. Have I cried about it? Yes, I have. Do I cry through the night about it? Nope, not anymore. God has delivered me from a guilt relationship with my mom, a mom who continued to speak evil against me deliberately. He has set me free.

> Stand fast therefore in the liberty wherewith Christ hath made us free, and be not entangled again with the yoke of bondage. (Galatians 5:1 KJV)

I have soon after been delivered from a lifelong fight with depression. I no longer needed the heavy doses of antidepressants that were suggested by my physician for me to use.

I did follow up, go to my physician, and explain the miracle that God had executed in my life. As a born-again Christian himself, he was amazed and very supportive. I shared my experience with my local pharmacist, who was so moved by this miracle that she sent me a card in the mail, which she had written. In it, she shared her amazement of God's power in my life and expressed how proud she was of me that I kept pressing in for deliverance, never refusing to give up. No more huge copay!

Many people are in need of antidepressants; I definitely was for many years. The psychologist who originally gave me my first prescription explained to me that I more than likely would be on antidepressants for the rest of my life. Though he was not a Christian, I know that my sincere close relationship with God opened his eyes to other possibilities. He was able to experience the power of God through my life experiences.

It was very emotionally difficult to officially sever the ties with the person who had birthed me into this world. One day, when I stand before the Lord, I want to be able say, "I heard You speak, Lord, and I obeyed You."

Daily I pray for my mom, asking God for her salvation. I trust that He knows my heart and my desire. His will is for all to be saved and to come and know our Lord and Savior Jesus Christ. How far is the Lord's hand? Can He not stretch it just a small amount longer to include salvation for my mom?

Complete Me in Your Will

> The fear of the Lord is the beginning of wisdom: and the knowledge of the holy is understanding. (Proverbs 9:10 KJV)

Continually through the years, I would read the Word, over and over. Each time, I would desire to want to walk in God's will for my life. Read the Word daily.

Recently when I came to the knowledge that in order to walk in God's will, I had to surrender my will completely to Him. How can God perform His will in my life unless He is my breath, my heart, my one desire, my one true love, my one hope, my everything? That all required my surrendering over my will.

So as I drove on that windy road home one day, I said, "Lord, break my will. Not my will be done, but complete me in Your will." It was in this surrender that God took over.

Some who knew me might say, "How could you be any more sold out for the Lord?" but He did not have my complete will.

That day I prayed for my soul, "Lord, please hold on to me." I realized that day that I had not wanted to be broken. "I feel altogether now, and if I surrender my whole will over to You, then I will feel broken again." Who wants to feel broken?

Little did I know that it was in that brokenness that I am found, that I am walking in God's will for my life.

Some may think I'm weird that I believe in something that I cannot see, but that something created the entire universe; those same hands created me. So I no longer want to not fear God. For the fear of God is the beginning of wisdom.

In my life, God had repeatedly spoke the words, "Complete that in which I have called you to do." On this day when God yet again spoke these words to me, I knew. In that moment, I said, "Yes,

God, I will write a book I will proclaim. I may publish it as it speaks of in Psalm 26:7." As I spoke the words aloud to God, driving down the road, I felt a peace of finally giving in to God's will for me. What a release it was not to fight that calling, which I had felt on my life for years, any longer. God knows me. He knows that if I say I will do it, then I will do it. God is good all the time.

My will was to not ever be in this burnt body, never to have been molested, never to have been raped, to have a daddy in my home whose love I could feel, to not have been raised by my alcoholic mean mother. God's will at this point in my life is to turn all that filth into something productive for Him. I had persevered and become a very strong woman of God. I know God, He is my friend, and He knows me. When God calls my name, and my time on earth is gone, I want to graciously and obediently submit. I want to hear, "Enter in, thy good and faithful servant."

I always want to keep my heart wide open for what it is that God wants to do to me and through me. No more do I want to feel less in God's eyes. I want God to look at me and say, "Now this child of Mine, I can trust to carry My gospel to the ends of the earth." My "ends of the earth" may not mean all the way to Africa, like some people are called, but possibly in my little town ministering to the least of them, the brokenhearted and the burdened. That is perfect if it is perfection to God. Perfection to God is when we hear His voice, heed warning, and submit to His will.

Surrendering your will over to God is something that needs to be practiced each and every day. We as humans seem to take back our will, and God beckons us over and over again to resurrender our will into His hands.

God Sees Everything

Some may say that God does not see my scars, but I disagree. He does see the scars. He looks down and sees how I have suffered through the scars and lived. They have been my cross to carry.

Blessings to you for reading my story. I hope that it will inspire you to never be afraid to dream big, to change that in which you can change through Christ, love deeply, and to not be ashamed of your past. I encourage you to get everything under the blood of Christ and continue on your journey to spread the love of the Almighty God and Lord and Savior Jesus Christ. Keep looking up!

CHAPTER TWENTY-FIVE

Deliverance

Depression Fled

WHAT HAPPENED WAS THAT ABOUT four years ago from this writing, I woke up from a restful night of sleep, and there was something different. I turned to my husband and told him, "It's gone."

Having no clue what I was talking about, he responded, "What is gone?"

Still shocked that it had finally happened, I said, "The depression. It's gone."

I had always been told that more than likely, it would be there for the rest of my life.

Of course, he wanted to make sure that I went to see my doctor and did not do anything rash. I told him that I would.

Three weeks later, I entered my doctor's office and told him that I no longer needed antidepressants.

My doctor, who was well aware of my struggle with severe depression and anxiety, carefully said, "Okay, and how do you know this?"

I explained to him, "I quit everything three weeks ago. God has delivered me from being oppressed by depression."

The doctor, not expecting to hear this, backpedaled by saying, "Well, let's taper you off the medicine."

"No, I don't need to do that. I am already one hundred percent off my antidepressants," I proudly told him.

My doctor knows me well, and he knows that I have always been reluctant to take anything if it was not medically necessary, and then even sometimes after doing my own research, I would want a full explanation as to why I had to take it. He knew of my close relationship with the Lord and how much trauma the Lord had brought me through in my life. At that moment, it was clear that I was very serious. God had set me free!

He carefully said, "Okay, I believe you. Let us see you back every ninety days for the next year. Let's try no medication for now, but please call my office anytime if anything changes, and I will rewrite you whatever you need."

I am here to say that years later and until now, I am not taking any medication for either depression or anxiety. God has delivered me from the dark, demonic torment from the evil one. Praise God for His power and His infinite wisdom!

Now let us back up a second. I became medicated on antidepressants in 1994. I was entering into a very difficult time in my life. This time is enough for a book of its own, so for now, I am going to skim past this section of my life. What I am at a liberty to share is that it was so horrific that I ended up in a therapist's office. After a few separate therapists and a lot of intake questioners, I was finally persuaded to start antidepressant and anti-anxiety medications. Five therapists later, I was attending therapy sessions two times one week and three times the next for a total of ten visits per month. Try paying that copay.

I would stop seeing a therapist when I could tell that they could no longer deal with my pain. They would get their Band-Aid out before the issue was properly addressed and try to shove the issue away. I tried to get one therapist to walk me through the burns and skin grafting, but I could tell that he was nervous and afraid, because he continued avoiding the issue. Goodbye to that one. I was determined to get to the root of the pain, hatred, and bitterness, but I could not seem to get a therapist to walk me through it. But God always completes what He starts.

I was referred to a psychiatrist who was the top in his field. Number 7 in the nation at the time. He was a Christian and very concerned and genuine. He was aware that I was a very knowledge-able, self-taught, Holy Spirit–led, Bible-believing, and Spirit-filled Christian—whose soul was all bound up. Yet I came to him asking for help, asking him to explain to me how to get *untangled* from this nasty web of lies and destruction I had been caught up in. This Doctor helped me so much. Most importantly, at the time, was that he validated my pain instead of trying to minimize it. He actually actively listened to the life that I lived. He addressed issues and allowed me to apply scriptures to any given situation. He was God ordained. I believe that he had my best interests at heart and that God had placed him in my life "for such a time as this."

With the best of intentions, this doctor told me that due to the severity of my abusive childhood, and the trauma I tolerated, that I more than likely would need to be on some degree of antidepressant and antianxiety medications for the remainder of my life. Nothing short of a miracle could change this. Miracle happened.

Well, nineteen years later, on that early morning, I received my miracle.

I believe God places doctors in our lives for a reason. To help us. I believe that medication can be used as God continues His heal-ing and restoration. Some people need medication for the remainder of their life. I on the other hand understood that once I was able to get to the bottom of all of the fear, lies, abuse, neglect, exagger-ations, tall tales, and cover-ups, that I would be able to release my mother from being hostage to my unforgiving heart. Oh, destructive unforgiveness.

It was only when I obeyed God, and came to a final separation from my mom and her negative engrossment in my life, my daugh-ter's life, and my grandkids' lives that the tie of generational curses were broken.

Remember earlier how I mentioned that my mom entertained witchcraft into her life? Those demons that she entertained were con-stantly attacking me both to my face and behind my back. They would speak out of her mouth and would insult my character and accusing me of things that I had no part in. Those evil spirits would speak lies out of my mom's mouth. They would try to convince me that the way that I remembered an event was not accurate. Ironically, the issues she had with my memory were all related to areas where she had dropped the ball. They feared being revealed.

God had blessed me with intelligence, discernment, and honesty all through of course the Holy Spirit. I knew the truth about two very pivotal, life-changing events in my life. These demons were trying their best to (1) shut me up and (2) get me to change my truth. I refused. I will stand strong no matter the opposition. God gave me my strong memories, and I will honor them. Truth is truth. A lie is a lie. I can always stand upon the truth because it never changes.

I spoke up for myself regarding the early spring morning when I was so severely burned. I also spoke out about the death of my precious baby sister's unnecessary passing. It may have been an accident, but there was a forewarning. That forewarning was me, my voice, hollering at her. That I was yelling for help, I was on fire, and that her infant child was crying for help and needed her assistance. If my mom had just came for her helpless daughter as she repeatedly cried out for help instead of ignoring her and continued standing outside flirting with some insignificant man. My mom quite possibly could have had a different outcome for her fifth child's life. The consequences of sin run deep.

It may sound harsh of me, but those life-and-death twisted truths were the very reason that the depression I suffered from were familiar and comfortable to hang around.

Once I exposed the truth, as I lived it, the darkness and evil forces had no more hold on me. They must flee in Jesus's name. When truths are revealed, deliverance always accompanies or soon follows.

The depression was gone, God was on the move, and He is still on the throne. Amen.

I speak the truth in hopes that anyone out there who feels that they are losing the battle against depression will find strength in their own journey to get to the bottom of the false truths. That you might come to believe that a holy, magnificent power, much greater than yourselves, can and will restore you to wholeness. That you too can be liberated to serve God with all your heart, soul, and mind! Point made.

Jesus said unto him, Thou shalt love the Lord thy God with all thine heart, and with all thy soul, and with all thy might. (Matthew 22:37 KJV)

There Is Help—just Reach for It

In that same hour said Jesus to the multitudes, Are ye come out as against a thief with swords and staves for to take me? I sat daily with you teaching in the temple, and ye laid no hold on me. (Matthew 26:55 KJV)

Some may claim that I am just bitter. I say they are wrong. I have swam through my ungodly emotions and resentments more times than I care to talk about. I am writing the truth, as I lived it, in hopes that I can help people who have come to the Lord and have experienced and lived through similar childhood abuse, yet cannot seem to get over the hump and deep despair of their past. I want to help them to lay it all down. Let it go.

I truthfully want Christians to know that there is a point of deliverance; you just have to reach for it. Sometimes you have to keep reaching a little higher, further, longer. Do not give up! You do not have to carry the pain any longer than God allows it. Some may say God allows it? I say, He may not be the cause of it, but it still happened. He is in control of the whole universe. Nothing is done without His knowledge. He is powerful enough to move a mountain, then yes, He has to allow it. When you stop dealing with these issues with your worldview and start looking at them as good and evil in the world, you get a different perspective. The devil will do anything—from seemingly insignificant things to the very obvious, whatever it takes to get your mind off what really matters; and that is God and His will in your life. This earth is an eternal battlefield for souls. What is most significant is the end-result. The devil will use all his tricks in order to pull you away from the love of God. However, do not let him fool you, you are God's cherished child. God will turn all the evil from the devil into something good for His glory.

Chapter Twenty-Six

Soul

The Darkened Soul

WHEN YOU REMAIN IN THE darkness of your past, your soul can remain dark also. When you are depressed and tormented most of your days, your soul hardly has any chance to get well. You must be delivered from the pain from your past. Blackened memories weigh you down. They zap the energy right out of you. Holding on for too long can cause mental trauma, depression, low energy, physical illness, low drive for Christ, lethargy, and even suicidal satanic thoughts. Your mind and soul have to be delivered. For me, I had to take a time out in my life for healing. I am grateful that I had a husband who could work and make the bills while I had to go through my pain. The modern world tells you that you are a "new creature through Christ." While that is true, along your journey prior to your salvation, you were not living in the truth. You have a value to Christ, and you did not deserve to be violated, abused, or neglected. If you do not receive deliverance from your past, then your mind cannot have the freedom to break through those past ways in which the devil taught you to think, feel, and act. The mind cannot freely reason in a wholesome way because you are all tarred up with thick mucky dark oil this world throws your way—not the oil of the anointing of the Holy Spirit God pours out upon you.

2015, the Year of Completion

When my dad died, it was one of the most difficult pains that I have had to bear.

You see, my dad had a lot of pain in his life also. He chose to lean to the bottle. By the time he was fifty years old, he was a full-blown hard-liquor alcoholic. He had become a very mean, foul, and violent drunk, even toward me at times.

His death brought back a lot of painfully joyful memories.

Like it was in that wonderful year of 1992, when I received that incredible phone call from my dad, where he was ready to accept Jesus Christ as his Lord and Savior; that life—as he and I knew it—was going to change for the better. When he asked me if I would come and pick him up and take him to his different doctors in order to help him get off all the loads of prescription drugs that he and they had gotten himself hooked on, I knew life as I knew it was going to take a huge turn in the road. Eventually he quit all unnecessary drugs and alcohol completely. Thank You, Jesus!

Then months later, I was sitting up in the balcony at my regular church, and I heard someone calling my name. I was shocked when I turned and saw my dad, my stepmom, and my youngest half sister a few rows behind me. This sight brought a deep joy to my heart and tears to my eyes. My dad was finally in church; this was one of my first prayers upon getting saved. Wow!

From that point on in my dad's life, I was able to have the relationship with him that I had lain awake at night dreaming about. With Christ, all things are possible! He had become a new man, and I was so proud of him. We became fast friends again. God had answered my faithful prayers; He had done it for me!

After I gave my life to Christ, my dad and I started growing further and further apart, but I always knew that my dad loved me. He often told me, when we would speak, that he loved me. He would say to me that no matter what anyone tells me, I should always know that he loved me. Therefore, I have continuously kept those words close to my heart. Many different times, in a drunken rage, when he would hurt me with his words, I would always remember the kind words he had spoken when he was sober.

He had passed away, and I needed to accept it. I would never hear these words again, but I knew he was in heaven, and another cycle had been completed on God's agenda chart.

Your Merciful Touch Forever Heals My Soul

It is hard for me to express the joy that I feel now that I accepted the unknowing challenge of writing my story. I am no longer overwhelmed with feelings, but rather am now relieved. I am clear on what God has called me to do: to step up to the plate and deliver the answers that I have found in the Word of God and to be an overcomer of child abuse, child neglect, and sexual abuse. As crazy as it might sound, forgiveness is the answer to undone emotions and feelings, and sometimes, if God instructs you to do so, separation from the family of origin members can be the answer too. There is true joy found in forgiving your enemies and those who have harmed you. In addition, this can be done from a distance when instructed.

You must first come to the place of true forgiveness and not the premature forgiveness that so many middle-of-the-road Christian churches are teaching about nowadays.

Ultimate forgiveness is what I was searching for. I could not experience it until I examined myself and went before the altar of God. Once I was able to spend time at the altar with God, He began to explain to me the different levels of forgiveness.

He showed me that there are levels to forgiveness. There is forgiveness in or of the mind, just a minor infraction. Like someone accidently scrapped you with his or her grocery cart in the store. They say "I am sorry." "No biggie," you say, "I forgive you."

Then there is an even deeper level: forgiveness of the heart. Where, say, a friend or family member or teammate or even a coworker kind of got in there and hurt you, quite possibly deliberately caused you harm. Such as gossiping about you or maybe having false accusations being made against you, or say even trying to get you fired from your job due to jealousy or envy or strife, because they want the position you hold. Now this goes deeper into the heart of man. This usually takes longer and takes a bit more understanding of the offense to release it to God and to get free from it, then say it's just a minor mind infraction. Not to be misunderstood, these heart wounds can and do run real deep. They are often difficult to detect. This is where a God-anointed therapist can truly come in handy.

Then there is a forgiveness of the soul. Where they have tried to soul-murder you. Where someone in your life has deeply and most deliberately harmed your soul. Such as someone who is, say, demon possessed, oppressed, or pursued by dark evil forces. They are being used of the devil or a dark satanic force to "on purpose" bring you awful harm. Quite possibly they try and convince you through demonic persuasion to harm yourself; or even commit suicide; or to run away, convincing you nobody loves you anyhow, so they are no longer responsible for feeding or clothing you, making you think it was your idea to leave in the first place; or they give you away as a child as if you were just a ten-pound sack of potatoes, with no after-thought as to the grave soul harm that one may endure. Their goal is to cause you soulful harm, to demolish you in your soul. *Period.* Soul murdering is their primary task. This is the level of forgiveness in my life I was at with many different people in my life. There are people out there in this world who are influenced by lies and spirits, and they do such evil. This is a deep infraction, and it takes the Holy Spirit's intervention, once acknowledged, for healing to take place. This is most often a lengthy process. For me it took years of healing. But healing does come, praise God! With God's merciful hand, I was able to release forgiveness to those who had harmed me.

So just to forgive them can be slightly more detailed then a perfectly worded one-minute prayer. Forgiveness can and will take time and will depend on your willingness to obey the Lord. It takes a point of deliverance oftentimes and a willingness to want to be *free* from the bondage of unforgiveness. Yes, the bondage we—in a very dysfunctional way—get used to, carrying around all of other people's baggage. Once we are ready to "release it," God is sitting there wait-ing to *remove it* all from you! God is in the free-delivery business. He will deliver your soul if you just *ask.* God is good.

I love the fact that through the cross, I am reconciled. Life goes by far too quickly. Get your past under the blood so that you can begin to experience and serve God to the fullest. Let God gently break you so that you become so lost in His love. In your brokenness, you will fall deeply in love with God, to such a depth that you will eventually look back and see that God had put you back together again when you did not even know you were not whole! Even when you are still in pain, continue pressing in.

At this point, I believe, is when you can truly love others. You can finally genuinely minister the love of God through true love and kindness. The same volunteered love and benevolence that God extended toward you. It is when you have forgiven those who have hurt, harmed, or hindered you that you can release them back over to the Almighty.

For me, God oftentimes would show me to separate myself from these people in order to prevent more damage. There will be times, for specific situations, when it is better to reconcile with the one who harmed you. Look at the fruits of your offender; do you see growth and beautiful plump full fruits and healthy branches? Well, then it may be possible that you can allow that person into your life again. However, if you can see that their fruits are rotten or moldy, you are probably best to stay away for a season. I would check in on that offender, whomever it may be, like, periodic checkups in order to determine if their branches looked freshly cut or recently pruned; if not, then I would step back for another season until it was time to do another review. There were many times God would tell me to just go on; I would have to obey His voice. God's grace is strongest in the deepest waters. His spirit will lead you if you will keep your heart pure and listen for His voice.

My Final Hope

I hope as you have read only a portion of my life here on earth, that it will help you to see that there is a way to wholeness; it is called deliverance from your pain or past. There is deliverance for those who have been tormented, abused, neglected, ignored, teased, mocked, laughed at, stared at, or even denied love.

For me, I am complete when I lay down my pride and shame and tell my story.

Victory is final, and there are no more stings. Once you reach your final destination of laying down your past and forgiving, it is at that point you can truly enter in to the destiny that God has been preparing you for all along: to walk in God's divine will for your life!

I will run my race victoriously, for I am running after the only true one who really matters. My gracious Jesus.

SECTION III

Launch Forth, My Child

***

THIS SECTION INCLUDES PRACTICAL BIBLICAL solutions that I have found helpful while walking through my healing and restoration.

CHAPTER TWENTY-SEVEN

Understanding Your Hurting Hating Heart

HATRED IS ALWAYS MEAN; IT is never kind. Hate is the opposite of love. Once hate has grabbed on to your mind, it takes ownership of your heart. It feels it has every right to do so. It tries every day of your life to suffocate you and to bring harm your way. Hatred is an extremely dark emotion to be consumed with or oppressed by. Hatred is never calm. It is ever violent. Its ultimate goal is to try to consume your very soul. Hatred is always abrasive, always cruel, and is most often out of control and rude to others. Hatred separates you from God. Hatred is a loud obnoxious demanding sound in one's head and heart. It pounds and pounds on your thoughts, trying its best to also destroy your mind.

> For God hath not given us the spirit of fear;
> but of power, and of love, and of a sound mind.
> (2 Timothy 1:7)

It tries to consume your every breath, every thought, and every comment. Hatred turned inward is the destructive force that Satan uses to try to destroy you. Hate repeats scenarios of itself over and over again in your mind, hoping that if it plays the same hate-tapes long enough, you will grab on to them and agree to become lifelong friends with them. Hate never forgives, which is the opposite of what God would have you to do. Along with hatred comes envy; envy carries with it jealousy. These two eventually invite bitterness to tag along, and of course, bitterness finally requests strife to join the party. This combination can be lethal. Hatred is never ever a good thing, unless of course it is the hatred of sin. The end-result of holding on to or responding to hatred and its cult following is inevitably rage. The most destructive of all emotions is rage. Rage held inward will, in the end, destroy you.

Once God brought it to my awareness of how I had hung on to the emotion and memories of hate, I felt moved to bring a peace offering to the altar of the Lord, because in the recognition I realized I was angry at God. Once I realized this, I could lay it *all* down and repent for my "held-on-to hostility" toward God. This was not a one-time deal. This took several different times and several years, and a lot of patience from my standpoint. I had to plead continuously with God for His merciful hand to heal me; it was deeply imbedded in me. I asked God if He could replace my hate with joy. There were so many times I would feel compelled to separate myself and to go to my closet and take a time-out from society. It was a must in order for me to be completed in Him.

I would always begin praying to God in the same old way, pleading with God, saying, "God, please take this sin of hatred and cast it as far as the east is from the west. Have mercy upon me, O Thou Son of David." I would then begin worshipping God and praising God, for it seemed to be the only force that could break the hold hatred had upon me. As I would be worshipping and praising God, His presence would draw near to me; and as He would draw near, He would also convict me of the sin of hatred. He then would gently prick my heart and ask me to let go of this very shaming and destructive emotion. It was at this very volatile time before the Lord that I would petition Him. I would ask, "God, have mercy upon me, a sinner that is saved by grace." This was a rhythmic and recurrent pattern that I had to repeat over and over again, sometimes day in and day out. After years of the same pattern, and the hatred did not seem to be all the way broken, it was at that time I began begging God to "break me" and to "break my will." My will was very strong, yet I knew in my soul I needed and wanted God to break it. I could feel a very dark force oppressing me that did not want to surrender. It took many years for "my will" to be broken. I can honestly say it was a remarkable yet embarrassing experience. Oh, the strength of our own will.

> Hatred stirreth up strife, But love covereth
> all sins. (Proverbs 10:12 KJV)

God's love is ultimately revealed in us and to us when we are willing to release, or let go of, any or all hate, bitterness, and malice. It is at this place where love can enter our lives, ultimately pushing out all the darkness. His power overpowers all bitterness, hatred, or malice. His love is unfailing and amazing.

Consulting Your Past

Learning how to decipher what you may need to deal with.

Usually in everyone's life, there are things that bring unrest to your soul, your innermost being where wisdom resides. When dwelt upon, they remain unsettled, uncomfortable, and somewhat irritating to your mind. These things need to be dealt with, especially if you were raised in total dysfunctional chaos, alcoholism, or possibly the loss of a parent through divorce or death. On the other hand, perhaps you lost a sibling or watched them being abused. It could be any number of situations that could be afflicting you. What is most important is that you search your heart and soul for any defective drama-like scenarios that are still undone on your insides. Pray for God to set you free from it all. Pray for God's holy protection as you swim through these issues.

When you have had such severe crippling occur in your life, if you allow the crippling residency or space in your soul and do not surrender these crippling over to God to walk you through, then you are in exchange allowing them to take up prime real estate; and in turn, darkness resides where light should have ultimate prime residency.

I knew that I had so many events that had adversely affected my life. I had no choice but to open up my soul to God and allow Him to help me. This took years. I needed God's help big-time. I believe that anytime a child is raised in a home where there is active alcoholism and deliberate rebellion toward God, that child is inevitably in grave danger. Alcoholism mixed with direct defiance toward the hand of God brings along with it sorrow, much depression, and despair into the entire home. Rebellion is as the sin of witchcraft, and it needs to be carefully and prayerfully rooted up and out. Demolished in the name of Jesus!

> For rebellion is as the sin of witchcraft, and stubbornness is as iniquity and idolatry. Because thou hast rejected the word of the Lord, he hath also rejected thee from being king. (1 Samuel 15:23 KJV)
> And Jesus said unto him, No man, having put his hand to the plough, and looking back, is fit for the kingdom of God. (Luke 9:62 KJV)

If that is the case for the parents, then imagine what a horror the poor child is living in and being subjected to. This is not fair to a child. It is spiritual child abuse in my eyes.

My best suggestion for such a child is to quickly accept Jesus Christ as their Lord and Savior.

> That if thou shalt confess with their mouth the Lord Jesus, and shalt believe in thine heart that God hath raised Him from the dead, thou shalt be saved. (Romans 10:9, 10 KJV)

Commit To

I knew enough of the word to know that in order for this dark satanic force to leave my presence, I was going to have to make a commitment to fasting and praying. I finally made that commitment to the Lord. As I began a series of fasting and praying and pleaded for the blood of Jesus Christ to cover me, changes began taking place. The blood of the Lamb was the only force that could break the hold of the sin of hatred that oppressed me. I knew it would take a tilling up of some very stony ground that surrounded my very embittered heart. This hatred was so strong, only the power of Jesus could break it.

Repentance was necessary. A must that had to come forth out of my *own* mouth, and it was then that God could begin to wash me clean with His Word. I was persistent; I was definitely thirsty for God's word to the fullest. I wanted so desperately to experience what the Bible said about love. I knew that what the word had spoken about love was true, and I wanted to experience that sweet feeling of love coming back at me from the Almighty. It was nothing I could do on my own. I knew I had to surrender *all* of me, every ounce of me, and that God would *do* it. I needed God to cast it far far away, and for good this time—permanently. I had had many a breakthroughs, on and off all through my years of salvation, but this time I needed a final deliverance from the dark force of hatred, which had tried so methodically to consume my life. I thank God for the power of deliverance. God in His wisdom can look in to our innermost being and see the sincerity of our soul!

Determined to become more Christlike, and from what I had been reading in the Bible, hate was not included in that description so notably known in the book of Corinthians! Being delivered from the spirit of hate, which was so comfortable in oppressing me, was a miracle I would never take lightly. I thank God daily for His deliverance power He so preciously chose to use on me.

No Lowering Here

I have tried hard to never lower my understanding of the Bible to my less-knowledgeable understanding in flesh. I try to allow God all of the leeway or movement that He wants in my life for Him to enlighten, encourage, and escort me into the depths, heights, and heavenly measurements of His word for my life and my destiny.

I want nothing more than that I may be pleasing to my Father in the remaining years of my life. I can do this by being as open to

Him as possible and by being obedient to His voice, His call, and His destiny for my life.

Propelled Determination

I have always been the sort of individual who wants more for others too. I have been on fire for God ever since I gave my life to Christ, believing the entire Word of God. I feel this is what propelled me into areas of the movement of the Holy Spirit in my life. I read in the scriptures where it says that "greater things shall ye do because I ascend to the Father" (John 14:12), and I believed what the Word of God was saying. God placed a fire under me to go hard for Him for a reason.

I look back, and I see all that has happened in my life. I am determined to turn all that was meant for my harm into thankfulness for God's glory. I thank God daily for the victories in my life and for my husband and my three children and my eleven grandchildren, who daily stand by my side.

I am always seeking and never satisfied with who I am in Christ. I want to mature daily. I was determined to claim my deliverance and healing. I had to learn to confront situations and people, sometimes causing offenses as my flesh would interfere. Those offenses were not intended, but merely a byproduct of the process that I needed to battle to complete to become whole. I was treading territory that God says in His word that is mine to tread.

When things in life have been stolen from you, like your virginity, your ability to love freely, your right to sober and present parents, and less than what was needed to get by, then you are going to have to load up your spiritual guns and fight for your God-given inheritance.

Jesus said, Son, thou art ever with me, and
all that I have is thine. (Luke 15:31 KJV)

In the Bible, in Exodus 20:12, it says to "honor your father and mother: that thy days may be long upon the land which the Lord thy God giveth thee." I have a responsibility to put my spirit before the

Holy Spirit and get things right in my heart and soul so that I can rightly honor them. If you just act as if you honor them, but in your heart, you cannot stand them, then the Lord knows your deceit. It is a sin in God's book. I have done this.

I honor the fact that they birthed me into this world, but I do not honor the life they so rebelliously chose to live.

I say all of this to say I despised both my parents. In this, Satan had won. I had a duty, an obligation, and a commitment to get to the bottom of the stack as to why I despised them both so much.

I make no excuses for myself. I had a responsibility as much as possible to live at peace. I have done this.

> If it is possible, as far as it depends on you,
> live at peace with everyone. (Romans 12:18 KJV)

The scriptures say in Acts 10:34, "God is no respecter of persons" (KJV).

I was looking around seeing many Christians walking in joy, peace, and love. I was not. It was my obligation to figure out why I had no true joy.

In my journey to spiritual increase and peace, I needed to expose the root of my depression, anxiety, fear, and lack of love. Not to mention hatred, jealousy, bitterness, and shame.

God knows what I am capable of. He created me with a strong mind, an aggressive personality, and a straitlaced—as some would call me—character. I had to look at myself honestly in a mirror and challenge my character defects, asking God what it is that I needed to do in order to get rid of these unclean thoughts of hate and discontent toward my parents and others. God began to call me to confront my feelings and issues, and to teach others to do the same in order to have victory in their lives.

My goal in my life is to bring to others knowledge of who the God of the Bible is. How wonderfully good He is to us, if we will just allow Him to deliver us. God knows your potential, what is inside of you, more than anyone else. He knows how I hold His power inside of my being and that I walk in a faith that few walk in. He knows because He planted that faith within me. Often people have a difficult time being around me because of their own conviction of sin, sin they are not willing to repent of or to change. Though hurtful sometimes to my flesh, I understand that it is all in God's hand. If I can make the slightest impact on their lives when they are around me, then I have done what I am called to do.

I truly believe that there are thousands of injured victims out there in the world who truly do want to draw closer to God, Jesus, and the Holy Spirit. These are the people I hope to reach. I am willing to speak out. Over time, I have come to realize that when God unravels Himself to me, showing me some new truth, something fresh, and vibrant gospel truth, it is for me to digest it, process it, and live it. Many times, it is also for me to pass on to the body of followers who can use it and apply it in their lives. God has shown me to share the truths derived from His word to His sheep. The words "Feed my sheep" have resounded in my soul as I have dug through my pain. I cannot tell you how many hundreds of times that the Holy Spirit has led me to read the parable of the ten virgins or the scripture of the three workmen and their talents. I would absorb these scriptures and pray on them for hours. God has shown me to give away what He has given to me, and He will give me more—more truth, more gospel truth, more principles, more knowledge, more wisdom, more understanding, and more love for His body of believers. He has shown me to not be concerned of what people think or say about me. None of that really matters anyway. What does truly matter is my obedience to the Lord. I am accountable when the bridegroom comes, for all that the Lord has asked me to do.

Jesus spoke to his disciples in John 15:4, saying, "Abide in me, and I in you. As the branch cannot bear fruit of itself, except it abide in the vine; no more can ye, except ye abide in me" (KJV).

Who am I that scripture would not pertain to me? In order for God to abide in me to the full, I must walk in truth. In order for me to walk in truth, I had to address all the lies in my life and all the hidden, closeted sins past and present. God is not to be mocked. He is a holy God. He expects His people to walk a clean life expounding in His joy.

Commanding Darkness with Power

Light and dark cannot dwell in the same vessel. Hence, I began by trying to address all of my generational family's stronghold, sin, dysfunction, betrayal, and spiritual sickness. I found victory in my life and soul when learning in Jesus's name I had the power to command this evil to flee.

I learned that I could live by the Ten Commandments. Loving God with all of my heart, soul, and mind. Loving my neighbors, parents, friends, and family as I love myself. Regardless if they loved me back. I did not need them to love me back to be complete in Jesus Christ. He was my completeness.

Following Philippians 2:5, I let the mind of Christ be in me, learning to treat others with love and concern for their best welfare. Jesus was direct, and yet He was extremely loving. I was learning to love others without allowing others to use me or walk all over me. I can show them the way that God has shown me to be. Many have tried to use me as a go-between for them and God. I have no desire for this position. I no longer allow this to happen in my life. It is up to each individual to have a love relationship with the Lord. It is up to each person to go directly to the Father.

I try to remain in Him. I try to always keep myself prepared to hear from God. It is just who I am. I can do it much more confidently now.

Matthew 5:6 says, "For blessed are they, which do hunger, and thirst after righteousness for they shall be filled" (KJV).

Well, I finally feel full. I am now doing my best to remain full so that when called upon, I can feed God's sheep God's Word.

Begin to Serve God

For with the heart man believeth unto righteousness; and with the mouth confession is made unto salvation. (Romans 10:10 KJV)

Next, you need to seek God for the baptism of the Holy Spirit. Therein lies your strength and your power to overcome. To receive salvation is only the beginning of life. Your new spiritual life in Christ will help you to cope. For me, there were so many unanswered questions about the whys of my life, how come this and how come that? Having salvation on your side is really the best way to live on this planet. Without salvation in Jesus, you only remain lost.

God knows your innermost being. He loves you, you are now His precious child, and He is your king. He can and will help you to file through any past unresolved issues in your old life and get them under the Blood, as you shall quickly learn.

Being raised by an alcoholic, there are so many hidden secrets. Some parents will tell you directly not to repeat to anyone what has happened or what goes on in your home. Some parents will just give you the look. You know the one that threatens you with no words; do not say a word, or you will be harmed! In *harmed*, I mean punished, hit, beaten, ignored, starved, verbally abused, sent to your room for thirty days, or stand in a corner for two hours. It could be any number of abuses—whatever it takes to shut you up and keep the family secrets. The alcoholic parent learns very quickly how to manipulate their children into not speaking out. After all, almost all alcoholics have one thing in common: unresolved or hidden emotional issues of their own that they have never dealt with.

Once you can untangle the issues that you need to walk through and receive deliverance from, find yourself a good Christian Holy Spirit–filled counselor. Make a covenant with the Lord to read His word regularly, pray frequently every day, and to journal much. When you begin the road to recovery, it is a long journey. Keep your covenant, and it will pay off. God will not fail you. God cannot fail; He is God.

Hearing the Voice

There is something about the correlation of a pure heart and hearing from God. It is called getting your sin under the blood, desiring the presence of God more than anything this world can offer at any cost.

Eventually, as I moved closer and closer to God, through much washing and watering of the Word of God, my trust increased, and He began to engulf more and more of my being and my life. The magnitude of God's presence would sweep me away into hours of worship. It was so strong, so powerful, so beautifully spirit-filled and so love-charged. I realized He had been loving on me all along. I had been so unloved in my past that I had nothing to compare it to, except the love from my husband and children and of course my awesome grandchildren—all eleven of them. I could not compare God's love to anything even remotely close to what this world had to offer. While my husband loved me in the flesh, there is nothing to compare to being loved on by God.

Walking in my divine destiny has been the greatest reward of all. There is such a true genuine peace. There is such an all-encompassing presence of the Lord. I had no idea that all of the tears, all of the hurting, all of the scars and the offenses and violations to my body and mind were a part of making and creating me into who I am today. Through all the trials, God's ultimate purpose was to bring me into His divine destiny for my life and for the glory of God. To fulfill His will and to be used for God's glory and not mine, lest I should boast. His power was carrying me through to bring me to such a time as this. To God be the glory for all that He has done for me.

Chapter Twenty-Eight

Becoming a New Creature in Christ

SWIMMING THROUGH THE MIRE IS important for each and every believer. It does not truly matter if you want to or not. God will make an opportunity for you to go through your past; it is up to you if you obey or not. I chose to obey.

If you choose to disobey, then you will find that almost every given situation you experience in life will continue to move you closer to the place of dealing with your past and your past pain, or even the current pain you are remaining in. God commands you to remain in Him. Not to remain in your sorrow. He told you He would replace your sorrow with joy, but you have to surrender your past sorrows over to Him first. So allow God to put on your beautiful garments and go forth! Shake yourselves from the dusty garments and remove the filthy clothes, sackcloth, and garments and put on the spirit of victory and rejoicing. For it is Satan who wants you to remain in him, in your past, in your pain; but God wants you to put on clean clothes, with pureness from God. So bow down to the Almighty God and sing praises, be cleansed, ye sinners, and weep no more. Let the tears you shed cleanse you inwardly. Be brave and surrender your past over to God. He can set you free from all pain, all sorrow, and all hurt from your past. He can make you a new creature in Christ. Let God plead your case for you. He can shake off anything that is continuing to hang on to you.

There are consequences for hanging on to your past: death, depression, anxiety, fear, torment, unaccomplished goals, low drive to succeed, sorrow, sadness, and pain. Also, there is a higher chance that you will return to the vomit and repeat all that was done to you.

Surrender Your Thoughts to Him

Test yourself by asking yourself what is on your mind most of the time? Are the answers God? Bible? Scripture? Or is it your past experiences? Offenses? Abuse? Hatred toward your violators? Are you consumed by what you had to suffer? Or are you living in the now? Is your mind being refreshed daily through the washing of the Word of God? Let your prayer be "God, I need You." This keeps you in a humble and repentant form so you can hear above the noise of your past. Keep yourself in a place of needing God. Remember, though you walk through the shadows of the evil one, the darkness cannot touch you, for God is with you. No evil shall harm you unless God allows it, and if He allows it, He has a reason for it; usually it is to bring you to a place of total surrender. God will plead your cause. He can calm and break any past pain or thought pattern with His presence.

Nevertheless Be Thou Healed

No matter how horrific your past or your childhood has been, it is still your responsibility to deal with any repercussions that the past may or may not be causing you in your adult life. Each person is accountable before God. Each person is responsible to fix any loose ends that are still open-ended and hanging out unprotected for the world, the devil, the evil one to come and harm. In a paraphrase, it is like a bunch of open-ended electrical wires that have been left out raw and exposed. Your job, with God's help, is too cautiously and carefully, one wire at a time, put something over each exposure and protect it one situation at a time. Each piece of wire—unresolved situation—usually has a different remedy for closure.

Let us say you were severely beaten as a child. Each time you try to discipline your child, you cannot bring yourself to properly discipline the child, even in the simplest way. By ignoring the problem your child caused and not disciplining them accordingly, you essentially carry on the dysfunction. However, you need to confront the pain or cover up the raw exposed wires. You may need counseling, therapy, psychotherapy, healing sessions with the Lord, or even confronting your abuser. Whatever the course is, you need to follow it to complete the healing that God is leading you through. Then when approached with a problem, like dealing with a disobedient child, you as an adult can deal with the issue with a healthy mind-set. No exposed wires dangling around ready to spark. Completing the process in turn stops the unhealthy dysfunction from passing down to the next generation.

Be Content

> As for me, I will behold thy face in righteousness: I shall be satisfied, when I awake, with thy likeness. (Psalm 17:15 KJV)

Some would say, "Oh, you should just be satisfied and content where you are at in your life. Doesn't the Bible say to be content in whatsoever state you are in?" To this, I say, "I am content when I am most like Christ. In there I find full satisfaction!"

I knew that the drive behind me desiring change was Holy Spirit inspired. What I did not know was that all the delays, all the stop signs in the road, all the time-outs, and all of the dead ends were all at the allowance of God.

All these years, I was giving the devil points for something that he had nothing to do with. It was the Lord each time. He was stopping me in my tracks. He was causing me to deal with my life before Christ would release me fully into my destiny. During all the lost careers, all the job failures, failed friendships, all the closed bridges, I had tried to forge my way through; God was on my side the entire time.

God was trying to slow me down so that I would deal with all the issues I was trying to run from. All the emotions I had neatly tucked down in my soul were not as neatly filed away in my mental library as I thought. In reality, there was mold and mildew growing in between each and every one of those files I had tried to seal closed. He was going to answer my prayers, just not the way I had planned.

Absolutely watch how you pray because God is all hearing. Beyond your words, God feels your heart. He knows your deepest filed-away memories and emotions. He knows what you have tucked away even long after you have forgotten.

One thing that I know is that if there is any unsettled pain, unresolved negative emotions, or dark circumstances that you have tucked away, in God's eyes, it is still unsettled for you too. God is no respecter of persons. Darkness separates you from God, our maker.

To become the person God has planned for you to become, you must deal with it: analyze it, pray about it, and fix it if you can. Make it right if possible. You cannot change it; however, you must be delivered from anything about that issue, abuse, neglect that has caused you separation from God. Whether it was you being sinned upon or against or if the circumstance caused you to also sin. Not dealing with it, or acting as if it no longer is in your life, will not make it go away. This is what I tried to do, and God would not let me get away with it. If you have an ought against your brother, the Bible tells us to leave your gift at the altar (in other words, you are saying, "Excuse me, God, I will be right back.") and go and make peace with your brother, mother, father, friend, cousin, whomever and make peace. If you do not, the devil's ultimate pleasure is to destroy you (Matthew 5:23).

Yes, I know that we are new creatures in Christ; of all people, I get that. However, you cannot put new wine into an old bottle. The bottle will rend and break (Mark 2:22 or Matthew 9:17).

God expected me to deal with all my past unresolved issues. Once dealt with, I in good conscience could drop the issue in my soul and memory.

Let us be honest; issues, life experiences, and ungodly sinful situations that you never resolve will remain unresolved until you resolve them within your soul.

Now, granted there are certain situations that no matter what you do or say you feel you just cannot seem to get right before the

Father. You may have to let God settle these when He comes again in all his glory, but the resolved ones you can get under the blood.

From my salvation, June 17, 1980, to when my dad died, I was swimming through these issues. My past was constantly kicking it up in my face. I am so sorry to God that it took me all these thirty-five years to figure it all out. So God, who loved me through the process, showed me that His grace is sufficient for all of me.

Voyage Covenant

The length of your journey will depend on the depth of issues that you have lived through and suffered in and, of course, God's timing. He can speed things up, and He has been known to slow things down. Ha ha ha. Everyone's excursion is unique. It is therefore important to seek God daily concerning your road to healing. Just as He has a plan for your life and destiny, He also has a plan for your healing. God is a healer. You will need some internal healing, God-ordained, soulful, and emotional healing and deliverance. I will not lie it can be quite painful emotionally at times; however, God will give you reprieves every so often. At least He did for me.

That is why I mentioned having a covenant with God as to this entire voyage. In the making of a covenant, you are placing your trust in the Lord to see you through so that you can reach a point of living for Christ in the present and in the now and not always having to "dip" back into your past and deal with something.

God began a few years back speaking this saying to me repeatedly, "There must be a point of deliverance." and "Where is the point of deliverance?" It took me a while to understand the meaning behind those words. God was telling me that people need to receive deliverance for their pasts, their addictions, and their deep dark repetitive patterns of sin. Elsewise, they will and do pick it back up. Which in turn makes your healing process take all the while longer. Thus, wasting time on planet earth.

You are God's special child. He created you with His own hands. Those same hands created everything around you. If He cares so much about the beautiful flowers, how much more does He care about you?

Consider the lilies, how they grow: "They toil not, they spin not; and yet I say unto you, that Solomon in all his glory was not arrayed like one of these" (Luke 12:27 KJV).

God cares if your conscience is clean. He cares if you are in bondage to your past. He cares if you are unable to function in this world as a whole individual. He cares enough about you to bring you to a place of humility. You are His child. He knows you far better than you know yourself.

Jesus died and rose again, ascending to the heavens, so that you can live. He gave you life abundantly; you just have to find it. It is hidden in Christ. God wants you to live in the here and now, not in your past. Yet you have to sort through your past to find ultimate healing.

In the process of waiting for God to complete your healing and deliverance of your past, keep looking up because He is the only one who can sustain you. He will bring your healing to completeness when you totally surrender and be honest with Him. It is then that God can finish that in which He started within you.

> Being confident of this very thing, that he
> which hath begun a good work in you will perform
> it until the day of Jesus Christ. (Philippians 1:6 KJV)

You see, it has been my experience that when we receive salvation, God begins a journey within us to make us whole. It is we who pull away from God, for a lack of knowledge of His word or fear of exposure of our pain. Jesus said, "My people perish due to lack of knowledge." He provides the knowledge, we just have to apply it to our lives.

> My people are destroyed for lack of knowl-
> edge: because thou has rejected knowledge, I will
> also reject thee, that thou hast forgotten the law of
> thy God I will forget thy children. (Hosea 4:6 KJV)

The Holy Spirit is a comforter and a gentleman. Jesus said that He would bring in to remembrance all things for your gain. I learned to listen carefully to the whispers of the Holy Spirit. He would speak soft words, comforting words of instruction to me. Words that I needed to hear to bring me immediate peace. He would show me what I needed to lay down, to pick up, or to be set free from or of.

So therefore seek Him for wisdom as to what you need to be delivered from so that you can go forth and carry the torch of healing to the next generation. God's sheep need restoration. It is imperative you pray daily while on this journey. Pray for the covering of the blood of the Lamb. Pray for the shield of faith to cover you, the breastplate of righteousness to fight for you, and the helmet of salvation to protect your mind while on the journey to ultimate healing. Only God can be your strength, your source of healing, and your deliverer.

Enter into the Joy of the Lord

This joy can only be achieved if you are truly willing to accept the challenge of entering into the greater things God is calling you to or toward. You cannot enter into the joy of the Lord unless you understand that God has not forsaken you, and you cannot bring your past with you if you want to enter into the joy of the Lord. Because where love is, there can be no hate. If you have not dealt with your past and are still living in it, you cannot truly enter into the full joy of God.

God is able to keep you from suffering if you will hand Him your past. By handing your past completely over to God, you are allowing Him to deliver you so that you can walk in joy. Again, I say, where is the point of deliverance?

Through it all, I have learned that God does love me. He does care about all the suffering, trials, and tribulations that I have been forced to walk through and bear. I have also learned that God has a special anointing upon my life. I am aware that just being a Christian is enough to get a person to eternity; however, that has never been enough for me. I want all that God has for me.

Grace by Worthiness

Grace, grace, God's very giving grace. Though there will and have been divisions in diverse places, your wonderful grace covers any and all the ditches that I may have fallen into. Though I fall short of loving all those who have caused me adversity, You, O Lord, have granted me the grace to forgive and let go of those who walk in cloudy darkness. I thank my God always for all of the adversity in my life; for through it I have learned that I am much stronger than I thought I was. Thank You, God, for all of the haters in my life, for through their lies and talebearing, I have grown more than I ever would have without them and their unkind words of encouragement.

Resources

Adult Children of Alcoholics
www.adultchildren.org

Alcoholics Anonymous
www.AA.org

Childhelp National Child Abuse Hotline 24/7
www.CHILDHELP.org

National Sexual Assault Hotline
www.RAINN.org

National Association of Anorexia Nervosa and Associated Disorders
www.anad.org

About the Author

Cynthia Reffner

CINDY HAS BEEN MARRIED FOR thirty-seven years, has three adult children and eleven beautiful grandchildren. She is a born-again, Spirit-filled lover of God who has had to overcome a tumultuous childhood.

Her desire as a first-time author is to share her story in hopes that others who remain dangling in their "undoneness" can find healing within their soul. Cindy is fully aware of the struggle that one must go through because of her own long journey to seek ultimate healing in her personal life. While others would suggest that she should just "let it go" and "move on," her inner knower kept telling her that God had more. Don't give up. Go forth. Propel.

Her unrelenting, and sometimes seemingly inconvenient, passion to use her God-given gift of discernment to help bring ultimate healing, deliverance, and wholeness to the wounded body of Christ falls close to her heart. The life-breathed words that Cindy speaks have been known to impart wisdom and transform many people's trajectories in their lives.

Her journey to wholeness included Spirit-filled journaling for over twenty-five years. She documented her life's ups and downs throughout the healing process. Many of these journals helped her for the basis of this book. She knew that one day she would write a book—if not two or three. She has always diligently sought the Holy Spirit's inspiration.

You can reach Cindy on Facebook @ No Soul Lost.

Deana Reffner

Deana is a mother of five unique children. Growing up, she witnessed a lot of the contents of this book, so who better to step up and help write it! She was raised in the house of the Lord, but through her own will, she chose a much rougher road to travel. The closer she drew to God's truths, the straighter her path became as she experienced God's pure love and grace for her own self. Seeing life through her children's eyes was what God used for her ultimate awakening. She never realized that God had an intended purpose for all those endless nights she spent reading, writing the story that needed telling.

CPSIA information can be obtained
at www.ICGtesting.com
Printed in the USA
FSHW010703250421
80814FS